Financial Accounting: An Introduction

Arthur HINDMARCH
Mary SIMPSON

MACMILLAN

First published 1991 by
THE MACMILLAN PRESS LTD
Houndmills, Basingstoke, Hampshire RG21 2XS
and London
Companies and representatives
throughout the world

ISBN 0–333–54729–2 (hardcover)
ISBN 0–333–54731–4 (paperback)

A catalogue record for this book is available
from the British Library

Printed in Hong Kong

Reprinted 1992

Contents

Acknowledgement

The authors and publishers acknowledge with thanks permission from Marks & Spencer Plc to reproduce extracts from their 1989 *Annual Report and Financial Statements* in Appendix B.

Introduction

Financial Accounting is concerned with how a business measures, records and communicates information to a range of potential users.

An earlier, related book, *Accounting: An Introduction* by Hindmarch, Atchison and Marke, published in 1977, attempted to cover both financial and management accounting in one volume. Subsequent experience suggests that, with the expansion of material in each of these areas of accounting, an adequate treatment of the subject now requires two books. We have decided in this new book to develop the financial accounting content of the earlier book. The book is designed to meet the needs of:

- undergraduate degree courses which include a study of accounting – these will include degrees in accounting, business studies, economics, etc.
- those studying for the foundation-level examination of the professional accountancy bodies.
- others who wish to have an understanding of how organisations prepare and use financial accounting information.

The book provides a foundation in accounting for those interested in analysis as well as description. There are many books which deal predominantly with the technical aspects of accounting. We believe that the logical method of teaching the subject is to introduce the conceptual foundation of the subject before building the superstructure of accounting methods and techniques. Thus we have written an introductory text which does not avoid the difficult conceptual problems but which attempts to present them in a language and style which will be easily understood by those unfamiliar with accounting. We have taken as our starting-point the well-known definition of accounting as 'the measurement, recording and communication of economic data'. Accounting has evolved from the needs of business so that its concern is essentially with the solution of business problems. Financial accounting is the means by which a business measures, records and communicates information for a range of potential users such as shareholders, lenders, managers, employees, suppliers and customers. Our objective is to help the reader understand the potential of accounting to meet the needs of this range of users but also to recognise the boundaries of the subject and the possible limitations of accounting measurement.

As experienced teachers we recognise that one of the major obstacles to understanding accounting is its use of terminology, which in many areas is imprecise and ambiguous. We have attempted to be consistent in our use of terminology, and as a learning and teaching aid the first of the questions at the end of each chapter provides a review of the significant terms introduced in the chapter. In addition we have attempted to meet the criticism of the earlier related book, referred to above, by increasing the number of examples and diagrams and by attempting to simplify the style of presentation. The inclusion of additional questions and problems at the end of each chapter should facilitate the use of the book in a teaching programme which includes seminar discussion and accounting workshops.

ARTHUR HINDMARCH
MARY SIMPSON

1
Introduction to Accounting

1.1 Introduction

The purpose of this introductory chapter is to attempt to provide the reader who is new to accounting with an idea of what accounting is about:

- What is its **importance** in society?
- What **problems** is it concerned with?
- What **methods** are adopted to solve these problems?

I have often asked students to tell me what they think accounting is concerned with. The range of answers usually includes 'something to do with money'; 'concerned with taxation'; 'keeping the books' or 'checking up on how money is spent'.

To some extent, all these answers are correct, but they do not provide an overall picture, and we need to identify a more general and formal definition. We have taken as our starting point the definition of accounting as a subject concerned with the process of:

Identifying, measuring and communicating economic information to permit informed judgement and decisions by the user of the information[1]

and we will use this definition to discuss further the nature and scope of the subject of accounting.

1.2 Organisations using accounting information

The relevant economic information to be accounted for will depend to a large extent on **who is going to use the information**, which in turn will be determined by what type of individual or organisation we are concerned with.

It will be useful for our purposes to classify organisations into **three** categories:

(1) *Government – both local and central government*
  Here we are concerned, for example, with accounting for

1

national or local income and expenditure, with issues regarding
the balance of payments, government borrowing and, at the
local level, income from rates, the community charge and
local authority expenditure.

(2) *Non-business (or 'not for profit') organisations*
Here we are concerned with organisations which may have a
variety of objectives, but whose main aim: is unlikely to be
solely to earn profits, for example, schools, hospitals, armed
services, emergency services, etc.

(3) *Businesses*
This category includes organisations operating in the **private
sector**, from the small one man business to the very large
organisations such as British Leyland (BL), Imperial Chemical Industries (ICI), or Marks and Spencer; and those in the
public sector such as the National Coal Board (now British
Coal)

The reasons for identifying these three categories is that each poses **different problems for accounting**, and consequently separate branches of accounting have developed to meet their separate needs. The focus of this book is on
what might be called 'mainstream accounting' – that is, accounting for
business – however, a great deal of the accounting principles and practices
discussed will be applicable to all types of organisations. It must also be said
that these categories cannot be precisely defined: for example, local authorities may privatise some of their activities such as refuse collection so that
they are operated as a profit making business; private schools or private
hospitals can also be operated as a profit making business.

1.3   Identifying, measuring and communicating accounting information

Much of the content of this book is concerned with an explanation of what is
meant by the title of this section. The following brief initial explanation is
intended to provide sufficient information to enable students to start asking
questions, while acknowledging that the issues are in reality extremely complex and that a proper understanding will be achieved only much later,
probably only after reading the rest of this book!

Identifying What is 'Accounting Information'

Of all the possible information about a business, what constitutes 'accounting
information'? We can use the business of Marks and Spencer, whose financial
statements are given in Appendix B to discuss this question. Marks and
Spencer Plc is a large retail business with sales of over £5000m, profits of

around £350m and more than 60 000 employees. The company appears to have a reputation for having well trained staff, good products and good relations with its customers. All of these pieces of information are relevant in depicting an overall view of the company, and each will contribute to the company's performance. If one of the tasks of accounting is to **identify, measure and communicate** information about the performance of companies such as Marks and Spencer, can we then say that all the above information concerning the company is accounting information? This question is not an easy one to answer, but the position will be clearer if we consider the nature of **accounting measurement**.

Measuring Accounting Information

'Accounting measurement' is essentially concerned with transforming information into **monetary terms**. If qualitative information about a business is not capable of expression in monetary terms, then it is by this definition not accounting information. However, this restriction does not necessarily set a clearly defined limit as to what might constitute accounting information. In the list of pieces of information about Marks and Spencer above, the sales and profit data is clearly capable of expression as accounting information because the monetary value is given. The reputation for training, products and customer relations are more difficult; they are examples of aspects of the company where it is conceivable that a monetary value could be measured, but it would be difficult to isolate the value of each to the overall performance of the company. We will discover that accounting is a pragmatic subject, so that the **practicality and cost** of its implementation must always be considered; we can therefore elaborate on our earlier statement by saying that:

> Accounting information is that which it is possible, with reasonable ease and cost, to express in monetary terms.

We shall see that in the current state of the art of accounting, the particular attributes of Marks and Spencer's reputation for training, products and customer relations would **not** be identifiable as accounting information.

Communicating Accounting Information

Having identified and measured the accounting information, the next issue is how it should be **communicated** to those who need to use it. Much of the time of accountants in recent years has been spent in considering how best to package and present accounting information in the most effective way – that is, so that it can be understood by **users of the information**. The financial statements of Marks and Spencer in Appendix B are an example of such a form of communication. Questions we attempt to answer in the course of the book will be: are the systems of communicating accounting information adequate and, if not, how can they be improved?

1.4   Users of accounting information

We have said that accounting is concerned with providing information to permit informed judgement and decisions by the user of the information. The information required may **vary with the type of user**. An individual may wish to discover his (or her) personal financial situation, for instance, when reviewing the family budget or deciding to buy a new car. If he runs his own small business he is even more likely to require such information. If instead of the individual or one man business, we consider a large organisation such as Marks and Spencer or ICI, then not only is the information likely to be more complex, but the groups of users interested in that information are also likely to be much larger.

1.5   Types of business organisation

Before we go on to discuss the types of users and their needs, it will be useful to identify **three** types of business organisation which are commonly found in the UK, and which will be used for illustrations throughout the book: the sole trader, the partnership and the company.

The term **sole trader** is commonly used to describe a business **owned by one person**: there may be several employees involved in the business, but the ownership is in the hands of one person. Typically these are small operations – shopkeepers, builders, window cleaners, etc.

A **partnership** consists of a number of people who **own a business jointly**. As with the sole trader, there is no legal distinction between the partnership and the individual members of the partnership. Solicitors, doctors and accountants are examples of people who often organise themselves into partnerships.

Although there is no legal distinction between the affairs of the sole trader and the owner or the partnership and the partners, it will be necessary to make such a distinction between their **private** and **business** activities when preparing the accounts of the business.

Large organisations usually operate as a **company**. A company is an artificially legal person; to become a company a business must be **incorporated** by registering with the Registrar of Companies. In the UK the importance of the company developed in the nineteenth century when the Industrial Revolution generated large scale organisations requiring large amounts of finance. The creation of the company and the related development of **limited liability** enabled finance to be raised from a wider range of sources. 'Limited liability' refers to the restriction of the liability of shareholders so that they cannot be held responsible for amounts **in excess of the finance they have provided to the company**. Without limited liability it would be very difficult to persuade investors to provide finance for a company.

1.6 Users and their needs

In a complex business organisation the users of accounting information can be many and varied. If the business has a number of owners (usually called **shareholders**) who have invested in the business they will be concerned about the progress of their investment. Similarly, if the business has borrowed from banks or from others, these lenders will have an interest in the performance of the business. We could extend this list to include employees, suppliers, customers and the government in their capacity as a tax authority, all of whom have some interest in the firm's activities. We can list these as shown in Table 1.1

The users listed in Table 1.1 have a legitimate interest in the affairs of the firm. As a result the firm may be said to be **accountable** to these users. The concept of 'accountability' has been an important factor in the development of accounting information.[2] We can see from the list of possible questions in Table 1.1 that users will have a variety of needs; if accounting is to provide an adequate service then accounting measurement of a firm's economic performance should be concerned with the needs of these users. One of the problems in achieving this is the capacity of accounting information to cope satisfactorily with such an apparently wide variety of needs.

The users in Table 1.1 are interested in having accounting information in order to **learn more about the firm**; they will usually be concerned to use the information to help in their decision-making – for example, whether to buy, sell or hold shares; whether to lend to the firm; whether to join the firm as

Table 1.1 Users and their needs

Possible users of accounting information	Possible questions asked about the business
Owners/Shareholders/Investors	IS THE BUSINESS PROFITABLE? WHAT ARE ITS PROSPECTS?
Lenders	CAN THE BUSINESS MEET ITS INTEREST CHARGES? WILL IT BE ABLE TO REPAY ITS DEBTS?
Employees	DO EMPLOYEES HAVE A SECURE FUTURE? ARE EMPLOYEES ADEQUATELY REWARDED?
Suppliers/Customers	DOES THE BUSINESS HAVE A SECURE FUTURE?
Inland Revenue	IS THE ACCOUNTING INFORMATION SUITABLE FOR USE IN ASSESSING TAXES?

employees or to ask for an increase in pay; and (for suppliers and customers) whether to continue to deal with the firm. An interesting feature of the users' need for information is that their decision-making would presumably be easier if they had information about the firm's **future performance**. This poses a further problem for accounting measurement: how well does it succeed in providing information which can be used to **assess the firm's future**?

It is thus apparent that accounting information can provide a basis for decisions and actions which have an important economic or political significance, stretching far beyond the boundaries of the individual company. This is a further reason why the way in which accounting information is produced should be properly understood, and not only by accountants.[3]

1.7   Introduction to the accounting information system

We saw in Table 1.1 that a variety of users might ask a variety of questions about a firm. However, to simplify the discussion we can say that they are all concerned with the 'health' of the firm. It is recognised that each user may have a different interpretation of what 'health' means, and the analogy can be extended. A doctor checking your current health is likely to ask questions about how well you have been in recent months, and from that information and a physical examination, he may be able to say (for example) that you are fit enough to return to work, to take up physical exercise, or he may be able to forecast that you will have a long life.

Similarly an analysis of a firm's current health will include questions on how well it has performed recently and how well it is likely to do in the future. This analysis is summarised in Figure 1.1, where the horizontal line represents the passage of time.

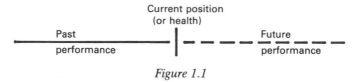

Figure 1.1

Figure 1.1 uses general terminology such as 'health' and 'performance'. We can now substitute terminology more specific to accounting to depict similar phenomena. This is shown in Figure 1.2.

Figure 1.2

Figure 1.2 includes the terms 'value' and 'profit'; we will investigate later in the book what these terms mean in an accounting context, and how they are measured by accountants. For the present we will merely say that a firm's value represents its position at a particular point in time and that profit is a term used to measure the firm's performance **over a period of time**. We can express this as a simple model:

$$Pt = Vt - V_{t-1}$$

where Pt represents the profit for the period t, Vt is the value at the end of period t and V_{t-1} the value at the end of the previous period.

Figure 1.2 also shows the horizontal line divided into time periods at V_1, V_2, V_3 and V_4. Just as an individual should visit a doctor periodically for regular check-ups, so the users of accounting information require **regular reports on the health and performance of the firm**. The most common means of communicating this information to users is by means of two statements:[4] the balance sheet and the profit and loss account. These are now incorporated into Figure 1.3, which is derived from Figures 1.1 and 1.2.

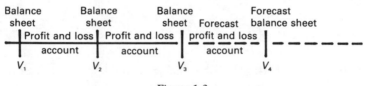

Figure 1.3

Figure 1.3 depicts balance sheets prepared at specified intervals and profit and loss accounts which cover the periods between the dates of the balance sheets. The length of time – and hence the **frequency of the preparation** – of these financial statements will vary in practice: a manager may wish to have weekly reports, whereas the tax authorities may be satisfied with annual reports. You can see from Appendix B that the Marks and Spencer balance sheet was prepared for 31 March and that the profit and loss account covers the year leading up to that date.

1.8 Financial statements

The term 'financial statements' is commonly used to denote the type of reports that are used to communicate accounting information, particularly in the context of the **annual reports** that companies have to produce under UK legislation. At this stage of the book we are restricting the meaning of financial statements to the balance sheet and the profit and loss account, although we will see later that other statements may also be included.

The Balance Sheet

The purpose of a balance sheet is to **report for a particular date** the following:

- The **resources** owned or controlled by the organisation (commonly referred to as **assets**).
- The **obligations** owed by the organisation (commonly referred to as **liabilities**).
- The **residual interest of the owner(s)** of the organisation (known as **net worth**, or alternatively **owners' equity**)[5]

What a balance sheet depicts is the **accounting valuation** of the firm's resources. If you deduct from the value of those resources the liabilities that the organisation has outstanding, you are left with what the **organisation is worth**. A simple example of a balance sheet would thus be:

Balance Sheet of ABC Company at 31 December 19X2

	£
Assets	30000
Liabilities	5000
Net Worth (or Owner's Equity)	£25000

The term 'net worth' denotes what the firm would be worth **after it had paid off all its liabilities**. If you are the owner of the firm it also denotes the value of your interest in the firm. This is the derivation of the expression 'owners' equity'.

The information contained in the balance sheet is often expressed in the form of a simple equation:

Assets − Liabilities = Owners' Equity

or

Assets = Liabilities + Owners' Equity

This equation is known as the **balance sheet equation** or simply as the **accounting equation**, and it will be referred to frequently in later chapters.

There are many problems associated with the preparation of a balance sheet, and we will be considering these throughout the book. However, two basic questions which we must deal with at an early stage are:

- What sort of items are **included** as assets and liabilities?
- How are these assets and liabilities **measured**?

These questions will be considered further in Chapter 2. At this stage it is necessary to explain that the value of the firm as depicted by the balance sheet is only one possible way of measuring its value. Before considering alternative approaches in Chapter 2 we must explore some other aspects of the balance sheet itself.

Referring to Figure 1.3 the ABC Company balance sheet could depict the company's position at V_2, where V_2 is 31 December 19X2. If we assume that V_3 is one year later, then the two balance sheets might be:

Balance Sheet of ABC company at 31 December

	19X2	19X3
	£	£
Assets	30000	37000
Liabilities	5000	6000
Net Worth (or Owners' Equity)	£25000	£31000

We can see that the company's net worth has increased from £25 000 to £31 000 over the year, an increase of £6000. Consequently the owners' interest has increased in value. We do not know at this stage **why** the net worth has increased, other than to say that the assets have increased by £7000 and the liabilities by £1000. Before we attempt to explain the increase, we must consider the profit and loss account.

The Profit and Loss Account

The name of this statement which we would prefer to use would be simply a 'profit statement'. However, the name 'profit and loss account' has been used in accounting practice in the UK for many years, and therefore we have used it throughout the book. The main purpose of the profit and loss account is to show the firm's performance in terms of **what it has earned from selling products or services**, and what **costs** it has incurred in relation to these earnings. The terms used here for these two aspects of the firm's performance are 'revenue' and 'expenses', with the excess of the former over the latter being 'profit'. The statement might thus be:

*Profit and loss account of ABC company for the year ended
31 December 19X3*

	£
Revenue	40000
Expenses	34000
Profit	£6000

We can see from this statement that the profit for the year to 31 December 19X3 is £6000, which is the same as the **increase in net worth** shown by the comparison of the two balance sheets for the beginning and the end of the period covered by the profit and loss net account. Is this a coincidence? Why should the increase in net worth be the same as the profit for the year? Figure 1.4 shows in a simplified form the relationship between changes in net worth of a firm and the profit it earns.

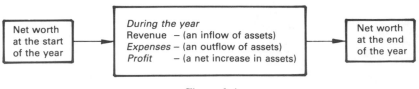

Figure 1.4

Figure 1.4 shows the worth of a firm at the beginning of the year, which we know consists of assets and liabilities held at that time. During the year the firm earns **revenues** (say, from selling products), and this will result in an **inflow of assets** to the firm in the form of cash (or its equivalent). The firm will also incur **expenses**, which might include the cost of the product sold and perhaps the wages of the salesperson. Meeting these expenses will result in an **outflow of resources** (or assets). If the revenue for the year exceeds the expenses, the firm will earn a profit which in our simple model will also represent a net increase in assets, which in turn mean that the firm's net worth will have increased. Earning a profit has thus resulted in an increase in the value of the firm, as measured by the balance sheet. In everyday language: the better the performance of the firm the higher the profit, and the better off the owner of the firm is at the end of the year.

Figure 1.4, however, oversimplified the situation in certain respects. Owners' equity or net worth is measured by **assets minus liabilities**, and 'assets' represents resources available to the firm. It follows that if the owner decides to increase these resources during the year by introducing more funds from his own private resources, then his owners' equity will increase, as will the net worth of the firm. Thus **not all** increases in net worth are the result of earning a profit. Similarly if the owner decides to **withdraw resources** from the firm, the net worth will decrease. In a small firm, this could occur where the owner takes cash out of the till as personal spending money; in a larger company this distribution of assets to the owner might be called a **dividend payment**. Figure 1.5 depicts the more complex – but more realistic – model of the part profit plays in changes in net worth.

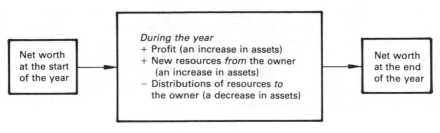

Figure 1.5

1.9 Summary

Our introductory Chapter 1 began by defining accounting and accounting information. It has suggested that the objectives of accounting should be concerned with meeting the needs of the potential users of the accounting information. The chapter also introduced the way in which the accounting information system is constructed, and showed how accounting information can be communicated by means of financial statements.

Notes and References

1. American Accounting Association 'A Statement of Basic Accounting Theory' (American Accounting Association, Evanston, Illinois) 1966).
2. For further discussion of the rights of users and the accountability of business, see 'The Corporate Report' (Accounting Standards Committee, 1975).
3. A report on accounting standards proposed that policy should be determined by 'a wide constituency of interests . . . to guide . . . on issues of public concern . . . and to act as a powerful proactive public influence for securing good accounting practice', 'The Making of Accounting Standards' (The Dearing Report) (London: ICAEW, 1988).
4. These statements have been the pre-dominant means of presenting accounting information throughout the world during the nineteenth and twentieth centuries; suggestions for their amendment or replacement have been made from time to time. The content of this book assumes that they will continue to be used, at least in the foreseeable future.
5. A more formal definition of the elements which make up a balance sheet is given in the statement issued in 1989 by the International Accounting Standards Committee (IASC), 'Framework for the preparation and presentation of financial statements':

(a) An asset is a resource controlled by the enterprise as a result of past events and from which future economic benefits are expected to flow to the enterprise.
(b) A liability is a present obligation of the enterprise arising from past events, the settlement of which is expected to result in a flow from the enterprise of resources embodying economic benefits.
(c) Equity is the residual interest in the assets of the enterprise after deducting all its liabilities.

Questions and Problems

1.1 What do you understand by the following terminology?

Accounting information	Balance sheet
Financial statements	Profit and loss account
Sole trader	Assets
Partnership	Liabilities
Company	Net worth
Limited liability	Owners' equity
Accountability	Revenue
Value	Expense
Profit	Distributions
Accounting equation	

1.2 What user groups do you consider have a legitimate right to information about a firm. What are these rights based on?
1.3 What are the main similarities and differences between accounting for:

(a) Government organisations;
(b) not for profit organisations;
(c) businesses?

1.4 What are the main similarities and differences between accounting for:

(a) Sole traders;
(b) Partnerships;
(c) Companies?

1.5 What in your view constitutes a 'healthy' company?
1.6 Discuss what constitutes 'accounting information'. Give examples of information about a company which could be classified as 'non-accounting information'.
1.7 There are various ways of measuring the success of a company. Suggest some of these, using the Marks and Spencer report in Appendix B as an Example.

1.8 Using the Marks and Spencer Plc annual report and financial statements from Appendix B:

(a) Identify the 'group' net worth at the end of the company's financial year.

(b) Identify the numbers that fit the 'accounting equation':

$$\text{Assets} - \text{Liabilities} = \text{Owners' Equity}$$

(c) Calculate the change in net worth from the end of the previous financial year to the end of the most recent year in the report.

(d) In some circumstances, the increase in net worth will be the same figure as the profit for the year. Why is this?

(e) Suggest reasons why this does not seem to be the situation in the Marks and Spencer financial statements.

2
Concepts of Value and Profit

2.1 Introduction

Chapter 1 introduced the two major financial statements used in accounting: the balance sheet and the profit and loss account. It also introduced the balance sheet equation:

Assets − Liabilities = Owners' Equity (or Net Worth)

It can be seen from this equation that the identification and measurement of a firm's assets and liabilities will determine its net worth. It was also explained that a change in net worth, over time, would usually be the result of **earning a profit**. There thus appears to be a close relationship between the measurement of assets and liabilities and the measurement of profit. Chapter 2 explores this relationship, and considers various ways in which the concepts of 'value' and 'profit' can be interpreted. The purpose of this early chapter is to present basic ideas of value and profit which we hope will enable students to adopt a questioning approach to later studies.

It is important to understand the difference between **value** and **profit** − for example, as illustrated by the model in Figure 1.3 (p. 7). In this context, 'value' is assumed to be a static concept, in that a monetary figure is placed on an item (or group of items) at a **particular point in time**. Values, may, of course, change, but these represent measurement made at **different points in time**. 'Profit', on the other hand, is a measure of **performance over a period of time**, often in practice the time period (known as the **accounting period**) between two sets of valuations. This idea of a **stock** (value) and **flow** (profit) forms the basis for major accounting statements such as the balance sheet and profit and loss account and for most accounting systems of recording events.

2.2 Concepts of value

An individual, asked what he is worth, would probably attempt to value his possessions, his house, car, furniture, etc. If he has borrowed money to buy his house or his car, then the amount he still owes would be deducted to arrive at his **net worth**. He is, of course, using the concepts of assets, liabilities and

14

net worth which form the basis of the balance sheet equation.

The dictionary defines an 'asset' as any possession, and also any useful quality. The idea of 'possession' is relevant to the value of a firm – for example, the firm may possess assets such as buildings, machinery and delivery vans. However, care must be taken over the distinction between **possession** and **ownership**. Normally both of these can be attributed to an asset. In the example above, the firm may both **possess and own** the buildings, machinery, office furniture and delivery vans. However, if an assets is on the firm's premises and thus in the firm's possession but actually belongs to someone else – for example, if it is a borrowed van, it should be **excluded** from the list of assets making up the firm's value. On the other hand, the definition quoted in Chapter 1, n. 5, includes assets which are **controlled by the enterprise**, and this implies that legal ownership is not essential. Property held on a lease could thus be included as an asset.

The definition of an asset used above included 'useful qualities'. How should these be included in the measurement of an individual's or a firm's value? Good health and a sense of humour are useful qualities, but there are obvious difficulties in calculating their monetary value! It might be possible to estimate a part of the value of 'good health' in terms of its effect on earnings from a particular occupation, but as there are many other benefits a precise, reliable value is unlikely to be obtained. Referring back to Section 1.3 we see that accounting information is that which can be expressed in monetary terms with reasonable ease and cost; it is doubtful whether good health could qualify as accounting information by this definition. If we extend the analogy to a firm, we can identify many similarly problematic areas – for example, qualities (favourable or unfavourable) such as customer relations, employer–employee relations, or a reputation for reliable products and service.

The previous paragraphs have been concerned with what might be included in a list of possessions or qualities which would constitute an overall value of an individual or a firm. A further problem is how to arrive at a **value** for items in the list.

If a number of people were asked to value a common object – say, a motor car – it is likely that they would reach different conclusions. This might be because they have different levels of knowledge about motor cars; it is also possible that they would adopt different approaches to the **process of valuation**.

Consider some of the possibilities:

	£
(1) Its cost – when new, two years ago	8000
(2) Its cost – when new, *less* an allowance for two years' use	5400
(3) What it would cost now to buy a similar two-year-old car from a car dealer	5300
(4) As for (3), but bought privately	5100

(5) What the car could be sold for now to a dealer	4800
(6) As for (5), but sold privately	5000
(7) The owners' estimate of the car's usefulness to him	5800

There are seven different values listed above, but it is possible to identify **four** approaches or concepts of **value** in common use:

(a) *Original (or historical) cost*
Where an asset's value is represented by its **original cost**. Values (1) and (2) are variations of this approach.

(b) *Replacement cost*
An approach which instead of considering only the original cost of the specific assets, updates the measurement by basing the valuation on the **current purchase cost of a similar item**. Values (3) and (4) are variations of this approach.

(c) *Realisable value*
An estimate of the **proceeds of selling the asset**. Values (5) and (6) are variations of this approach.

(d) *Value to the owner*
An estimate by the owner of the asset's usefulness,[1] as in value (7).

These four approaches are central to the consideration of 'value' in accounting. We will explore their application to accounting measurement in later chapters, but first it is necessary to note the significant characteristics of each.

(a) *Original cost*
Accounting is a pragmatic subject: it is concerned with the **provision of information for a variety of practical purposes**. This information must be **reliable** and **reasonably easy to obtain**. In this context some aspects of the original cost approach make it an attractive proposition.

Original cost is the only one of the four concepts which is based on an **actual transaction**. At least two people – the purchaser and the seller – have agreed a value for the asset when the transaction took place. In addition, there may be **documentary evidence** of the transaction which can therefore be used for verification at a later date. The value is not an estimate, but is based on objective and verifiable evidence which – as we will see later – are two of the cornerstones of accounting measurement.

The reliance on an actual transaction as a basis for measurement of value does, however, lead to two potential disadvantages. One is that by definition original cost arises **at the time**

of a transaction. If it is used to value a number of assets in a firm's balance sheet which have been acquired at different times in the past, the valuations will thus to varying degrees be out of date. Methods have been adopted to try to get around this problem by adjusting the original cost: the reduction in the original cost to allow for use given in value (2) in the motor car example above is a case of such an adjustment.

A second disadvantage arises from the reliance on the existence of a **transaction cost as evidence of value**. This leads to a tendency to exclude assets which have not been acquired by a means of a verifiable transaction. If a firm pays £1m for the patent to produce and market a new medical drug, the patent has an original cost of £1m and might thus be included in a firm's balance sheet. If, however, the same firm had discovered the formula for the drug in its own research laboratories at virtually no cost, could it then be included as one of the firm's assets? The answer is 'no' if the sole criterion is to be original cost.

We will see in later chapters that the original cost approach, usually termed 'historical cost accounting', is the one which in the past has been the most influential in accounting measurement.

(b) *Replacement cost*

Using the cost which would have to be incurred to replace an asset has the attraction of providing an **up-to-date valuation**. To some extent, it also involves **objective criteria**, especially if it is possible to use current widely accepted **market prices**, such as the dealer's list price for second hand cars.

There are areas where it is, however, difficult to apply replacement cost. Again using the example of a car, the particular model may have been discontinued, or it may have special features, low mileage, or accident damage, all of which make an accurate replacement cost difficult to estimate.

In a firm, there are further examples where replacement cost may be difficult to apply. Assets which have been made to perform a particular task – for example, an automated production line or a specially designed factory – will have no obvious existing market price which can be used. Replacement cost is also of little help in trying to value the 'useful qualities' discussed earlier – i.e., employee or customer relations and reputation for reliable products. Again, there is no market from which a replacement cost can be obtained.

Despite these difficulties, replacement cost has attracted a lot of support in recent years as an alternative to original cost for accounting measurement.

(c) *Realisable value*

The attraction of this concept is in some respects similar to that of replacement cost, in that both provide an **up-to-date value** and in some circumstances an **objective** one. Another feature of this concept which makes it attractive is that it conforms to an everyday notion of value – i.e., what you could obtain by selling something. It thus provides an indication of how much a firm's assets would realise **if they were sold**. This might be useful information – for example, if considering a take-over bid or changing the asset structure of the firm.

Where the asset has been acquired for a particular purpose, however, it may have characteristics which make it peculiar to the firm, and its selling price may not be an adequate measure of its value. For example, an asset which is an integral part of a firm's operation – such as a power plant or a piece of manufacturing machinery – would be difficult to sell **separated from the firm as a whole**. In general, the market selling price is least likely to be adequate where the purpose for owning the asset is to **use it in the firm**, rather than to resell it.

(d) *Value to the owner (see n. 1 at the end of the chapter)*

The three concepts considered so far have a common factor in that they are all variations of a **market price**, either buying or selling. The idea of value to the owner is different in that it attempts to value the asset by identifying its **usefulness**, and by placing a monetary value on the **benefits identified**.

An individual or firm will find an asset 'useful' if it is expected to produce some **future benefit**. This approach attempts to estimate the present value of these future benefits. The nature of the future benefits will depend on the type of asset being measured. If the asset consists of stock to be sold, such as dresses in a Marks and Spencer store, the future benefits will be similar to the realisable value in (c) above – that is, what they could be sold for. If, however, the asset is used in the firm (say, a piece of machinery or a motor vehicle), then the value to the owner will be a more complex calculation. If the machinery produces articles for sale, then the value will be based on the **proceeds from the eventual sale of the product** (after adjusting for costs such as raw materials). This value may be very different from the selling price of the machinery itself.

An illustration of a 'value to the owner' calculation is shown in Figure 2.1 (see n. 1 at the end of the chapter).

V is what we are trying to measure (i.e., the value of the asset using the future benefit to be enjoyed by the owner as a result of owning the asset). B_1, B_2, B_3, B_4, etc. are the benefits

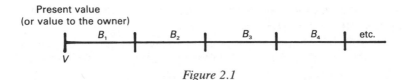

Figure 2.1

arising in future periods. A simple mathematical expression to calculate the value is $V = B_1 + B_2 + B_3 + B_4$, etc. However, in practice the values of B would not simply be added together without some form of adjustment. The adjustment is made necessary because the benefits received in later periods should be given a **lower weighting** than those received in the earlier periods. This is because the earlier the benefits are received, the sooner they can be used **to earn a return elsewhere**.

This approach ensures that the asset is valued using the benefits as defined by the owner, as opposed to values determined by market prices. This, it is said, makes this concept the most relevant, and achieves the most satisfactory values. However, because it is based on estimates of future benefits it is inevitably the most **subjective** of the four concepts we have considered. This creates difficulties in applying it in accounting measurement. Once market based values are discarded and replaced by individual estimates of potential benefits it will be more difficult to achieve a valuation which is generally acceptable by a variety of users.

2.3   Concepts of profit

Sect. 2.2 introduced alternative concepts of value. We have seen from Figure 1.3 the relationship between value and profit, Sect. 2.3 explores further the idea of 'profit'. In particular, we will see that although it is basically a simple concept it becomes complex when applied to the measurement of a firm's operations.

Single Transactions

In its simplest form, most people would be able to identify the nature of a profit: it occurs when something is sold for **more than was paid for it** – if I buy a squash racket for £50 and sell it for £70 I have thus made a profit of £20. From this simple example of a single transaction we can explore further the ideas, introduced in the early part of this chapter, of value and profit being likened to 'stocks' and 'flows'.

If we assume that the £50 was my only possession then my balance sheet equation before the transaction is:

Assets	–	Liabilities	=	Owner's Equity
£50	–	0	=	£50

I first converted the £50 into a squash racket, but this did not change the equation, it merely changed the **type of assets** owned. When the racket is sold the equation becomes:

£70	–	0	=	£70

The owner's equity now includes the £20 profit and has increased from £50 to £70. The 'stock' of value for the two points of time – before and after the transaction – is £50 and £70 respectively. The profit of £20 represents the measurement of the 'flow' of events between these two points in time, as in Figure 2.2.[2]

Figure 2.2

Multiple Transactions

If I decide to continue to buy and sell squash rackets then I might use the proceeds of the first sale to buy another racket for resale, and continue to trade in this way. Suppose that I do this for several months, recording the details of the purchases and sales. My records show that during these months I have bought and sold 40 rackets and that the total cost was £2000 and the total selling price was £2800. From this information, I can produce a profit and loss account:

	£
Revenue	2800
Expenses	2000
Profit	£ 800

If I assume that a separate bank account has been used for the cash purchases and sales, and that no other use has been made of the account, then the balance will have risen from £50 at the beginning of the trading period to £850 at the end. In other words the 'stock' of value has increased from £50 to £850 as a result of a 'flow' of profit of £800, or as in Figure 2.3.

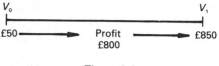

Figure 2.3

More Complex Situations

The analysis of profit using single or multiple but simple transactions can now be expanded to the more complex situation of the measurement of profit for a firm. The basic principles of profit and value are unchanged; however, the simplicity of the principles is often obscured by the existence of two additional complications:

    (1) The **variety of transactions** entered into.
    (2) The **timing** of the measurement of value and profit.

    (1) *The variety of transactions*
        In the final analysis, firms attempt to earn profits by **selling something**, whether it be products such as squash rackets or motor cars, or services such as legal advice or banking facilities. However, in order to sell their products or services they may have to undertake transactions which are only indirectly related to the central activity of selling: for example, in order to sell my squash rackets I may have to advertise, or I may have to pay someone to change the grips on the handles of the rackets. If I open a sports shop then I may have to acquire a lease on suitable premises, install shop fittings and employ a shop assistant. All of these activities will result in expenditure in addition to the purchase of the items of sports equipment I intend to sell in the shop.

        The example now includes a variety of different transactions, and it can be imagined how this variety would be extended if we were analysing the activities of Marks and Spencer, ICI or BT.

        Let us assume that I intend to operate the sports shop for five years, and that I take a five year lease at a cost of £30 000, install shop fittings at a cost of £10 000 which will last exactly five years and employ a shop assistant on a five year contract at an annual salary of £4000. During the five year period my total cash sales amount to £200 000 and cash purchases of sports equipment are £60 000. At the end of five years I can calculate the profit and change in value as in the earlier simpler examples, as shown in Figures 2.4 and 2.5.

Profit and Loss Account for the Five Years

	£	£
Revenue (proceeds of sale of sports equipment)		200000
Expenses		
Sports equipment purchased	60000	
Lease purchased	30000	
Cost of shop fittings	10000	
Assistant's salary	20000	
		120000
Profit		£80000

Figure 2.4

If we assume that the business was started with an inheritance of £50 000 then the stock and flow diagram would be as in Figure 2.5, where $V_0 - V_5$ represents the five year period with the £50 000 at V_0 being the opening cash figure and the £130 000 at V_5 the closing cash balance.

Figure 2.5

Even with the additional complication of the costs of operating the shop, we have been able to calculate profit and the change in value in an apparently straightforward manner. However, it is obvious that the example is based on several naive assumptions. First we have assumed that the life of the business was **exactly five years** and that each of its components lasted **precisely for that period** with no necessity to measure any residual value for the shop fittings or for unsold sports equipment. With an on-going business it is not possible to identify a date on which all its activities come neatly to an end – for example, Marks and Spencer buy and sell products daily, they buy or construct department stores and equipment from time to time and they dispose of unwanted buildings and equipment. These activities **overlap each other**, and there is no precise cut-off date when they all end, as in our example. Perhaps the nearest analogy in practice to a situation where all activities end at the same time is where a firm ceases trading, goes out of business and sells all its assets. This, of course, is a comparatively rare occurrence and it thus cannot be used to solve the general problem of measurement in accounting.

This leads us to the other naive assumption made in the earlier example, that it is acceptable to **wait until the end of**

five years to discover how well the shop is performing. This leads to the second complication referred to earlier.

(2) *The timing of the measurement*

In practice, one of the main reasons for measuring value and profit is to discover how well a firm is performing. We saw in Sect. 1.6 a list of potential users of accounting information, and also an indication of the needs of these users. The needs included the use of financial statements to report on the firm's profitability, to check the security underlying the firm's debts, and to assess the firm's taxation liability. Clearly these users will not be prepared to wait until the firm goes out of business before it discovers its profitability, security or taxation position. It is apparent that firms will have to report on their activities at regular intervals during the life of the business – in practice, firms will report at least annually by means of a profit and loss account and balance sheet.

The requirement for regular reporting makes the calculation of value and profit more difficult than in our earlier examples. To explain why, take the example of the sports shop and depict its expenditure as in Figure 2.6.

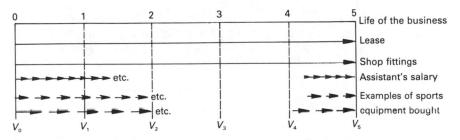

Figure 2.6

In Figure 2.6 the top horizontal line represents the life of the business. With an on-going business there would be no terminal point, but this example made the simplifying assumption of a five year life. The lease and the shop fittings were purchased at the beginning of the business and are represented by unbroken lines. The assistant's salary is a series of short arrows depicting that he was paid at regular intervals. The two examples of sports goods purchased for resale have arrows of varying length, showing that batches were bought at irregular intervals in response to the needs of the business. The vertical dotted lines at V_1, V_2, V_3, V_4 represent artificial cut-off points in the life of the business at the end of year one, two, three and four.

In the earlier version of the profit and loss account shown in Figure 2.4, the computation covered the five year life of the business. It would be more realistic to assume that the owner, his bank manager, or perhaps the inland revenue, would wish to have a report on the business at the end of the first year – i.e., at V_1. If we assume that the sales of sports equipment in the first year generated revenue of £40 000 and that the purchases of sports equipment cost £18 000, then the profit and loss account for year one might be as in Figure 2.7.

Profit and Loss Account for Year One

	£	£
Revenue		40000
Expenses		
Sports equipment purchased	18000	
Lease purchased	30000	
Cost of shop fittings	10000	
Assistant's salary	4000	
		62000
Loss		£22000

Figure 2.7

The firm thus appears to have made a loss of £22 000 in its first year, and its value to have changed as in Figure 2.8.

Figure 2.8

The fall in value can be explained more clearly if the data is analysed as in Figure 2.9.

	£	£
Value at the start of the year		50000
(cash in the bank)		
Cash receipts during the year		40000
		90000
Cash payments during the year:		
Sports equipment	18000	
Lease	30000	
Shop fittings	10000	
Assistant's salary	4000	
		62000
Value at the end of the year (cash in the bank)		£28000

Figure 2.9

The statement in Figure 2.9 is in fact a form of **cash flow statement**, and we will refer to it again later in the chapter. First we need to go back to the loss of £22 000 shown in the profit and loss account and consider it in conjunction with Figure 2.6. Figure 2.6 depicted some transactions, such as the buying of the lease and the shop fittings, as having a use which **lasted the life of the business**, whereas others, such as the monthly salary payments, had a use which **lasted for only the month in question**, and therefore had to be repeated frequently. Similarly the usefulness of the sports equipment ended when the equipment was sold and had to be replaced.

If we consider the idea of 'usefulness' and relate it to the **benefit derived by the business from its possession**, we are close to the definition of an asset from Sect. 2.2. For example, at the end of the first year the benefit to the firm from the use of the lease had not all been used up and therefore 4/5 of its cost could be said to constitute an asset. The same argument can be made in respect of the shop fittings. Also the initial purchases of £18 000 includes £6000 of stock which was not sold during the year. It follows that the value of the firm at the end of the year consists of more than the cash balance of £28 000. We can now redraft the profit and loss account, as shown by Figure 2.10.

Profit and Loss Account for Year One

	£	£	£
Revenue			40000
Expense:			
Sports equipment purchased		18000	
less unsold stock		6000	
		12000	
Lease purchased	30000		
less value at the end of the year	24000		
		6000	
Cost of shop fittings	10000		
less value at the end of the year	8000		
		2000	
Assistant's salary		4000	
			24000
Profit			£16000

Figure 2.10

The loss of £22 000 has become a profit of £16 000. In terms of the value diagram, it is as shown by Figure 2.11.

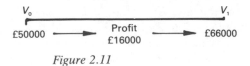

Figure 2.11

From Figure 2.11 the value at the end of the year is seen to be £66 000. This value consists of:

Cash	28000 – as calculated in Figure 2.9
Stock	6000
Lease	24000
Shop fittings	8000
	£66000

The value of £66 000 includes what may be called 'uncompleted transactions' in respect of the stock, the lease and the shop fittings. The necessity to report on the performance on a regular basis by means of an annual profit and loss account and balance sheet will mean that many such uncompleted transactions will have to be valued at the end of an accounting period. This sort of **end of period adjustment** is illustrated further in Example 3.5. The principles and rules which accountants use in making such judgements are developed and explained in Chapter 5. In effect, the balance sheet is merely an **interim value of a business**. The final definitive value can be obtained only when the business ceases to operate. For most firms, that date is unknown and perhaps it may never arrive. However, it would clearly be absurd to wait until a company such as Marks and Spencer ceased trading before attempting to prepare its balance sheet!

2.4 Profit and cash flow

The profit and loss account in Figure 2.7 ⌐howed a loss of £22 000 which in turn led to the fall in value from £50 000 to £28 000 shown in Figure 2.8. This fall in value was explained in Figure 2.9 as a decrease in the cash balance over the year. In other words, the loss of £22 000 was exactly matched by the fall in the cash balance of £22 000. However, this equivalence of cash flow and profit was made possible only because of the simplifying assumptions in the example, and once these assumptions were dropped the loss of £22 000 became a profit of £16 000 which did not equal the change in cash. In practice, the complex relationship between profit and cash flow causes a great deal of difficulty for those interpreting the meaning of accounting information.[3]

There are two main reasons why annual accounting profit may differ from cash flow:

(1) *The classification of some expenditure as assets*

We saw in Sect. 2.3 that the profit for the sports shop for the first year was £16 000 and not a loss of £22 000. This was because we decided that the stock, the lease and the shop fittings had a value at the end of the year and that the expense in respect of these items in the profit and loss account should be only a proportion of their expenditure. Immediately we have a discrepancy between profit and cash flow, because the total expenditure was regarded as an outflow of cash in year one. There is a general lesson to be learnt from this specific example. Cash expenditure will always affect the cash flow in the period in which it is incurred, but the initial recognition of some of that expenditure as an asset will always result in a **difference between profit and cash flow in the current period**. The asset will then be treated as an expense in a future period, when there will be no related cash outflow. There will consequently also be a difference in that future period.

(2) *Credit transactions*

The other reason why profit and cash flow will tend to differ is because of the widespread use of **credit** in business transactions. Goods will be bought (and sold) not for an immediate cash payment, but on the understanding that the cash will be paid (or received) at some future date. Accounting generally recognises these credit transactions at the time the **possession of the goods changes hands**. The result is that the profit and loss account will include sales and purchases made on credit, for some of these transactions the cash will be received or paid within the same accounting period as the sale or purchase. However, at the end of any accounting period there will usually be a proportion of transactions where the cash has still not been paid or received. Clearly in this situation there will again be a **divergence between profit and cash flow**.

Financial accounting

2.5   The balance sheet revisited

Sect. 1.8 in Chapter 1 introduced a simple form of balance sheet:

Balance sheet of the ABC company at 31 December 19X3

	£
Assets	37000
Liabilities	6000
Net Worth (or Owners Equity)	£31000

Sect. 2.2 of this chapter discussed alternative concepts of value which could be used in measuring the elements in such a balance sheet. The subsequent discussion of profit in Sect. 2.3 adopted a form of asset measurement calculated in relation to the **amount spent on its acquisition**. The reason why this particular form of asset measurement is popular in accounting is considered in Chapter 5. We will continue by applying it to the examples of assets used in this chapter, which together with the explanation of credit transactions in Sect. 2.4 allows us to restate the balance sheet above in more detail, and to introduce more terminology.

Balance Sheet of ABC Company at 31 December

Assets	19X2	19X3
	£	£
Land	10000	10000
Buildings	8000	13000
Stock	4000	6000
Debtors	3000	5000
Cash	5000	3000
	30000	37000
Liabilities		
Creditors	5000	6000
Net Worth (Owners' Equity)	£25000	£31000

This balance sheet shows more detail of the assets and liabilities owned and owed by the company. It can be assumed for the present that the assets 'land', 'buildings' and 'stock' are valued by the amount of expenditure used to acquire them. The asset labelled 'debtors' and the liability labelled 'creditors' arise from the use of credit transactions. Debtors are the amounts still owed **to** the company at the date of the balance sheet in respect of sales to customers on credit. Creditors are the amounts still owed **by** the company for purchases made on credit.

The discussion in Sect. 2.4 on the distinction between profit and cash flow is underlined by the details of company ABC. During the year to 31 December

19X3 its profit is £6000. This is confirmed by the increased net worth of the company over the year, and by the profit and loss account shown in Chapter 1. However, during the same period the cash balance has fallen from £5000 to £3000. The explanation of the discrepancy of £8000 (profit £6000 + fall in cash £2000) can be linked to the explanation in section 2.4 – i.e.:

Cash expenditure treated as assets:

		£
Buildings		5000
Stock		2000
		7000

Affect of credit transactions:	£	
Increase in debtors	2000	
less increase in creditors	1000	
		1000
		£8000

2.6 Summary

Chapter 2 has explored the concepts underlying the accounting financial statements. It considered alternative approaches to value that can be adopted in a balance sheet. It also analysed the calculation of accounting profit. The necessity of measuring profit for relatively short periods in the overall life of an organisation was explained as being one of the major problems in the satisfactory measurement of accounting profit. The relationship between profit and cash flows in both the short term and the long term was also explained.

Notes and References

1. This type of valuation model forms the basis for the calculation of value in economic analysis. In that context it is usually depicted as the 'present value of future cash flows'. This approach to value is used, for example, in the classic analysis of economic income by J. R. Hicks which is referred to again in Sect. 14.2. One of the main differences between accounting and economic measurement of profit and value is that economics uses this forward looking subjective model for measuring value, whereas accounting – which has to be more concerned with **reliability** and **objectivity** – relies on historical or market based values.

2. In this example and throughout the remainder of this chapter we have deliberately ignored the problem of **changing prices**. For example, what if in the time between the purchase and the sale of the squash racket there had been an increase in general prices (inflation) or an increase in the specific replacement cost of the squash racket? These and other problems of changing prices are dealt with in Chapter 14.
3. Over a short period the relationship between accounting profit and cash flow may be difficult to identify. However reference to Figures 2.4 and 2.5 show that for the five year period the profit of £80 000 is equal to the £80 000 increase in cash. It has been suggested that one of the strengths of accounting profit is that it may be an indicator of the **long run cash flow** of the firm.

Questions and problems

2.1 What do you understand by the following terminology?

Accounting period	Objective evidence
Original cost	Verifiable evidence
Replacement cost	Stock and flow concepts
Realisable value	Credit transaction
Value to the owner	Debtors
Present value	Creditors

2.2 Characteristics attributed to assets in accounting literature have included the following:

'Items of value owned.'
'Future economic benefits'.
'The results of past transactions'.

Explain what you think is the reasoning behind these three definitions.

2.3 Four alternative approaches to valuation suggested in this chapter are:

Original cost.
Replacement cost.
Realisable value.
Value to the owner.

Discuss how these might be applied to the valuation of the following assets:

(a) A car.
(b) A computer.
(c) A First Division footballer.
(d) A company's reputation for efficient service.

2.4 How would you calculate the value to the owner of the following assets:

(a) A taxi.
(b) Stock.
(c) A car production line.
(d) A Marks and Spencer store.
(e) All the assets owned by Marks and Spencer Plc.

2.5 Why is it necessary to produce financial statements annually, or even more frequently'. What measurement problems can arise because of the need for such regular reporting?

2.6 Explain the relationship between accounting profit and the cash flow for a firm for:

(a) The total life of the firm.
(b) One year in the firm's life.

2.7 A firm borrows £10 000 on 1 January. During January it buys goods for £6000 and sells half of them for £5000. All transactions are in cash, and the firm has no other assets or liabilities. What is the net worth of the firm at 1 January and at 31 January? What is its profit for the month? Show that it is possible to calculate the profit in two ways – i.e., by using either a stock approach or a flow approach.

2.8

(a) Prepare a balance sheet from the following information, which is for the Barratt company as at 30 June 19X3:

	£
Creditors	5000
Debtors	6000
Stock	4000
Bank Overdraft	2000
Machinery	5000
Buildings	4000

(b) The Barratt company has been in business for two years only. It started on 1 July 19X1 with £4000 cash borrowed from the bank. On 30 June 19X2 it had stock of £2000, debtors £3000, machinery £4000 and a bank overdraft £2000.
   What was the company's profit for each of its first two years?

2.9 Using Figure 2.11 as a basis, construct balance sheets for the sports shop at the beginning of the first year and at the end of the first year.

2.10 What difference would it make to the sports shop balance sheet at the end of year one and the profit and loss account for the year if the shop:

(a) Had £8000 of unsold sports equipment?
(b) Had sold all of its sports equipment during the year?

2.11 If the sales for the sports shop in year two amount to £55 000 and the sports equipment purchased was £16 000, prepare a profit and loss account for year two and a balance sheet at the end of year two, assuming:

(a) That the unsold stock at the end of year one was £6000 and at the end of year two was £5000.

(b) That there was no unsold stock at the end of year one or year two.

2.12 Calculate the profit for the year ended 31 December 19X2 from the following information;

(a)

	1 January 19X2	31 December 19X2
Property	10000	10000
Machinery	5000	7000
Debtors	2000	5000
Cash	1000	2000
Overdraft	4000	5000
Creditors	3000	2000

(b) The owner withdrew £3500 during 19X2.

(c) Additional capital introduced by the owner during 19X2 was £4000.

3
The Structure of Accounting Data

3.1 Introduction

The application of the concepts of value in Chapters 1 and 2 relied on the ability of the firm to collect data to provide evidence for increases or decreases in its value or net worth. The preparation of such financial statements as the balance sheet and profit and loss account in order to show this data in a coherent manner is an integral part of accounting. The accounting concepts on which these statements are prepared were introduced in Chapter 2, and are examined further in Chapter 5. Chapter 3 now examines some of the **procedures for their preparation**.

It has been emphasised that because of the accounting concepts used in the accounting framework, not all economic events will be reflected in the balance sheet and profit and loss account. This in turn implies that the preparation of these statements will be based mainly on an analysis of **historical data** which reflects original costs and the benefits from past transactions. Chapter 3 examines some of the interrelationships between assets, liabilities and owners' equity first introduced in Chapter 1, and Chapter 4 provides an examination of the problems of processing accounting information for preparation of the profit and loss account and balance sheet.

3.2 The accounting equation

The analysis of procedures for the preparation of financial statements will begin by considering some simple transactions and their effect on the firm. If we assume for simplicity that the first resource that a firm receives is cash, we can see that the effect on the financial position of the firm is twofold. Not only does the firm now own an **asset** – namely the cash – but it has also established a relationship with the person **from whom the cash came**: the provider of the cash can be thought of as having a **claim against the firm**. This twofold effect on accounting data is termed 'duality'. If the cash was provided by one of the firm's owners, the owner would have a financial interest in the firm equal to the amount of cash. It is conventional to refer to this as the owner(s)' claim or owners' equity. Although the owner now has a claim against the firm it is not normally termed a liability because of the restricted legal claims which owners have against a firm's assets. If the cash was obtained by borrowing, the firm would owe the lender that sum; the lender's interest in the firm would be a **liability**. The underlying contrast in these different forms of providing a business's assets are discussed in Chapter 10. At this stage, it is sufficient to note that the firm will find it useful to distinguish between the qualitatively different relationships of owners (owners' equity) and lenders (liabilities).

Chapter 1 (Sect. 1.8) introduced the concept of the 'accounting equation', i.e.:

Assets = Liabilities + Owners' Equity

It was explained that the traditional meaning of these terms[1] is:

Assets	– Resources **owned or controlled** by the organisation; the assets also represent the use made of available funds or resources
Liabilities	– Obligations **owed** by the organisation; liabilities also represent details of the providers of funds or resources
Owners' Equity	– The accounting measure of the **interest of the owner(s)** in the organisation; this also represents details of funds or resources provided by the owner(s) either by a direct injection of cash or by not withdrawing profits earned by the organisation.

The above definitions emphasise the concept of **duality** already referred to. This derives from the inclusion in the equation of both the provision of resources (liabilities and owners' equity) and the uses to which the resources are put (assets). This explains why a balance sheet **balances**. In effect, the balance sheet lists the same resources twice (i.e., **provision** and **use**). It also provides the basis for the system of **double-entry book-keeping** which is used throughout the world and which will be explained further in this Chapter and Chapter 4.

The following sections illustrate the contribution of duality and the accounting equation in the analysis of accounting information.

3.3   Examples of analysis using the accounting equation

In Sects 3.3, 3.4 and 3.5 we will examine the relationship between assets, liabilities and owners' equity and we will see how their respective values change as a result of a firm's transactions. Examples 3.1, 3.2 and 3.3 provide an initial illustration of simple transactions and their implications for assets, liabilities and owners' equity. We will see how accounting information which is collected about changes in value is reflected in accounting statements.

Example 3.1 Changes in Assets and Owners' Equity
Cotton Company commences business on 1 January 19X1, and the owner immediately provides £5000 in cash. The balance sheet for the firm at the end of 1 January would be:

Balance Sheet Cotton Company at End of 1 January 19X1

	£
Assets	
Cash	5000
Total Assets	£5000
Owners' Equity	
Capital	5000
Total Owners' Equity	£5000

We can see from this example the duality effect, and how the analysis maintains the equality of the accounting equation. The owners' equity on commencing business is described as capital (see Sect. 3.4). It is convenient to continue our analyses by using the data and balance sheet of Ex.3.1

Example 3.2 Changes in Assets and Liabilities
On 2 January Cotton Company borrows £9000 in cash from the bank as an interest-free loan, which is provided on the same day. This information could be reflected in a revised balance sheet:

Balance Sheet Cotton Company

	At End of 1 January 19X1	At End of 2 January 19X1
	£	£
Assets		
Cash	5000	14000
Total Assets	£5000	£14000
Liabilities		
Owed to bank	---	9000
	£5000	£5000
Owners' Equity		
Capital	£5000	£5000

In Ex.3.2 we can again see the duality effect operating, and that the equality of the accounting equation still holds.

The results of Exs 3.1 and 3.2 can be summarised as follows:

	Assets £	=	Liabilities £	+	Owner's Equity £
Ex.3.1	+5000	=			+5000
Ex.3.2	+9000	=	+9000		
Total	£+14000	=	£+9000		£+5000

There will clearly be a series of other combinations of changes which affect assets, liabilities and owners' equity, but the principles can be illustrated by considering a limited set of combinations.

Example 3.3   Changes in Assets Only
The following is a summary of the transactions of Cotton Company during the rest of January 19X1:

1. Pays £3000 in cash for stock.
2. Lends £2000 in cash to Mr Morris as an interest-free loan.

The balance sheet for the end of the month can now be calculated as:

Balance Sheet Cotton Company

	At End of 2 January 19X1 £	Transactions £	£	At End of 31 January 19X1 £
Assets				
Cash	14000	−3000	−2000	9000
Stock		+3000		3000
Debtors			+2000	2000
	£14000			£14000
Liabilities				
Owed to bank	9000	no change		9000
Owners' Equity				
Initial	5000	no change		5000
	£14000			£14000

The transactions in Ex.3.3 alter the amounts of assets that are classified into particular categories: again we can see that the equality in the accounting equation is not changed.

3.4 Owners' equity

As explained already, the owners' equity represents the owners' interest in the firm – i.e., the **net worth**, or assets *less* liabilities. Figures 1.4 and 1.5 in Chapter 1 provided a simplified analysis of the change in net worth. This analysis is developed further in this section.

The changes in owners' equity over time can be classified into capital and profit changes such that:

Owners' Equity = Capital + Retained Profit

A firm will receive assets from its owners **at its inception**, and may periodically receive further assets from its owners **during its life**. These direct flows between the owners and the firm are normally termed 'capital inputs'. It is possible that assets which were formerly associated with capital inputs may be returned to the owners, perhaps when a firm no longer requires the assets, or ceases its activities. Although the term 'capital' has many uses in accounting we will restrict its use to this context.

The change in the value of the firm which is associated with changes in capital can be distinguished from the circumstances in which value changes as a result of earning a profit, or a loss. When the value of the assets and liabilities changes, to reflect profits or losses (see Sect. 1.8), the owners' equity will absorb the change. This analysis reflects contemporary legal, social and economic considerations as a result of which the owners' claim extends to **profit**. The legitimacy of the claim to all profit may be challenged when parties other than owners consider that all or part of the profits is available for their claim – e.g., employees in a profit-sharing scheme.

Clearly, then, the net worth of the firm will increase when profits are earned over time. The firm may decide to distribute part or all of the profits earned in a period to its owners. These distributions – termed 'dividends' in the case of companies – are **flows of assets from the firm to the owners**, and thus the owners' equity will be correspondingly **reduced**. The **retained profit** of a period is the excess of a period's profit over distributions; where a firm earns profits over several periods and not all are distributed the amount of retained profit for past and current periods will accumulate into the total retained profit. The net worth of a firm will thus consist of capital and retained profits for all periods in the past. In Chapter 10 we examine the factors which will affect a firm's decisions about its distributions of profit.

It is important to distinguish between capital and profit when a firm transfers assets to its owners, who must be able to decide whether they are receiving a **payment of capital** or a **distribution of profit**. This may be useful in their evaluation of the performance of the firm, in the same way that it is useful to distinguish between a bank deposit and its associated interest.

Furthermore, as a means of reassuring creditors that the owners have a continuing and non-withdrawable financial interest in a company, it is illegal for a company to **repay capital to shareholders**, except in liquidation. The separation of capital and retained profits is thus a legal disclosure requirement under UK company legislation. This apparently simple proposition gives rise to difficult theoretical and practical issues which are often discussed under the heading of '**capital maintenance**.' This concept is referred to again in Chapters 5, 10 and 14.

Some of the changes in net worth of a firm during an accounting period may thus be the result of capital introduced, profit earned and distributions made. The profit model first introduced in Sect. 1.7 must now be modified to:

$$C_t + (P_t - D_t) = V_t - V_{t-1}$$

rearranged to

$$P_t = V_t - V_{t-1} + D_t - C_t$$

where D_t and C_t are, respectively, the distributions and new capital for a period.

Where profit can be said to be equal to the change in value over a period, it is assumed that D and C are both zero.

Revenue and Expenses

Assuming that D and C are zero, the profit of a period is the net result of increases and decreases in the firm's assets *less* liabilities – i.e., its net worth. It is useful to separate the profit into those elements which cause **increases** (+), termed 'revenues', and those which cause **decreases** (–), termed 'expenses'.

Example 3.4   Revenues and Expenses
The following is a chronological summary of the transactions of Cotton Company during February 19X1:

1. Paid £6000 in cash for stock.
2. Received £12 000 in cash for selling all stock – i.e., opening stock and the month's purchases.
3. Paid £800 in cash to an assistant for working during February.

The balance sheet for the end of February could now be calculated:

Balance Sheet of Cotton Company

	At End of 31 January 19X1	Transaction			At End of 28 February 19X1
		1	2	3	
Assets	£	£	£	£	£
Cash	9000	−6000	+12000	−800	14200
Stock	3000	+6000	− 9000		—
Debtors	2000				2000
	£14000				£16200
Liabilities					
Owed to bank	9000				9000
Owners' Equity					
Capital	5000				£ 5000
Profit:					
Revenues (note 1)			+12000		= 12000
Expenses (note 1)			−9000	−800	= −9800
Retained (note 2)					2200
					7200
	£14000				£16200

Notes:

(1) Revenues are shown as positive (+) as they are increases in profits, and expenses are shown as negative (−) because they reduce profits.

(2) No profit is distributed during February and therefore all is retained.

It will be useful to examine these transactions in more detail, to see their effect on the firm's net worth.

Transaction 1 An exchange of assets: cash for stock, therefore **no change in net worth**.

Transaction 2 There are two aspects of this exchange: the generation of revenue of £12 000 which **increases** the assets and **increases** the profit (owners' equity) and the use of stock, an expense which **reduces the assets** and the profit (owners' equity).

Figure 3.1 illustrates the two-directional flow.

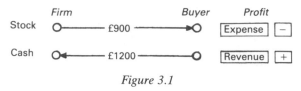

Figure 3.1

Transaction 3 The cash payment of £800 for wages was in exchange for the resource of labour provided by the assistant; if it is assumed that this payment related to services for February only, there would be no further services owing to the firm at the end of February, and hence no assets at that time. The value of the firm's assets would thus **fall by £800** during February.

We can see within the balance sheet of 28 February that the excess of revenues over expenses is £2200 (all retained within the firm, as no distribution of profit was made). In this example we have summarised the increases and decreases of profit within the balance sheets, information about the causes of changes in profit would however, normally be sufficiently important and contain enough items to warrant a **separate profit statement**, which would show details of the calculation of the £2200 retained profit.

To indicate that this approach to calculation of profit is identical in principle to that described in Chapter 1, we can calculate valuations at two points in time. Using the data from Ex.3.4 we can see that:

$$P = V(28 \text{ Feb } 19X1) - V(31 \text{ Jan } 19X1), \text{ with } D \text{ and } C \text{ as nil}$$

$$P = (£16\ 200 - £9000) - (£14\ 000 - £9000)$$

$$P = £7200 - £5000$$

$$P = £2200$$

However, if the profit of £2200 was calculated in this manner in practice it would not provide sufficient information about the **causes of the changes in value** of the firm during February 19X1.

Although the previous process of profit computation may appear a routine arithmetical manipulation, the **conceptual framework of accounting** has been used implicitly in limiting our analysis to information which is considered **relevant for purposes of profit computation and valuation of net worth**. The data in Ex.3.4 thus reflects those historical events which are considered as falling within the accounting framework, and ignores other information which might have been relevant for valuation purposes had some of the other concepts of value been applied – e.g., alternative uses for the stock which were foregone, or the effect of the transactions on the reputation of the firm.

3.5 Assets and expenses

Sect. 3.5 analyses the inherent relationship between the **assets** and **expenses** of a firm. In Chapter 1 we saw that a major problem of valuation of assets was in estimating the extent to which a firm would derive **future benefits** from owning an asset. The discussion of Figure 2.5 showed that measurement was easy if a sufficiently long period was taken over which to calculate profit; this is because all asset lives would have ended within the period, and there would be no need to estimate future benefits. In Sect. 3.4 the process of profit calculation involved, *inter alia*, the valuation of assets. Where assets fall in value over time, this fall is a **reduction in profit**. As was explained there, the reduction in the profit of a firm is termed an **expense**.

For certain assets – whose useful life for the firm is longer than the period over which profit is measured – it will be necessary to calculate an **interim valuation** for the asset at points in time between acquisition and disposal. For example, if a firm acquires a van which it expects to use for three years, and it wishes to calculate its profit annually, it will be required to value the van after one year to enable it to calculate its profit for the first year. The fall in value of the van during this first year is an expense of the firm during the first year of the van's ownership.

Other types of assets which the firm acquires – such as the assistant's commitment to work in Ex.3.4 – may be without value at the end of the period over which profits are calculated. Where assets are acquired and used up within the period, no asset exists at the end of the period for which profit is measured. Because of this, the payment is considered as an expense **at the time of payment**. This latter treatment is essentially a shortened form of analysis; at the time the payment is made (let us assume for simplicity it is payment in advance for wages) an asset exists in the form of a requirement by the assistant to provide future service. A balance sheet prepared at that point would thus consider the wages paid as an asset. The period of time over which profit was calculated in Ex.3.4 was of such a length that the asset was completely used up by the end of the period. The analysis thus recognised the payment of £800 wages as an expense rather than as an asset which later became an expense. This can be shown as:

	Assistant's Wages
Underlying flow	Payment ------------> Asset --------> Expense
Assumed flow	Payment ----------------------------- > Expense

There are many transactions which are often recognised as expenses at the time of payment (e.g., rent, wages and salaries and insurance premiums).

The accounting concepts discussed in Chapter 5 provide some additional guidance on the accounting analysis of a firm's acquisition of assets. A firm may incur costs (as payments or accruals) in exchange for expected future benefits which may not be classified as assets in the valuation of net worth because of the accounting concepts used. These costs may thus be considered as expenses when incurred, rather than as assets. Some examples discussed in later chapters are costs of research and development (Chapter 6) and costs of production (Chapter 7).

Costs classified as long lived assets are sometimes termed 'capital expenditure' by accountants, and those which are classified as expense are 'revenue expenditure'.

It has now been established that the relationship between assets and expenses is that the cost of most assets will eventually become expenses. The initial classification of costs will depend on the length of time over which profit is being calculated, and the application of the accounting concepts.

3.6   Analysis of accounting data for financial statements

The processes adopted so far in this chapter for measuring the effect of the firm's transactions during an accounting period have required the calculation of a new balance sheet, through the addition and subtraction of amounts from the previous balance sheet. This method as presented in Ex.3.4 will become increasingly difficult as the number of transactions to be processed increases. In Ex.3.5 a more complex problem is considered, where the number of transactions precludes the methods of Ex.3.4. As a more useful and generally applicable alternative to representing the effects of transactions horizontally, a **vertical** system is adopted. This change in the system helps to solve the problem of processing data, and does not require any changes in the principles previously established.

Example 3.5
Crisp Company commenced business on 1 July 19X1, and the following transactions occurred during July:

Transaction	Date	Description
1	1	Received £10 000 in cash from owners
2	2	Purchased van for £6000 in cash
3	8	Purchased stock for £2000 in cash
4	10	Sold all stock for £3000 in cash
5	12	Paid £500 in cash for clerical labour
6	20	Purchased stock for £5000 in cash
7	23	Sold all stock for £8000 in cash
8	27	Purchased stock for £5000: £2000 in cash and £3000 to be paid in August

9   31   £1000 paid in cash to the owners of the firm as part of the estimated profit for July

Notes:

(1) The van's useful life is estimated as five years, and will have no sale value at that time, and will be disposed of.
(2) The firm owes £500 for the rent of the shop which it used during July.

As in Ex.3.4 we can calculate the profit for July by an analysis of the transactions of the firm, and by using the other information which the firm may have available to enable it to carry out its valuation procedures. In this simple example we are using the analysis developed in Chapter 2. In practice, an accountant would need to apply the accounting concepts which are described in detail in Chapter 5. This information can be systematically processed as shown in Figure 3.2.

The two-part analysis indicates that the process of profit calculation involves an initial analysis of the **transactions data**, followed by inspection of – and recalculation through an analysis of – any **adjustments** to the valuation of assets and liabilities so calculated, to establish whether they conform with all the accounting concepts. In terms of Ex.3.5, the total valuations given to assets after the transactions' analysis proposes a valuation of £6000 for the van and £12 000 for the stock. Liabilities are also understated by £500 at this stage. The adjustments' stage reflects the application of accounting concepts in the form of adjustments to the primary data.

Explanation of the Analysis in Ex.3.5

Each transaction or adjustment was analysed to show the effect on the various classifications within the accounting equation. If the processing of the data has been arithmetically correct the **equality of the accounting equation** will hold. This accuracy is illustrated by the check total.

The separation of the effects on individual categories of assets, liabilities, or owners' equity as shown in the columns (or accounts) in Figure 3.2 is the basis of what is termed the **accounts of a firm**. The nature of the accounts and the accounting systems for processing data are examined in Chapter 4. In Ex.3.5 we assumed that the Crisp Company had just commenced business and there were no assets, liabilities or owners' equity at the beginning of the period. In the subsequent period the starting point of the analysis will be the amounts of assets, liabilities and owners' equity at the end of the previous period.

Transactions Analysis

Analysis of transactions 1 to 9 in Ex.3.5 can be understood with the knowledge of the accounting equation previously established. Further explanation may be useful for transactions 4 and 7: the receipt of cash in both transactions is an increase in the assets of the firm and the revenue (owners' equity). The stock expense of generating this revenue is calculated as adjustment 1. In practice this procedure may be necessary because the expense is not known at the time of sales (see Chapter 7). The £1000 distribution of profit of transaction 9 is not considered as an expense of the firm, but rather as a payment to owners which reduces their claims against the firm. A full analysis of the accounting data from Ex.3.5 is given in Figure 3.2.

Adjustments Analysis

The need for **end of period adjustments** was first introduced in Chapter 2 (Sect. 2.3 and Figure 2.8). The adjustments recognise that some assets **no longer exist** (in an accounting sense) or that some assets should be **revalued**. The various accounting concepts explained in Chapter 5 are used in practice to make these adjustments.

Adjustment 1 The stock obtained in transaction 8 is still available, and, as an asset, will be included in the balance sheet. Stock acquired in transactions 3 and 6 (£2000 + £5000 = £7000) has been used up and is hence an **expense**. Further discussion of the flow of costs in stock follows in Chapter 7. This adjustment **reclassified the asset as an expense** – i.e., cost of sales.
Adjustment 2 The van purchased under transaction 2 was estimated to have a life of five years. It is assumed that one month later the van has an estimated life of five years less one month; 1/60 of its life will have expired, and hence 1/60 of its original cost of £6000 is an expense of July 19X1 – i.e., £100. This type of expense is termed '**depreciation**'. Further discussion follows in Chapter 6.
Adjustment 3 The firm owes £500 for rent: as benefits have flowed from renting the shop, even though they have not been paid for, there is an **expense flow** though there is no **associated cash payment**. The opposite treatment is necessary for **prepayments**.

3.7 Presentation of the balance sheet

The numbers used in the balance sheet below correspond with the totals of the columns presented in Figure 3.2.

   The presentation of balance sheets that are clear and informative is important for the process of **communicating** accounting information to the **users** of financial statements. There is no universally accepted standard way of pre-

	Assets				= Liabilities + Owners' Equity		Profit (see note 1)		
	Cash	Van	Stock		Creditor	Capital	Revenue	Expense	Distribution
Transaction									
1	+10000					+10000			
2	−6000	+6000							
3	−2000		+2000						
4	+3000						+3000		
5	−500							−500	
6	−5000		+5000						
7	+8000						+8000		
8	−2000		+5000		+3000				
9	−1000								−1000
Sub-total	+4500	+6000	+12000	=	+3000	+10000	+11000	−500	−1000
Adjustments									
1			−7000					−7000	
2		−100						−100	
3					+500			−500	
Total	+4500	+5900	+5000	=	+3500	+10000	+11000	−8100	−1000

Check total

$$+15400 = +3500 + 11900$$
$$+15400 = +15400$$

(Profit: Revenue +11000 and Expense −8100 bracketed = +2900)

Figure 3.2

Note: (1) The negative sign attached to expenses and distributions under this system of processing indicates that they are reductions in owners' equity.

Financial accounting

senting information in the financial statements, but the terminology and structure of the examples shown below are typical of those in common use. The UK Companies Acts specify a standard format to be followed for financial statements that are required to be published annually in the UK (see Sect. 5.4 for the meaning of 'published'). Details of this standard format are given in Chapter 11.

Two alternative presentations of the data from Ex.3.5 are given below:

Horizontal Presentation

Though historically the most popular form, this form of presentation is frequently now being replaced by a vertical form.

Balance Sheet of Crisp Company at 31 July 19X1

	£	£		£	£
Owners' Equity			*Fixed Assets*		
Capital	10000		Van at Cost (note 1)	6000	
Retained profit	1900		*Less* Accumulated Depreciation	100	
		11900			5900
Long Term liabilities		---			
Current Liabilities (note 3)			*Current Assets* (note 2)		
Creditors		3500	Stock	5000	
			Cash	4500	
					9500
		£15400			£15400

Note:

    1. For notes on the balance sheet, See p. 47/48.

Vertical Presentation

Presentation of the balance sheet vertically is now widely adopted, as comprehension of data so presented is considered easier.

Balance Sheet of Crisp Company at 31 July 19X1

	£	£
Fixed Assets		
Van at Cost (note 1)	6000	
Less Accumulated Depreciation	100	
		5900
Current Assets (note 2)		

	£		
Stock	5000		
Cash	4500		
		9500	
Current Liabilities (note 3)			
Creditors		3500	
Net Current Assets			6000
			11900
Long Term Liabilities (note 4)			---
			£11900
Financed by			
Owners' Equity			
Capital		10000	
Retained Profit		1900	
			£11900

Terms used in Balance Sheets

A brief summary of some of the terms used in balance sheets will be useful at this state.

Term	Definition	Examples	Considered further in Chapter
Fixed asset	Asset acquired by firm for use rather than sale	Buldings Machinery	6

continued

Term	Definition	Examples	Considered further in Chapter
Current Asset	Asset acquired by firm, but retained for short periods, conventionally up to one year	Stock Cash	7
Current Liabilities	A liability which will normally be repaid within a short period, conventionally one year	Wages payable	9
Net Current Assets	Assets and liabilities which are frequently changing – i.e., current assets *less* current liabilities: sometimes known as working capital		9 12 13
Long Term Liability	A liability which will normally be repayable after more than one year	Five year loan	10

Notes on Presentation

(1) The **original cost** and the **accumulated depreciation** associated with fixed assets are shown **separately**. The accumulated depreciation is the amount of the asset treated as an expense up to the date of the balance sheet. The balance sheet will then show which assets have been depreciated. By examination of the balance sheet it may then be possible to obtain an estimate of the **age structure** of the fixed assets, and perhaps gauge the extent of the assets' **future usefulness**.

(2) The sequence of current assets is in order of **increasing liquidity** (closeness of conversion into cash); **current** assets are separated from **fixed** assets.

(3) **Current** liabilities are separated from **long-term** liabilities.

(4) If this company did have long-term liabilities they would be deducted from the £11 900 to give the firm's net worth.

The type of presentation chosen should be based on an understanding of the **needs of users** of the financial statement. The **format** of statements will vary greatly, according to whether they are for use within the firm by its management, or are for external users such as shareholders. As stated above, where statements are published they have to satisfy the legal reporting requirements laid down by the Companies Acts. Chapters 5 and 11 explain further the factors which determine the form and content of financial statements. An example of a published balance sheet is included in Appendix B.

3.8 Presentation of the profit and loss account

The analysis of profit in Figure 3.2 does not reveal sufficiently clearly the **causes** and **details** of revenues and expenses. The profit and loss account is an additional statement which is usually provided to give an analysis and presentation of this information.

The revenue, expense and distribution data from Figure 3.2 can be formed into a profit and loss account by rearranging the relevant items.

Profit and loss account of Crisp Company for One Month Ended 31 July 19X1

	£	£	Notes
Sales Revenue		11000	
Less Cost of Sales (stock expense)		7000	
Gross Profit		4000	(1)
Less Other Expenses:	£		
Clerical	500		
Depreciation	100		
Rent	500		
		1100	
Net Profit		2900	
Distributions		1000	(2)
Retained Profit		1900	
Retained Profit from Previous Periods		-----	
		£1900	

The classification used in the profit and loss account will depend on the proposed use of the report. In Chapter 4 we discuss the problems of classification of accounting data, and Chapter 11 explains the relevant format required by the UK Companies Acts.

Notes on Presentation

(1) The terms 'gross' and 'net' profit are used to distinguish between different categories and classifications of profit, the former **after deduction of the cost of sales**, and the latter **after other expenses have been deducted**.

(2) The profit retained from previous periods is often most conveniently incorporated into a period's profit statement, so that we can show the effect on the **cumulative retained profits** of a period's profits and dividend. The total of retained profit for the period and the previous periods will be part of the owners' equity in the balance sheet. As Crisp Company commenced business in the period under consideration, there was no retained profit from the previous periods.

Comparison With the Financial Statements of Marks and Spencer

It will be useful at this stage to examine the statements shown in Appendix B (pp. 319–49).

3.9 Profit and cash flow

Sect. 2.4 analysed the difference between the measurement of profit and the underlying cash flow for the example in Sect. 2.3. It may be useful to an understanding of the nature of profit to compare again the **amount of a firm's profit** with the **flow of cash into and out of the firm**. The cash flow of a firm can be measured by the comparison of the cash position at the beginning and the end of a period of time. The **cash flow into** the firm will normally comprise the receipt of cash from owners, lenders, and those who purchase the firm's goods and services. The **cash flow out** of the firm will be the payments of cash for assets and expenses provided to the firm, payments to the creditors, and also any distribution of profit or capital to the owners.

The net cash flow of Crisp Company during July 19X1 can be calculated as:

	£
Cash at commencement of business	Nil
Cash on 31 July	4500
Net cash flow **in** (into firm)	4500

An analysis of the cash transactions indicates:

Cash flow *in*	£	Cash flow *out*	£
From owners	10000*	Purchase of van	6000
From sales	3000	Purchase of stock	2000
From sales	8000	To obtain clerical services	500
		Purchase of stock	5000
		Purchase of stock	2000
		To owners; profit distribution	1000*
	£21000		£16500

The net cash flow is £4500 inward to the firm

Further examination reveals that:

	£	
Cash flow relating to capital and distribution of profit	+9000	(marked *)
Cash flow relating to operations	−4500	(all others)
Net Cash flow **in**	**£4500**	

The accounting profit was £2900; the difference of £7400 between profit (+£2900) and operations cash-flow (−£4500) could be explained thus:

	Transactions and Adjustments	Cash £	Profit £	Difference £
			Expenses	
Purchase of van	TR2 AD2	−6000	−100	−5900(1)
Purchase of stock	TR3 AD1	−2000	−2000	−
Clerical services	TR5	− 500	− 500	−
Purchase of Stock	TR6 AD1	−5000	−5000	−
Purchase of stock	TR8 AD1	−2000		−2000(2)
Rent	AD3		− 500	+500(3)
			Revenues	
Sales of stock	TR4	+3000	+3000	−
Sales of stock	TR7	+8000	+8000	−
		£−4500	£+2900	£−7400

Notes on Differences

(1) –£5900: this reflects the **unused future life of the van**, which the accounting concepts adopted recognised as an asset.
(2) –£2000: as this stock has future use, and thus value (because it can be sold to earn revenue), it will be an **asset**.
(3) +£500: the rent is included because **benefit has been received**, even though there has been no cash flow.

The importance of the relationship between these two measurements of the changes in the firm's position is that the measurement using accounting concepts gives a clearer guide to the total change in the value of the firm and includes **all the firm's assets**, while the cash flow position is closely related to a firm's **liquidity** – e.g., its ability to pay its creditors (see Chapters 10 and 13 for a fuller analysis). The performance of the firm must satisfy several criteria, and these two analyses have useful, though complementary, roles to play. An objective of the firm may be to earn profits, but it may also wish to maintain its liquidity. To provide a full measure of a firm's health, both liquidity and profitability are important.

3.10 Summary

Chapter 3 has provided an introduction to some of the problems of the analysis of financial information in preparing accounting statements. The selection of events which are of concern to the accountant is limited by the accounting concepts, at least in his evaluation of performance, although not in a decision-making context. Their effect can be analysed within the framework provided by the accounting equation. The format of accounting statements should be determined by the needs of users, as well as by convention or legal considerations. The problems of developing a system to process accounting data are examined in Chapter 4.

Note and Reference

1. See Note 5 to Chapter 1 on p. 11.

Questions and Problems

3.1 What do you understand by the following terminology?

Owners' equity	Revenue
Duality	Expense
Accounting information	Transaction
Capital	Adjustments
Retained profit	Accounts
Distribution	Fixed asset
Dividend	Current liability
Depreciation	Net current assets
Long term liability	Cost of sales
Working capital	Liquidity
Accumulated depreciation	Gross profit
Cash flow	Net profit
	Accounting equation

3.2 The following are transactions relating to Cram, a retailer for November 19X0:

(a) Commences business with £10 000 cash provided by Cram, the owner
(b) Uses £4000 cash to buy stock
(c) Borrows £7000 from the bank on an interest-free loan
(d) Buys £5000 of stock on credit
(e) Paid rent in cash £600 for November and December
(f) Cram withdraws £2000 in cash for his own use
(g) Sells all stock on credit for £16 000

Analyse the information using the accounting equation and prepare a profit and loss account and balance sheet. Explain the relationship between the cash flow of the business and its profit or loss for November 19X0

3.3 The following are transactions relating to Crow, a wholesaler, during January 19X1.

(a) Commences business with £4000 of his own cash, and £6000 borrowed at an interest rate of 12% per annum payable at the end of the year
(b) Purchases a van for the firm for £8000 on credit
(c) Purchases stock for resale for £4000 on credit
(d) Sells three-quarters of stock for £10 000, £5000 on credit and £5000 for cash
(e) Purchases stock for £2000 in cash
(f) Pays rent for first six months of £6000
(g) Pays wages of £1800 in cash, but in addition still owes £500 at the end of January.
(h) The depreciation expense for the van for the first month is £500
(i) Withdraws £600 as a share of the anticipated profit for January

Analyse this information using the accounting equation and prepare a profit statement and balance sheet. Explain the relationship between the cash flow of the firm and its profit for January 19X1.

3.4 Crab Ltd is already in business and has prepared its balance sheet and profit and loss account for 19X1. The following data has not been reflected in these statements. Explain what effect there would be on the profit and loss account and balance sheet if the data were included:

(a) Debtors are valued at £1000 in the balance sheet but 10% are expected to be unable to pay
(b) A vehicle is valued in the balance sheet at £600 but its resale value is nil
(c) The firm owes £200 for purchases of goods which it did not use during 19X1
(d) £586 was entered in the 'cash' and 'revenue' accounts for a transaction in error; the correct data is a credit sale of £865

3.5 Should a company be required to have a permanent minimum amount of capital?
3.6 An accountant values a firm at two points in time:

$$V_0 \text{ £1000} \qquad V_1 \text{ £1500}$$

What assumptions are necessary to calculate the profit for the period? If you were informed that £300 new capital had been introduced and distributions were £200, would this affect your calculations?
3.7 What criteria should determine the format of the balance sheet and profit statements?
3.8 'The owners' equity concept is redundant in the analysis of the accounts of nationalised industries and local authorities.' Do you agree?
3.9 On 1 January 19X1, J. Wall used his savings of £25 000 to open a shop. He transferred his £25 000 to a business bank account and on 2 January bought equipment for the shop for £4000 and a van for £10 000. He did not maintain proper accounts but he provides you with the following information relating to his situation on 31 December 19X1:

(a) He has a stock of goods which cost £4000
(b) Customers owed him £3000
(c) The balance on the business bank account was £15 000
(d) He owed suppliers £5000 for goods purchased.
(e) He owed £500 rent to his landlord.
(f) His rates which are £200 a month have been paid up to 31 March 19X2.
(g) It was agreed that the shop equipment should be valued at £3500 and the van at £7500.
(h) Mr Wall had withdrawn £4500 for his own use during the year

Required:

(i) Show the calculation of profit for 19X1.
(ii) Produce the accounting equation as at 31 December 19X1.

3.10 B. Robson opened a sports shop and invested his world cup bonus of £5000 in it. Shown below is a summary of the activities for September, the first month of business.

(a) Robson opened a business bank account and put £5000 in it
(b) He paid September's rent on the shop of £200

(c) He bought a small computer for £1400 (cash) for use in the shop
(d) He bought the following goods for resale:

  – 50 pairs of football boots for £10 each (by cheque)
  – 10 squash rackets for £20 each (by cheque)
  – 10 pairs of running shoes for £30 each (on credit)

(e) He sold all the football boots for a total of £1000 cash
He sold all the squash rackets for a total of £300 cash
He had not sold any of the running shoes by the end of the month
(f) Robson drew £180 from the bank for his own use
(g) At the end of the month Robson had not yet paid for the running shoes he had purchased; he also owed £100 for the rates on the shop for the month

  Required: Show the accounting equation for the end of September.

3.11

(a) On 1 October 19X3, Fred Green decides to open a fruit and vegetable stall. He uses his life savings of £3000 to start the business.

  Required: Set up an accounting equation to represent the above. (identify his capital and his assets).

(b) On 2 October Mr Green uses some of his £3000 to buy a stall and stock of fruit and vegetables for resale. The stall cost £2000 and the fruit and vegetables £750. He drew £50 out of the bank for petty cash and left the rest in the bank.

  Question: Does the accounting equation in (a) need amending, if so, show revised equation.

(c) At the end of his first day's trading (3 October) he has sold half of his fruit and vegetables in return for cash receipts of £500.

  Required: Show Fred Green's position at the end of 3 October by means of the accounting equation.
  Identify the change in net assets from 2 to 3 October.
  Identify the profit made on 3 October.

(d) Mr Green decides to celebrate his first day's trading so he withdraws £60 out of cash receipts and takes his wife out to dinner

  Question: How does this affect the accounting equation?
(e) Consider Mr Green's activities and draw parallels with those shown in the Marks and Spencer accounts in Appendix B.

4
The Processing of Accounting Data

4.1 Introduction

Chapter 4 continues the analysis of the preparation of accounting statements begun in Chapter 3. The discussions of Chapter 3 involved an underlying assumption that the data required in the accounting process was available in the **necessary form**, and with **sufficient frequency**. We will see now that the required data will emerge from an **information system** which is designed to enable us to prepare the financial statements. An information system has **three** identifiable components – data **collection**, data **processing**, and data **communication** – and it is in this form that we will examine methods of translating accounting data into financial statements. We begin by considering the most widely used method of analysis of accounting data.

4.2 Double-entry book-keeping

The double-entry book-keeping system has long been considered as the central and most important procedure for processing accounting data. The term 'double-entry' is an alternative term for the idea of duality described in Chapter 3: the **twofold** effect on the firm of **transactions** (and **adjustments**). The reference to the term 'book-keeping' is, however, perhaps now an anachronism; the processing of accounting data with the use of books and clerks which was the forerunner of the modern accounting system has largely been replaced by mechanical and electronic techniques. However despite this, the term continues to be used both in the UK and elsewhere.

Procedures

The procedures of double-entry book-keeping require the same analysis of transactions and adjustments as was outlined in Chapter 3. These could formally be stated as:

(a) The identification of which **components** of the accounting equation are affected: assets, liabilities or owners' equity?
(b) The identification of which **classification** within a component is affected: e.g., within assets – cash?; within owners' equity – sales revenue? The individual classification is usually known as an 'account' or a 'ledger account'
(c) The identification of the direction of **change** in an account – i.e., an increase or a decrease?

The account referred to in (b) is a detailed analysis of the results of transactions and adjustments relating to that classification: the **accounts of a firm** are central to any accounting system.

In a double-entry book-keeping system an account is not usually represented by a column as in the solution to Ex.3.5, but by a column divided down its centre; this is termed a 'T' account, because of its physical similarity to the letter 'T'. As shown in Figure 4.1 the description of the classification that the T account represents is written along the top of the T. The account will show a detailed analysis of all **increases** and **decreases** of the **relevant classification**.

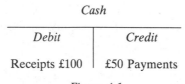

Cash

Debit	Credit
Receipts £100	£50 Payments

Figure 4.1

Increases or decreases in an account are denoted by entering the details and amount of the transaction on either the left or right, according to a set of rules explained below. These are not normally presented or thought of as a set of rules, but as we are considering a systematic approach to the analysis of transactions it is useful to consider them in this way.

Rules for Recording Transactions and Adjustments in Accounts

The rules of double-entry book-keeping are best understood in relation to the accounting equation:

Assets = Liabilities + Owners' Equity

It should be explained that in our presentation of the accounting equation the assets have been shown on the left of the equation and liabilities and owners' equity on the right. This is arbitrary and the validity of the equation would not be reduced by reversing the sides. However, it is useful to show the equation as above because it helps in the explanation of the book-keeping rules which are themselves arbitrary.

> *Rule 1* Entries on the left side of any account are termed 'Debits' (commonly abbreviated to **Dr**) and entries on the right side are termed 'Credits' (commonly abbreviated to **Cr**).

As was stated above, this is an arbitrary rule which is followed world-wide but which could operate equally successfully by having debits on the right and credits on the left. It is similar to the UK rule that cars must drive on the left side of the road: it is arbitrary but it works because we obey the rule.

> *Rule 2* Increases in the values of the various assets, liabilities and owners' equity accounts are entered on the side of the T accounts **corresponding to their side in the accounting equation** – i.e., increases in assets on the left, increases in liabilities and owners equity on the right.

> *Rule 3* Decreases in the value of the various asset, liability and owners' equity accounts are entered on the side of the T account **opposite to their side in the accounting equation** – i.e., decreases in assets on the right and decreases in liabilities and owners' equity on the left.

Summary of Entries in Accounts From Rule 1.2 and 3

Assets	= Liabilities + Owners' Equity
Left (Debit)	*Right (Credit)*
Increase in assets	Increase in liabilities,
Decrease in liabilities	Increase in owners' equity
Decrease in owners' equity	Decrease in assets

We have seen in Sect. 3.4 that owners' equity consists of the capital provided directly by the owners plus the profit earned and left in the business by the owners, i.e.:

Owners' equity = Capital + Profit – Distributions

We also saw in Sect. 3.4 that profit is the net result of increases termed 'revenues' and decreases termed 'expenses'. We can thus now restate the above equation as:

Owners' Equity = Capital + Revenue – Expenses – Distributions

and by substituting this into the basic accounting equation:

Assets = Liabilities + Capital + Revenue – Expenses – Distributions

We also saw in Sect. 3.5 that assets and expenses are derived from similar activity – i.e., the use of resources to acquire benefit for the firm. The difference between assets and expenses is simply one of the **timing of when the benefits are used up**. Similarly distributions are using resources of the firm by returning them to the owners. Because of this we can finally adjust the equation to show:

Assets + Expenses + Distributions = Liabilities + Capital + Revenue

Representing:

Use of Resources   = Sources of Resources

The representation of the accounting equation showing the **sources** of resources made available to the organisation on one side balanced by the **uses** to which those resources are put on the other side may be helpful in justifying and explaining the similar treatment of the three items on the left and the three items on the right. The idea of sources and uses of resources will be developed further in other chapters, particularly Chapter 12.

We can now repeat the summary of entries in accounting from Rules 1, 2 and 3:

Assets + Expenses + Distributions = Liabilities + Capital + Revenue

Left (Debit)	*Right (Credit)*
Increase in assets	Decrease in assets
Increase in expenses	Decrease in expenses
Increase in distribution	Decrease in distribution
Decrease in liabilities	Increase in liabilities
Decrease in capital	Increase in capital
Decrease in revenue	Increase in revenue

Supplementary Rules

Rules 4 and 5 are an explanation of the **consequences** that flow from applying Rules 1–3:

Rule 4 For each recorded transaction or adjustment the **total value of the debits will equal the total value of the credits**. Without this rule the accounting equation would not maintain its equality. This in turn constitutes one of the strengths of the double-entry system – it is **self-balancing** provided Rule 4 is followed. Failure to follow the rule is one of the common reasons why students have difficulty in producing balance sheets which 'balance'.

Rule 5 The 'balance' on an account is the **numerical difference between the sum of the debit entries and the sum of the credit entries**. If the sum of the debit entries exceed the sum of the credit entries the account is said to have a *debit balance*, or a *credit balance* if the sum of the credit entries is higher.

Because of the application of Rules 2 and 3:

Asset, expense and distribution accounts will have **Debit balances**

and

Liability, capital and revenue accounts will have **Credit balances**

Two examples of accounts, one with a debit balance and the other with a credit balance are shown below:

Cash				*Creditors*			
Dr			Cr	Dr			Cr
Receipts 100		Payments	50	Cash Payment 50		Purchases	200
" 200		"	150	" 150		"	300
" 300						"	250
£600			£200	£200			£750
Balance £400				Balance			£550

Cash, being an asset account, is increased by debiting it with cash receipts, and decreased by crediting it when cash is paid out leaving a cash balance of £400 in the account.

The creditors'[1] account is increased by crediting it with purchases made on credit and reduced by debiting it with cash payments made to creditors, leaving a balance of £550 which represents a liability owed to the firms creditors.

Note that it is necessary to distinguish between a debit or a credit entry **in** an account and a debit or a credit balance **on** that account. Every account may contain both debit and credit entries, but each account will have only **one balance**. Whether it is a debit or credit balance will depend on what type of account it is.

The Use of Double-entry Procedure and T Accounts

The use of T accounts and the rules of double-entry offer us many advantages over the method of processing data discussed in Chapter 3. In industrial or commercial accounting it will be necessary to provide classifications of assets, liabilities and owners' equity into many accounts to produce useful accounting statements. Furthermore it is necessary to control the processing of information to ensure accuracy in the data and to eliminate as far as possible the need for correction of errors. Large volumes of data will often be processed by many methods within an organisation, and control becomes more difficult as the operation of the accounting system becomes decentralised.

The procedures we have explained in this chapter will enable those responsible for preparing accounting statements to use as many accounts as they find necessary by creating (often termed '**opening**') a T account for each classification necessary. Where there is a large volume of data the tasks of entering (often termed '**posting**') data into particular accounts may be split up among several individuals – e.g., Mr A responsible for cash, Mr B for stock data. In modern data processing some of the accounts may be prepared by computer, and some by manual methods. All these requirements will make the procedures used in the previous chapter inappropriate as the system described there would not be sufficiently flexible to satisfy the demands that would be made on it, nor would **control of accuracy** be maintained. Increases in the volume of data and decentralisation of account preparation increase the likelihood of errors.

A major source of error may be where data is given an incorrect sign before it is entered in the accounts, such as could occur using the system of Chapter 3. In Chapter 3 we decided on the sign of a number in an account according to whether it was an increase or a decrease in assets, liabilities or owners' equity. Thus, for example, if we increased an asset (+) say by buying stock we could either decrease another asset (–) by paying cash or increase a liability (+) by buying on credit. Therefore:

+ followed by – is correct
+ followed by + is correct

It would not be possible for someone unskilled in understanding the accounting equation to tell whether a + entry should be followed by a + sign or a – sign unless he knew whether the first and second accounts were assets, liabilities or owners' equity. If instead of an unskilled human operator we substitute a machine such as a computer, then the same problem arises. This raises the possibility of error – e.g., a message such as: 'Cash + £50, Debtors + £50', which the unskilled person or machine would not recognise as incorrect unless it was known that both cash and debtors were assets.

The use of the term 'debit' and credit' in accordance with the rules of double-entry book-keeping acts as a filter to eliminate the errors referred to above. For any transaction (or adjustment) we will know that the sum of the debit entries into accounts will equal the sum of credit entries:

'Dr Cash £50, Cr £50 Debtors'
'Dr Cash £50, Cr £50 Creditors'

are correct messages. The incorrect message:

'Dr Cash £50, Dr Debtors £50'

would be immediately recognisable as incorrect by anyone, irrespective of their knowledge of the component of the accounting equation being altered. The elimination of this type of error is of considerable importance in an accounting system as the costs of correcting errors are high, and errors are difficult to identify in large and/or decentralised systems. It is equally important that the numerical accuracy of entries can be checked by calculating that the **total debit** and **total credit** entries for a transaction are **equal**. The correct application of the rules will not, of course, eliminate all errors from the system. The description of the procedures of double-entry book-keeping at the beginning of this section stated that it is first necessary to identify **which account is affected** by the transaction or adjustment, and then the **direction** in which the account is changed must also be identified. Some errors in the process of identification will not be automatically highlighted by the double-entry system. For example the purchase of machinery for £5850 cash should result in the accounting instruction:

Debit Machinery Account £5850
Credit Cash Account   £5850

Incorrect entries which will be automatically picked up by the system are:

Debit Machinery Account £5850
Debit Cash   £5850

or

Debit Machinery Account £5850
Credit Cash Account   £5550

But the following are examples of entries which are incorrect but which will not upset the **self-balancing** nature of the system mentioned under Rule 4:

Debit Cash Account £5850
Credit Machinery Account   £5850

or

      Debit Machinery Account £5580
      Credit Cash Account   £5580

or

      Debit Machinery Account £5850
      Credit Creditors   £5850

In other words, the double-entry book-keeping system provides a system for processing large amounts of data. If the initial identification of the required accounting entries is correct the data can then be processed satisfactorily by unskilled operators or by machines such as computers.

4.3 Accounting systems

In the introduction to this chapter, we said that the accounting information system had three identifiable components: data collection, data processing and data communication. The double-entry book-keeping rules and procedures are essentially concerned with the **data processing stage**. In Sect. 4.4 we illustrate the application of these rules and procedures using the data from Ex.3.5. Before we do so, it will be useful to place this data processing stage in context by considering further an example of an accounting information system, such as depicted in Figure 4.2.

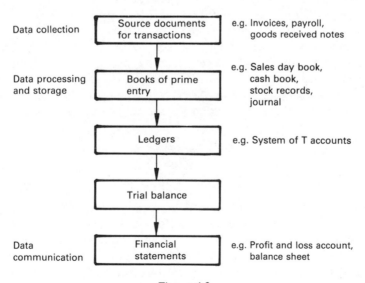

Figure 4.2

Data Collection

The term 'data collection' involves the **identification** of the information that is required and the means by which it is to be **collected**. In Sect. 1.3, it was emphasised that not all possible information about a business constitutes 'accounting information': the data to be collected in the accounting system will be determined by the contemporary definition of what constitutes 'accounting information'. The means by which the data is collected will vary from firm to firm, but it will typically include such items as **invoices**, **cheques**, **payroll** and **goods received notes**, some invoices being created externally and the others internally by the firm itself.

Data Processing and Storage

Data once collected will need to be **processed** in a form suitable to the needs of the potential users. The procedures explained in Sects 4.2 and 4.4 fall within the concept of data processing.

Storage of data is an important part of an information system. A firm will store data because it is not required immediately, and stored data may be **retrieved** and **updated** from time to time. From Figure 4.2 it can be seen that the data collected is originally stored in what is known as 'Books of prime entry'. These consist of listings and records of data on accounting transactions or adjustments organised into classifications useful to the firm. The books of prime entry are likely, for example, to include a 'Sales day book', which provides a daily listing of **sales invoices**, or a 'Cash receipts book', which (as the name suggests) lists details of **cash received each day**.

The books of prime entry store detailed information on these transactions which in a well designed system can be easily retrieved for audit and reference purposes. The information is then processed, using the rules from Sect. 4.2, into the **ledger accounts** which are central to any accounting recording system. The ledger accounts constitute a further means of storing accounting data, but in this case classified into accounts based on the **components of the accounting equation**. The trial balance shown in Figure 4.2 will be explained further in Sect. 4.4.

Data Communication

Data can be communicated in a variety of ways, the major determinant being the **requirements of the users of the data**. In this chapter we are concentrating on the use of financial statements – i.e., the balance sheet and profit and loss account – as a means of communicating accounting data about the firm. Accounting systems can, however, be used to communicate data in a variety of ways for a variety of purposes, such as the **planning** and **control** of an organisation.

4.4 Application of double-entry book-keeping procedures

In Sect. 4.4 we give an illustration of the data processing component of the accounting information system, by applying the double-entry book-keeping rules and procedures explained in Sect. 4.2 to the data in Ex.3.5. Before we process the data it will be useful to set out clearly the **steps in the process** to be followed.

(1) **Identify** transactions
(2) **Record** transactions in books of prime entry
(3) **Transfer** (or post) details of the transactions into relevant **ledger accounts**
(4) Periodically calculate the **balance on each ledger account**
(5) Prepare a **trial balance**
(6) Identify **end of year adjustments** (repeat stages (2), (3) and (4) to include adjustments)
(7) Prepare a **further trial balance**
(8) Use the trial balance in (7) as a basis for the preparation of the **profit and loss account** and **balance sheet**
(9) **Close** those accounts which apply only to the **current accounting period**

Step 1   Identify Transactions
The transactions to be used are those detailed in Ex3.5 which are for convenience repeated here:
   Crisp Company commenced business on 1 July 19X1, and the following transactions occurred during July:

Transaction	Date	Description
1	1	Received £10 000 in cash from owners
2	2	Purchased van for £6000 in cash
3	8	Purchased stock for £2000 in cash
4	10	Sold all stock for £3000 in cash
5	12	Paid £500 in cash for clerical labour
6	20	Purchased stock for £5000 in cash
7	23	Sold all stock for £8000 in cash
8	27	Purchased stock for £5000: £2000 in cash and £3000 to be paid in August
9	31	£1000 paid in cash to the owners of the firm as part of the estimated profit for July

Notes:
(1) The van's useful life is estimated as five years, and will have no sale value at that time, and will be disposed of.
(2) The firm owes £500 for the rent of the shop which it used during July.

Step 2   Record Transactions in Books of Prime Entry
The most common books of prime entry are:

Cash book
Sales day book[2]
Purchase day book[2]
Journal

In practice, the journal is used only for **unusual transactions** which are not covered by the other more frequently used 'day books'. However, the format of journal entries provides a useful way of explaining the basic elements of recording a transaction and they will be used in the example here and in others throughout the book. The typical format of a journal entry is

Date	Debit	Credit
Account to be debited	£xxx	
Account to be credited		£xxx

A brief **narrative** to explain the nature of the transaction (note that this narrative has **not** been included in the journal entries below).

Journal entries for transactions in Ex.3.5 will be:

19x1				Debit £	Credit £
July 1	TR1	Cash		10000	
		Capital			10000
2	TR2	Van		6000	
		Cash			6000
8	TR3	Stock		2000	
		Cash			2000
10	TR4	Cash		3000	
		Sales Revenue			3000
12	TR5	Clerical Expense		500	
		Cash			500
20	TR6	Stock		5000	
		Cash			5000
23	TR7	Cash		8000	
		Sales Revenue			8000
27	TR8	Stock		5000	
		Cash			2000
		Creditor			3000
31	TR9	Distribution		1000	
		Cash			1000

The journal entries have identified which accounts are **affected** by the transactions, and the **amounts to be debited or credited** according to Rules 1, 2 and 3. The **asset accounts** (cash, van,), clerical **expense** and **distribution** have been debited when they are to be increased and credited when they are to be decreased. The **liabilities** (creditors), **capital** and sales **revenue** have been credited to increase them and debited to decrease them.

Step 3   Transfer (post) the Journal Entries Relating to the Transactions into the Ledger Accounts

Step 4   Calculate the Balances on each Ledger Account
From the information in the journal entries we can see which accounts need to be **opened**, and these are shown below:

Assets

Cash

July 1	TR1	10000	July 2	TR2	6000
10	TR4	3000	8	TR3	2000
23	TR7	8000	12	TR5	500
			20	TR6	5000
			27	TR8	2000
			31	TR9	1000
		£21000			£16500
Balance		£4500			

Stock

July 8	TR3	2000
20	TR6	5000
27	TR8	5000
		£12000
Balance		12000

Van

July 2	TR2	6000
Balance		£6000

Liabilities

Creditors

	July 27	TR8	3000
	Balance		£3000

Owners' Equity

Capital

	July 1	TR1	10000
	Balance		£10000

Sales Revenue

	July 10	TR4	3000
	23	TR7	8000
	Balance		£11000

Clerical Expenses

July 12	TR5	500
Balance		£500

Distribution

July 31	TR9	1000
Balance		£1000

Steps 3 and 4 have been carried out to produce the above **ledger accounts**. The ledger accounts include the date and reference number of each transaction; this makes it possible to trace the **documentation** behind each transaction, and to check for possible **errors** in the accounts. The procedure used to calculate the balance on each account was simply to **add** the transactions on each side and to **carry down** the difference between the two sides as a balance on the side with the larger total, thus creating either a debit or credit balance. An alternative method which is also commonly used can be explained by using as an illustration the cash account in our example:

Short Form Method Used Above

Cash

July 1	TR1	10000	July 2	TR2	6000
10	TR4	3000	8	TR3	2000
23	TR7	8000	12	TR5	500
			20	TR6	5000
			27	TR8	2000
			31	TR9	1000
		£21000			£16500
Balance					
July 31		£ 4500			

Balancing and Carrying Forward

Cash

July 1	TR1	10000	July 2	TR2	6000
10	TR4	3000	8	TR3	2000
23	TR7	8000	12	TR5	500
			20	TR6	5000
			27	TR8	2000
			31	TR9	1000
			Balance carried		4500
			forward		
		£21000			£21000
July 31 Balance					
brought forward		£4500			

As can be seen from this example, the only difference in the two methods is that the more conventional 'balancing and carrying forward' method places the balance on the *opposite side* (i.e., on the credit side if it is a debit balance, in order to make the two sides agree (balance)) and then carries this balance forward to its **correct** side to show in the case of cash a debit balance. Both methods, of course, produce the same balance, and either can be used in practice, throughout the book we will use the short form method. It should be noted that the balances at the **end of the accounting period** (or in this case, one month) also represent the **starting balance for the next accounting period**: opening balances for August 1 will be £4500

Step 5   Prepare a Trial Balance
A trial balance is a list of the **accounts and their respective balances** which have been used in the double-entry procedures. Using the data from Steps 3 and 4 of our example, the trial balance would be:

Trial Balance at 31 July 19X1 (before adjusting entries)

	Debit £	Credit £
Cash	4500	
Stock	12000	
Van	6000	
Creditors		3000
Capital		10000
Sales Revenue		11000
Clerical Expenses	500	
Distribution	1000	
	£24000	£24000

The equality of the trial balance totals arises because of the application of Rule 4 – i.e., that the sum of debit and credit entries for each transaction will be equal. This provides a mechanism for ensuring the arithmetic accuracy of the entries in the accounts and ensures that all accounts have been listed. However, as we noted at the end of Sect. 4.2 some errors in the book-keeping process will **not be revealed** by the trial balance: for example, where the wrong amount is entered in the system on both the debit and credit sides, or where the current debit and credit amounts are entered on the opposite sides to where they would be under the correct treatment.

Step 6   Identify End of Period Adjustments
We saw in Sect. 3.6 that adjustments are essentially entries made at the end of an accounting period to **correct errors**, or to **improve the information content** of the ledger accounts by increasing or decreasing the value of assets or liabilities or recording the existence of assets or liabilities which for various reasons have not been recorded by the book-keeping system.

The adjustments identified in Sect. 3.6 were:
ADJ 1   The balance of stock shown in the stock account of £12 000 which represents the total purchases of stock during July. However, we know that the only stock left at the end of July is the £5000 bought

on July 20; the other £7000 has been used up to generate the sales revenue.

ADJ 2   The van is show at £6000 in the accounts which is its purchase cost on July 2. The information is Sect. 3.6 is that July represents $\frac{1}{60}$ of the van's useful life, and therefore $\frac{1}{60}$ of £6000 (or £100) should be written off the book value of the van as a form of **depreciation**.

ADJ 3   The firm owes £500 rent for July. This is at present not recorded, and requires an adjustment to correct the situation.

The journal entries to record these adjustments are:

		Debit	*Credit*
		£	£
July 31 ADJ 1	Cost of Sales	7000	
	Stock		7000

The cost of sales account is an expense account which records the cost of the stock used up in making sales; it is an example of the phenomenon described in Sect. 3.5 of an **asset** (stock) which becomes an **expense** (cost of sales) when it is used up and no longer exists within the firm.

July 31 ADJ 2	Depreciation Expense	£100	
	Accumulated Depreciation		£100

The depreciation expense is again an **asset** (or part of an asset) which becomes an **expense**. The credit could have been made direct to the Van account, thus reducing the balance on the account to £5900. However, it is convenient to accumulate depreciation in a separate asset valuation account which is normally simply called 'accumulated depreciation'.

July 31 ADJ 3	Rent Expense	£500	
	Creditors		£500

This entry records the fact that the firm has incurred an expense and that the payment is still outstanding and is therefore a **liability** (creditors).

The adjustments must now be entered in the relevant **ledger accounts**; only the accounts affected by the adjustments have been repeated below.

Stock				Cost of Sales		
July 8 TR3	2000			July 31 ADJ 1	7000	
20 TR6	5000			Balance	£7000	
27 TR8	5000					
	£12000					
Balance	£ 5000	July 31				
		ADJ 1	7000			
			£7000			

Accumulated Depreciation			Depreciation Expense		
	July 31 ADJ 2	£100	July 31 ADJ 2	£100	
	Balance	£100	Balance	£100	

Creditors			Rent Expense		
	July 27 TR8	3000	July 31 ADJ 3	£500	
	Balance	£3000	Balance	£500	
	July 31 ADJ 3	500			
		£3500			
	Balance	£3500			

Step 7   Prepare a Further Trial Balance

Now that the end of period adjusting entries have been made, a further trial balance can be prepared:

Trial Balance at 31 July 19X1 (after adjusting entries)

	Debit £	Credit £	(for step 8)
Cash	4500		B/S
Stock	5000		B/S
Van	6000		B/S
Accumulated Depreciation (van)		100	B/S
Creditors		3500	B/S
Capital		10000	B/S
Sales Revenue		11000	P/L
Cost of Sales	7000		P/L
Clerical Expense	500		P/L
Depreciation Expense	100		P/L
Rent Expense	500		P/L
Distribution	1000		P/L
	£24600	£24600	

*Step 8   Preparation of the Profit and Loss (P/L) Account
and Balance Sheet (B/S)*

The example we have been using to explain the double-entry procedure is of
course based on the data in Ex.3.5 in Chapter 3. The presentation of the
balance sheet from that example is shown in Sect. 3.7 and the profit and loss
account in Sect. 3.8. In a more typical situation, the trial balance after
adjusting entries would be used as the basis for the preparation of the
financial statements. As we have shown in the above trial balance each
balance should be identified to show whether it appears in the **balance sheet**
(B/S) or in the **profit and loss account** (P/L). The revenue, expense and
distribution balances are then presented as shown in Sect. 3.8. The 'bottom
line' figure of retained profit (in this case £1900) is transferred to the **owners'
equity section** of the balance sheet, which is shown along with the other
balance sheet items from the trial balance, as in Sect. 3.7.

Step 9   Closing Entries.

In Step 8 the profit and loss account and balance sheet were prepared, using
the balances from the trial balance. We did not at that time make any entries
in the ledger accounts. The balances on accounts which were designated as
balance sheet items remain in those accounts as the **opening balances** for the
next accounting period. Those balances on the accounts which were used to
calculate **profit** must, however, actually be **transferred to the profit and loss
account**. These accounts are often termed 'temporary' accounts because they
accumulate revenues and expenses for each accounting period and then start
the new account period with a nil balance. The procedure of closing these
temporary accounts is illustrated in Figure 4.3.

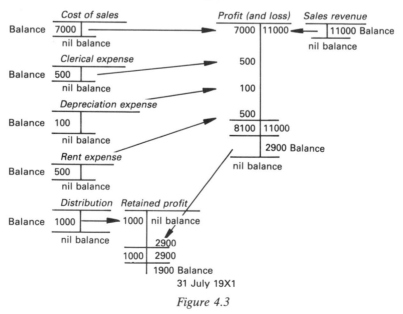

Figure 4.3

4.5 Classification of accounting data

In Chapter 1 we saw that the major purpose of accounting was to provide financial information about the firm to those who **required it**. In the preparation of the balance sheet and profit and loss account it was necessary to provide a classification of our information into various categories. In the balance sheet in Sect. 1.8 we classified assets into land, buildings, etc. In the profit and loss account we were also involved in the classification of revenues and expenses. The classification system we choose, as in all problems of taxonomy, should be designed to illustrate information in a form most useful to **a user's range of needs** – we could, for example, classify our fixed assets by geographical location, or age, if such information would be useful. The accounts used in the recording system will be designed around a certain predetermined classification system chosen in the light of anticipated requirements. Accounting data is thus concerned not only with recording financial values but also with their classification.

One useful way of classifying for the management of a firm is by identifying **parts of organisations** or **functions** which have been **responsible for incurring costs or expenses**. This is invaluable for purposes of **business control**. The profit statement in Sect. 3.8 used a 'natural expense classification' such as 'clerical' and 'depreciation'.

In Figure 4.4, we have reclassified the expense data formerly classified under natural accounts into a 'functional classification'. To enable us to reclassify we will need evidence, to determine certain criteria, which will help us establish an **equitable allocation of expense and costs to functions**. In Sec 8.2 we have paid special attention to the process of reclassification of data in determining the costs of production.

Natural		*Functional*[1]		
		Production (cost of sales)	Administration	Marketing
	£	£	£	£
Clerical labour	500		200	300
Depreciation	100			100
Rent	500		100	400
Cost of sales	7000	7000		
	£8100	£7000	£300	£800

Figure 4.4

Note:

1. Sect. 11.6 explains that the UK Companies Acts now require companies to classify expenses into **Distribution costs and Administration** expenses.

A profit and loss account using a functional classification could be:

*Profit and Loss Account of Crisp Company for One Month
Ended 31 July 19x1*

			£
Sales Revenue			11000
Less Cost of Sales (production)			7000
Gross Profit			4000
Less Other Expenses:			
Administration		300	
Marketing		800	
			1100
Net Profit			£2900

4.6 Summary

Chapter 4 has examined how the use of a system of double-entry accounting using T accounts has developed and improved the flexibility and reliability of the system of processing accounting data. The procedures leading to the preparation of the balance sheet rely on the collection and processing of data, all of which are ultimately determined by the needs of users of information. An understanding of the processing of data can be developed only in the context of an overall accounting system which in some firms may be related to other information systems. The mechanisms of particular accounting systems are likely to be substantially different between firms, though the underlying characteristics of the system should be the same.

We have now examined the problems of preparation and presentation of financial statements in the context of data analysis. In Chapter 5 we shall turn to the examination of some of the more important underlying conceptual issues and problems.

Notes and References

1. Many students understandably find the use of some terms in accounting confusing. In this sentence *creditor* refers to the amounts owing as a result of purchases made on *credit* which simply means that the cash payment is not made at the time of the purchase. The term *credit* introduced in Rule 1 should be understood in this context as merely having the meaning conveyed by Rule 1 – i.e., it describes entries on the **right hand side of an account**. It does not mean having things 'on credit', nor should it be used as a synonym for 'good', any more than a debit is 'bad'. Both are **neutral terms** which bear a meaning restricted to that described in Rule 1.
2. See Sect. 9.4 for details of these day books.

Questions and problems

4.1 What do you understand by the following terminology?

Double-entry book-keeping	Accounting system
T account	Ledger
Opening accounts	Temporary account
Debit	Balance
Credit	Functional classification
Posting data	Natural classification
Trial balance	Data collection
Information system	Data processing
Books of prime entry	Data communication
Journal	

4.2 Examine the advantages and disadvantages of the use of T accounts for the processing of accounting data.

4.3 Many firms use computers to process and record accounting data. Is the analysis of transactions into 'debit' and 'credit' still meaningful and useful under such a system?

4.4 Using the data from Question 3.2 for Cram, prepare the Journal entries, T accounts, trial balance, profit and loss account and balance sheet.

4.5 You are responsible for an accounting system which processes the following volume of data on a daily basis:

1000 cheques received
£5000 received in cash in 30 tills
300 cheques paid to suppliers
5000 items of stock received from suppliers

How would you ensure the accuracy and security of the system?

4.6 Explain any problems which may arise in a small transport firm in classifying the following expenses into functional areas:

(a) petrol for lorries and cars from the firm's pumps
(b) insurance
(c) electricity
(d) rent for garages, haulage yard and offices
(e) the accountant's salary
(f) the managing director's salary
(g) interest

4.7 The following balances were extracted from the ledger of T. Ford at December 31 19X5

	£
Purchases	121760
Trade Creditors	31980
Fixture & Fittings	2860
Stock	36940
Delivery Cost on Sales	6270
Delivery Cost on Purchases	11430
Trade Debtors	31380
Postage and Telephone	1400
Sales	199260
Delivery Vans	11250
Wages and Salaries	51400
Returns by Customers	3280
Advertising	11780
Returns to Suppliers	1140
Discounts Received	2190
Discounts Allowed to Customers	1740
Bank Overdraft	11820
Drawings	10000

You are required to calculate the balance on Ford's Owners' Equity Account and to prepare a Trial Balance at 31 December 19X5.

4.8 The following balances were extracted from the ledger of a sole trader, and you are requested to prepare a Trial Balance as at 31 March 19X1.

	£
Capital	30000
Premises	15000
Plant and Machinery	4000
Fixtures and Fittings	5000
Purchases	76400
Sales	105000
Goods Returned by Customers	1200
Goods Returned to Suppliers	1100
Creditors	12240
Debtors	34200
Drawings	3000
Bank Overdraft	3760
General Expenses	3250
Rents Received	1200
Rates	1350
Delivery Cost on Sales	750
Delivery Cost on Purchases	800
Wages	7300
Discount Allowed to Customers	2400
Discount Received from Suppliers	1350

4.9 The following trial balance of a sole trader, although it adds up to the same total on both sides, is incorrect:

Trial Balance as at 30 June 19X2

	Dr £	Cr £
Capital	8950	
Drawings		1050
Stock	3725	
Purchases	23100	
Sales		39425
Wages and Salaries	6205	
Lighting and Heating	310	
Equipment	3600	
Carriage Outward		230
Returns Inward	105	
Returns Outward		290
Provision for Bad Debts	350	
Discounts Allowed	285	
Discounts Received		315
Rent, Rates and Insurance	1115	
Motor Vehicles	1475	
Cash in Hand	110	
Creditors	4925	
Debtors		13920
Bank Overdraft	975	
	£55230	£55230

Draw up a corrected trial balance.

4.10

F. Hall PLC
Balance Sheet as at 31 December 19X1

	£	£		£	£
Owners' Equity		15800	*Fixed Assets*		
			Shop premises	40000	
Mortgage Loan		25000	Shop fittings	4500	44500
Current' Liabilities			*Current Assets*		
Creditors	3500		Stock	8000	
Bank overdraft	9600	13100	Debtors	1200	
			Cash	200	9400
		£53900			£53900

The following transactions took place during January 19X2

(1) The company had a cash sale of £6000. The stock sold had cost £4000
(2) The overdraft was increased for the following:

(a) to pay creditors £1500
(b) to distribute a share of profits £1000
(c) to purchase additional shop fittings £1200

(3) Replacement stock of £2500 was purchased on credit

Required:

(1) Prepare a profit and loss account for the month.
(2) Prepare a balance sheet as at the end of the month.

Note: The opening balance sheet (i.e., at 31/12/X1) shows the opening balances on the ledger accounts – show ledger accounts which are affected by the above transactions.

4.11 Mary Jones decides to open a hairdressing business on March 1 19X1 and invest her savings in it. She opens a bank account and puts in her savings of £1000. The following is a summary of the events for the first month of the new business.

(1) Rented a shop and paid a month's rent of £100
(2) Bought a hair dryer on credit for £150 and shop fittings for £500 cash
(3) Bought brushes and combs for £40 cash
(4) Bought, for cash, shampoo and dyes, etc., costing £90; all were used up during the month.
(5) Cash received from customers amounted to £400; this was paid into the bank
(6) Mary drew £80 from the bank for her own use
(7) At the end of the month she owed £60 in respect of the rates, and £50 for electricity

Ignore depreciation.

Required:

Show the above transactions in the form of journal entries. Write up Mary Jones's ledger accounts and show the profit and loss account for the month of March and the balance sheet at the end of the month.

4.12 Joe Brown commenced business as a baker on 1 January 19X3. The following is a summary of the transactions which took place during the first three months of trading.

(1) Brown paid £5000 into the business on 1 January and immediately paid a full years rent of £1000
(2) A delivery van was purchased on 1 January at a cost of £4000; it was agreed that it should be depreciated in equal instalments over four years, assuming zero residual value.
(3) Cash sales amounted to £4000
(4) Credit sales totalled £2000 and of this £450 was still outstanding by 31 March
(5) During the period suppliers had been paid £1800 and invoices totalling £800 remained unpaid at 31 March
(6) Sundry expenses paid amounted to £600
(7) At the end of the period Brown owed £400 for electricity used
(8) The stock of ingredients, bread, cakes, etc. at the 31 March was valued at £100.

Required: Show the above transactions in the form of journal entries. Write up the ledger accounts for Joe Brown.
Extract a trial balance.
Prepare a profit and loss account for the three months and a balance sheet as at 31 March.

5
Accounting Concepts

5.1 Introduction

In Chapters 1 and 2 we introduced the fundamental issues in accounting, the potential users of accounting information and the requirements of these users. We were also concerned with ideas of value and profit and with various ways of measuring them. Chapters 3 and 4 analysed how accounting information is structured, recorded and processed in order to produce, among other things, statements such as the profit and loss account and balance sheet.

The methods of processing data shown in Chapters 3 and 4 can be used to implement various approaches to the measurement of a firm's performance. The book-keeping systems used to process accounting data can be adapted to various alternative measures of value or profit, and if required can be adapted to produce financial statements other than the profit and loss account and balance sheet.

The purpose of Chapter 5 is to analyse the factors which determine the **particular type of financial reporting** that accountants currently use.

5.2 What determines the form and content of financial statements?

We need first to distinguish between what is commonly termed 'internal' and 'external' reporting. **Internal** reporting refers to that information which is prepared for an **individual's** or a **firm's own use**. Because this is essentially a private matter there need be no formal rules and regulations which must be applied. **External** reporting, on the other hand, is where an individual or a firm prepares information which may be used by an **outside party**. An individual, for example, may have to prepare financial information for the tax authorities, or when seeking a loan from a bank. A firm may be required to produce financial statements for its shareholders or creditors, or for the inland revenue. Although we have made the distinction between internal and external reporting, for most firms the distinction may not have significant practical implications – for example, if a firm has to prepare its accounting information in a particular way for external purposes it may be impractical to adopt a different method for internal reporting. However, there will be situations where the different objectives of internal and external reporting lead to **differences in the form and content** of the respective information.

There are **three** major influences on the form and content of financial statements for external reporting:

(1) **Theoretical** or **conceptual** considerations.
(2) **Legal** requirements.
(3) **Non-legal** regulations.

We will consider each of these in the following sections.

5.3   Theoretical and conceptual considerations

Here we are concerned with identifying the body of knowledge which underpins accounting measurement. Accounting is not like subjects such as physics or chemistry, in that it **does not have a recognised theoretical base**: it is difficult to set up hypotheses which can be properly tested, and there is no accounting equivalent of the physics laboratory. However, concepts have been evolved over time to meet contemporary needs; such concepts can be found in the academic literature on accounting and in reports and statements issued by the bodies representing the accounting profession. As mentioned above, it is difficult properly to test these concepts, and we will see that their use has usually been based on their **general acceptability** by accountants and users of accounting information.

Conceptual thinking may be concerned with general issues such as:

– What are the **objectives** of accounting reports?

Or it may be concerned with more specific issues, such as:

– How should elements such as **profit**, **assets** or **liabilities** be **measured**?

We will discuss in Sect. 5.7 what constitutes accepted thinking on accounting concepts, but first we need to identify recent developments in this area. No formal statement has been developed by the UK accounting profession of what constitutes the conceptual framework underlying accounting information. Two documents which reveal thought in this area are:

– 'The corporate report'[1] published in 1975 as a discussion paper commissioned by the ASC and with terms of reference 'to re-examine the scope and aims of published financial reports in the light of modern needs and conditions'.
– 'A conceptual framework for financial accounting and reporting'[2]

published in 1981 as a report by Professor R. Macve to 'Review the possibility of developing an agreed conceptual framework'.

In the USA, the Financial Accounting Standards Board (FASB) has since 1973 been working on an ambitious plan to develop a definitive conceptual framework which they have defined as: 'A coherent set of interrelated objectives and fundamentals that can lead to consistent standards and that prescribes the nature, functions and limits of financial accounting and financial statements'. An example of the way in which the FASB has approached this issue can be seen in Sect. 5.9.

In 1989 the International Accounting Standards Committee (IASC) published a proposed conceptual framework[3] to assist it in developing **international standards** for accounting information. The UK Accounting Standards Committee (see Sect. 5.5) agreed to recognise this framework, and an outline of its content is given in Sect. 5.10.

5.4 Legal requirements

In Britain the Companies Acts legislated by Parliament are the source of law which regulates the way in which a company **publishes its financial statements**. The object of law in general is to regulate society in an equitable manner; company law in particular is concerned with:

(a) The **rights** and **duties** of those **operating** companies.
(b) **Protecting** the **rights** of **individuals** or **groups dealing with** companies.

The guiding principle is that published financial statements should give a 'true and fair view' of the firm's position and performance. The Companies Acts do not specify what constitutes a 'true and fair view', and it is accepted that the interpretation should be left in practice to the accounting profession. This interpretation is discussed further in Sect. 5.7.

The mechanism by which the law attempts to achieve the objectives in (a) and (b) is chiefly by ensuring that companies make adequate minimum **disclosure** of relevant information in order to inform outsiders of what is going on within the company. The Companies Acts contain extensive rules governing the publication of financial statements. Among the items covered by these rules are requirements to ensure that:

- the company keeps **proper accounting records**
- the financial statements are **audited**
- the statements give a **true and fair view** of the firm
- the financial statements conform to **specified rules on format and presentation**

- there is the maintenance of a **minimum capital base**
- that **dividends** are **paid only out of distributable profit**

The last two items on the list are concerned with **protecting those dealing with the firm** against the possibility that the firm will distribute resources which should **properly be retained within the firm** to ensure its future operations. This is often referred to as 'capital maintenance', a concept we will return to particularly in Chapters 6, 7, 10 and 14.

5.5 Non-legal regulation

In addition to the legal rules the accounting profession currently impose a form of self-regulation.[4] The operation of this self-regulation from 1969 to 1990 was chiefly by means of the Accounting Standards Committee (ASC),[5]; it represented the major professional accounting bodies in the UK and operated by issuing Statements of Standard Accounting Practice (SSAPs) (a list of which can be seen in Appendix A) and Statements of Recommended Practice (SORPs). The purpose of issuing such statements was to improve the quality of published financial statements. The aims of the ASC were set out by the 'Consultative Committee of Accountancy Bodies' (CCAB), to which the ASC was responsible, as follows:

> The objects of the ASC shall be . . . to define accounting concepts, to narrow the differences of financial accounting and reporting treatment, and to codify generally accepted best practice in the public interest. These objects encompass:
>
> (a) fundamentals of financial accounting and their application to financial statements;
> (b) definition of terms used;
> (c) questions of measurement of reported results and financial position; and
> (d) the content and form of financial statements.

Companies whose shares are listed on the Stock Exchange have also to conform to **Stock Exchange** requirements. These include disclosure requirements in addition to those required by the Companies Acts. The Stock Exchange also requires companies to apply the SSAPs issued by the ASC. This latter requirement considerably strengthened the authority of the ASC.

5.6 The need for a conceptual framework

We have seen in the earlier part of this chapter the various influences and regulations which determine the form and content of financial reports. It would be possible in their absence for each accountant to work out his or her own solution to the problem of measurement, recording and communication of accounting information; however, in most circumstances this would be unacceptable. The basic reason for having an agreed conceptual framework is that if accounting is concerned with communicating information, it makes sense if there is an **agreed and commonly understood language** in which to communicate. There are **four** advantages which flow from such an agreed framework:

(1) Its use will encourage **consistency** in the **content** of different companies' financial statements. It should also result in **consistent treatment over time** by individual companies. Each of these factors will make **comparisons** of company information more effective.

(2) If there are agreed principles and rules, they can form a basis for the preparation of accounting information to be used by individual accountants and perhaps act as a sort of **manual**.

(3) The agreed framework can act as a constraint on the freedom of individual accountants to exert any bias in the preparation of accounting information; it thus limits the area of **discretion** open to the accountant.

(4) Accounting information should not only be reliable but it should be **seen to be** reliable, and having a well known agreed framework for its preparation should increase **users' confidence** in the information.

There are, however, some who argue that the characteristics listed above are not entirely desirable. The search for consistency referred to in (1), for example, could prevent the expression of genuine differences between the activities of different companies. The constraints on the accountant's ability to exercise his professional judgement implied by (2) and (3) can also be seen to be a negative factor.

5.7 Generally accepted accounting principles (GAAP)

In Sect. 5.4 it was stated that the guiding principle in UK legislation on published accounting information was that it should give a **true and fair view** of the firm's position and performance, and that the interpretation of the phrase was in practice left to the accounting profession. In general, it is assumed that the accounting information will give a true and fair view if it is prepared in accordance with **generally accepted accounting principles**.[6] These principles refer to those which are, at the time, **recommended** by the accounting profession and **accepted** by users of accounting information.

The terminology used to describe this aspect of accounting is unfortunately often confusing. It is ironic that in describing the content of what constitutes 'generally accepted accounting principles' there appears to be no generally accepted terminology. Terms which are commonly used include 'concepts', 'principles', 'conventions', 'rules', 'doctrines', 'postulates' and 'assumptions'. Attempts have been made by various writers to reduce the confusion by distinguishing between fundamental theoretical principles and applications or 'rules of thumb' which are used in practice. One such attempt was made in the ASC's 'Disclosure of accounting policies' (SSAP 2, 1971). The foreword to SSAP 2 states:

> It is fundamental to the understanding and interpretation of financial accounts that those who use them should be aware of the main assumptions on which they are based. The purpose of this statement . . . is to assist such understanding by promoting improvement in the quality of information disclosed. It seeks to achieve this by establishing as standard accounting practice the disclosure in financial accounts of clear explanations of the accounting policies followed in so far as these are significant for the purpose of giving a true and fair view.

In the statement a distinction is made between:

(1) *Fundamental accounting concepts*

These are defined as 'broad basic assumptions which underline the periodic financial accounts of business enterprises'. Their fundamental nature is, however, qualified by the further comment that 'they are practical rules rather than theoretical ideas and are capable of variation and evolution as accounting thought and practice develop'.

(2) *Accounting bases*

Defined as 'the methods which have been developed for expressing or applying fundamental accounting concepts to financial transactions and items'. We shall see in later chapters that because of the wide diversity of business situations there may be **several bases** for dealing with particular items and this is the reason for a third category.

(3) *Accounting policies*

These are 'the specific accounting bases judged by business enterprises to be most appropriate to their circumstances and adopted by them for the purpose of preparing their financial accounts'.

This terminology will be adopted for the remainder of the book to describe the accounting conceptual framework of principles and practices. The relationships between these aspects of the accounting framework is shown by Figure 5.1.

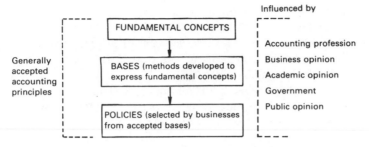

Figure 5.1

Figure 5.1 shows that what constitutes generally accepted concepts and bases is subject to a **variety of influences**. The relative effect of each of these is difficult to assess, but it is likely their influence will **vary over time** – for example, as governments change or as public attitudes towards the accounting profession vary.

SSAP 2 appeared to be the initial step in the development of an **explicit** (as opposed to an **assumed**) conceptual framework for the UK. However, although (as Appendix A shows) many SSAPs have since been issued, none have sought to develop the start made by SSAP 2. The content of SSAP 2 was given enhanced status by its inclusion in the Companies Act 1981, and in the consolidated Companies Act 1985.

SSAP 2 singled out **four concepts** for special mention: going concern, accruals, consistency and prudence. It is pointed out in a footnote to the Statement that it was considered expedient to recognise only these four concepts as having general acceptance at that time (1971), but that a more theoretical approach would include other concepts. Further evidence that these four concepts do not form an exhaustive list can be found, for example, in the publications of the American Institute of Public Accountants[7] and the Financial Accounting Standards Board.[8]

There is no universal agreement on the number and terminology applicable to these concepts, but the following list seems to have considerable support:

- Going concern
- Matching (or accruals)
- Consistency
- Conservatism ⎫
- Realisation ⎬ (or prudence)
- Entity
- Objectivity
- Materiality
- Money measurement (including an assumption of a **stable monetary unit**)

The first five concepts are similar to the four singled out in SSAP 2. Going concern and consistency survive with the same title; the accrual concept becomes the matching concept and the concept of prudence approximates to a combination of conservatism and realisation. An explanation is given below of each of the concepts listed above; as already stated, the framework consists of generally accepted concepts, bases and policies. The framework is thus an attempt to **specify the underlying ideas** which are believed to **guide** accountants in their **measurement of accounting data**.

5.8 The concepts defined and illustrated

We will now examine further the accounting concepts listed in Sect. 5.7.

Going Concern

It is assumed that, unless there is evidence to the contrary, the business will have a **continuing existence**. This is important in the valuation of assets, especially those which have little use outside the business. Such assets may have little selling price value, but with the going concern assumption their value in use is more significant.

Matching (or Accruals)

Profit has been defined as a change in value, expressed in the profit and loss account as revenue *less* expenses. Profit is usually measured and profit and loss accounts prepared at regular interval. The process of matching is an attempt to ensure that the **revenues** recorded in a period are matched with the **expenses** incurred in earning them.

Consistency

Accounting information should be prepared on a consistent basis from **period to period**, and **within periods** there should be consistent treatment of similar items. At first sight this seems too obvious to be regarded as a concept but it will be seen to be important when it is realised that there may be **several alternative bases** for dealing with similar situations.

Conservatism

This is difficult to define because it is an expression of a general attitude that it is thought should be applied to accounting measurement and reporting. It is equivalent to taking a **cautious or prudent approach** to valuation. It will be a matter of judgement and experience as to what constitutes a 'conservative approach' in a particular situation, but it is a concept which is firmly entrenched and underlines many of the other concepts. If it is possible to measure with accuracy, then conservatism has little impact, but there are many situations where **accuracy cannot be achieved** and in such situations this concept should prevent overoptimistic valuations.

Realisation

Increases in the value of assets should not be recognised unless they have been **realised by an exchange of assets**; this means that revenues and profits will **not be recognised until realised**. What constitutes 'realisation' is not always clearly definable – the sale of an asset for cash is clearly a realised revenue, for example, and a sale on credit will also be recognised as realised. However, where assets appear to have increased in value when judged by a market price, this will usually not be recognised as a realisation unless the asset is **actually sold**. On the other hand, a different view may be taken of assets which have fallen in value. These expenses may be recognised immediately, though the asset is not yet sold: this is an example of the realisation and conservatism concepts working together.

Entity

If accounting information for a unit of organisation is to be meaningful it is important to **identify the entity of the unit being accounted for**, and **distinguish it** from other units. An attempt must thus be made to define the boundaries of the entity so that it is possible to identify the basis for accounting information relevant to the entity, and what is not relevant or outside the boundaries of the entity. A sole trader's **business unit** should, for example, be distinguished from his **domestic activities**, and consequently information on his **domestic spending** should not form the basis for accounting entries for the business.

Information relevant to the entity can also be defined in terms of those economic events which have an **impact on the business unit**. If a factory pollutes a river and the cost of the pollution is borne by the community rather than by the company which owns the factory, then those costs do not effect the company – they are, in other words, outside the entity defined as the firm. In this example, the impact on the firm is being determined by the law which attributes the responsibility for the cost of pollution; if the law changed, the pollution costs might be redefined as being within the boundaries of the firm, and thus constitute accounting information relevant to the entity. It will be apparent from this example that what constitutes the identification of an entity and the accounting information relevant to it will in practice be determined by the **exercise of judgement and experience**, and not merely the application of simple rules.

Objectivity

Accounting information should be based as far as possible on **objective evidence**. This means that it should be free from bias, based on factual evidence, and capable of independent verification. It should be clear that this again is a matter of **judgement** whether these qualities are present. The importance of this concept is based mainly on the need for the information to be seen to be **reliable to those users outside the firm**.

Materiality

The accounting treatment of an item may be determined by its materiality – i.e., its relative value or importance. In Figure 2.6 it was shown that assets with a life longer than the accounting period would have to be valued **at the end of each period** to ascertain the total net assets, and thus derive the **profit** for the period. However, if an item is of small value in relation to the size of the organisation it may be treated differently – e.g., a spanner may last several years, but it might be regarded as an expense of the period in which it was purchased and its end of period value ignored, the resulting inaccuracy being ignored as immaterial.

Money Measurement

Accounting information is expressed in terms of **money**: money is the common denominator which enables diverse types of activity to be compared and combined. It follows that only those items or activities which can be expressed in **money terms** are included in accounting statements. This may exclude attributes such as the quality of the product, customer satisfaction, or employee dissatisfaction, which may be relevant information for running a business. Another disadvantage is that although money may be an adequate common denominator between diverse activities, it is a less than satisfactory common denominator between different **periods of time**, because of changing price levels and purchasing power. Nevertheless the next principle is used in many countries.

Stable Monetary Unit

At the present time, accounting statements are prepared using the assumption that the value of the monetary unit is **stable**. The development of this issue is discussed in Chapter 14.

We now need to look at an example of applying the above concepts. An illustration of such an application is shown in Figure 5.2.

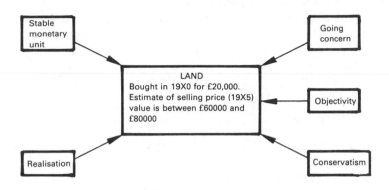

Figure 5.2

Assuming we were preparing a balance sheet at the end of 19X5, there are at least five concepts potentially influencing the valuing of land to be included in the balance sheet. The value of the land may have risen because there has been **general inflation**, or because it is sited in an area where building land is in **short supply**.

If the stable monetary unit concept is followed then increases in value due to rises in general price levels **should not be recognised**, and in any event the realisation concept may not allow unrealised gains to be included as profits where the land is still held by the company. If this seems unrealistic and misleading, it can be pointed out that the **going concern** concept assumes that the company will continue its existence, and may need the land for its own use, and any potential market value for the land is thus irrelevant to the balance sheet. A common counter argument to this is that if the potential market value of the land was shown, the owners might decide to discontinue the business as a going concern, sell the assets and use the proceeds to go into some other business.

The concept of **objectivity** can now be introduced into the argument, and in this example the most objective value is that based on the original cost of £20 000 paid in 19X0. This figure is based on a transaction which **actually took place**, and for which there is **verifiable documentary evidence**. Whether the varying estimates of current market value constitute objective evidence is a matter of judgement; for example, if an identical piece of land has recently been sold then the value of that sale might be taken as acceptable evidence. In recent years, it has also become increasingly common to accept the opinion of a **recognised valuer** as objective evidence of changes in land and property values. If, however, there are complicating factors – for example, where the land has factory buildings on it – then it may be impossible to estimate a market value for the land separate from the buildings.

Also underlying this discussion is the concept of **conservatism**, which may lead to the rejection of some estimates of market value where they cannot be ascertained with reasonable certainty.

Reference to the Marks and Spencer financial statements in Appendix B will reveal that the company does revalue property from time to time (see note 12 to the financial statements).

5.9 The FASB conceptual framework project

In Sect. 5.3 we referred to the work on the conceptual framework which has been carried out since 1973 by the Financial Accounting Standards Board (FASB) in the USA. A diagram illustrating the way in which the FASB has approached the task can be seen in Figure 5.3.

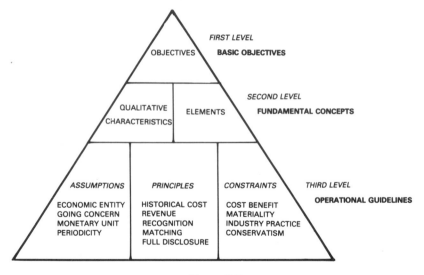

Figure 5.3

The work commenced with a statement of the **objectives of financial statements**,[9] and then went on to define qualitative characteristics desirable in financial statements.[10] The **basic elements making up conventional financial statements** were next defined. The third level of **operational guidelines** is as yet incomplete, but a comparison with the list of concepts discussed in Sects 5.7 and 5.8 will reveal considerable similarity with the operational guidelines identified there.

5.10 The IASC framework for the preparation and presentation of financial statements

In Sect. 5.3 we referred to the conceptual framework statement issued by the IASC and adopted by the UK Accounting Standards Committee. The content of the framework reveals that the committee were influenced by the work done by the FASB referred to in Sect. 5.9. The main areas covered in the statement are:

(a) The **objectives** of financial statements.
(b) The **qualitative characteristics** that determine the **usefulness** of information in financial statements.
(c) The **definition**, **recognition** and **measurement** of the elements from which financial statements are constructed.
(d) Concepts of **capital** and **capital maintenance**.

5.11 Summary

Chapter 5 has been concerned with an analysis of the three influences on the form and content of financial statements, particularly in the context of **external reporting**. These were identified as conceptual considerations, legal requirements and non-legal regulations. Each of these influences was discussed before returning to the further discussion of the conceptual framework, 'generally accepted accounting principles' (GAAP) and accounting concepts. Finally, the work of the FASB and the IASC on the development of a conceptual framework was briefly outlined.

Notes and References

1. ASC, 'The Corporate Report – A discussion paper' (London: Accounting Standards Committee, 1975).
2. Macve, R., 'A conceptual framework for financial accounting and reporting' (London: ICAEW, 1981).
3. IASC, 'Framework for the preparation and presentation of Financial Statements' (London: International Accounting Standards Committee, 1989).
4. The system of self-regulation has been frequently criticised as ineffective, and suggestions for a more formal, legally backed system have been proposed.
5. In 1988 a review committee recommended replacing the ASC with two bodies, a 'Financial Reporting Council' and an 'Accounting Standards Board', in order to separate policy from technical implementation: These two bodies formally took over from the ASC in August 1990. 'The making of accounting standards' (the Dearing

Report) (London: Institute of Chartered Accountants of England and Wales, 1988).
6. However UK legislation requires companies to depart from the accounting rules in the Companies Acts where it is necessary in order to give a true and fair view. A true and fair view must therefore in some situations involve **more than the mere application of accounting principles** or **legal rules**.
7. Accounting Principles Board Statement, no 4, 'Basic concepts and accepted accounting principles underlying financial statements of business enterprises' (1970).
8. FASB, 'Statements of Financial Accounting Concepts' issued since 1973 as part of the ongoing conceptual framework project.
9. SFAC 1, 'Objectives of Financial Reporting by Business Enterprises' (Financial Accounting Standards Board, 1978).
10. SFAC 2, 'Qualitative characteristics of accounting information' (Financial Accounting Standards Board, 1980).

Questions and Problems

5.1   What do you understand by the following terminology?

Internal reporting	Matching
External reporting	Accruals
Conceptual framework	Conservatism
True and fair view	Prudence
Capital maintenance	Realisation
FASB	Entity
GAAP	Objectivity
ASC	Materiality
SSAP	Money measurement
SORP	Stable monetary unit
IASC	Going concern
FRC	Concepts
ASB	Bases
	Policies

5.2   Outline the advantages of having an agreed conceptual framework. Which of the advantages do you think is most important?
5.3   What is the function of a professional accounting organisation?
5.4   Identify the major influences on the content of published financial statements.
5.5   What influence does the European Community (EC) have on UK financial statements?
5.6   What do you understand by the phrase a 'true and fair view'?
5.7   Give examples of where accounting concepts might be in conflict with each other.
5.8   Discuss the approach to financial statements and reporting revealed by the FASB conceptual framework project depicted in Figure 5.3.
5.9   Explain what you understand by the expression 'historical cost accounting'.

5.10 How should the following seven situations be accounted for? Identify what accounting concepts are involved in each situation. Each situation is independent of the others.

(a) As owner of a sports shop you withdraw five squash rackets from stock to give to friends as Christmas presents. Each racket cost £50, and had a selling price of £70.

(b) A shop keeper commences business on January 1. He bought 100 tennis rackets at £60 each. During the year he sells 70 rackets at £80 each. How should his profit for the year be measured at December 31, if:

  (i) He goes out of business at the end of the year and estimates that he will get only £40 each for the unsold rackets.
  (ii) He intends to continue in business next year.

(c) Land has been purchased for £100 000. The company has since had an offer of £150 000 for the land but it does not at present wish to sell because it might be needed as the site of a new factory. It is estimated that a similar site would cost £180 000.

(d) The auditors have discovered an error which overstates the assets by £10 000 in:

  (i) The fixed asset total of £3m.
  (ii) The stock value of £40 000.

(e) A building is left to the owner of a business by his aunt. He spends £50 000 converting the property and now lives in half, the other half being used in the business.

(f) Stock consists of 1000 units of a product which cost £60 each. The company has received an order for 600 units at £80 each. It anticipates that the remaining 400 will have to be sold off at a price of £40 each and even then it is not certain that all will be sold.

(g) A company is being sued by a former employee for wrongful dismissal. The damages could amount to £100 000 if the employee wins his case. The company believes that it will win the case.

6
Fixed Assets

6.1 Introduction

We saw in Chapter 1 (Note 5) that assets can be defined as 'a resource controlled by the enterprise as a result of past events and from which future economic benefits are expected to flow to the enterprise'. Assets are thus a **stock of benefits**, and over time the benefits usually get **used up**. Chapter 6 deals with the specific characteristics of assets, and looks particularly at **fixed assets** and the measurement problems which result from **using up the stock of benefits which they represent**.

6.2 Characteristics

Sect. 1.8 introduced **assets** as resources owned or controlled by the organisation, and Sect. 3.7 distinguished between **fixed** and **current assets**. Fixed assets are those acquired by the firm **for use**, in the pursuit of profit, **rather than sale**, and can be considered as a category of asset owned by the firm normally for more than a year. Examples of fixed assets are:

Land
Mineral Rights
Factory Building
Shop Premises
Ships and Aircraft
Motor Vehicles

Fixed assets are initially acquired to **provide the firm with the means of carrying on its operations**, rather than being held for processing and selling. Assets which are held for **processing and selling** are normally called **current** assets. Some of the items in our examples of fixed assets above might appear as current assets in some balance sheet: Marks and Spencer may record motor vehicles, under fixtures, fittings and equipment in their balance sheet. They will have been acquired to enable the company to distribute its goods between stores, and will generally be held for more than a year. However motor vehicles held by a BL dealer for resale will appear as stock in current assets in the dealer's balance sheet.

The list of fixed assets above covered just one type of asset, which in accounting terminology are called **tangible assets** because they have **physical properties**. Another group of fixed assets which an organisation might own are referred to as **intangible assets**.[1] These are assets which do not have physical substance, but the firm **controls the benefits that are expected to flow from them**. Examples of these non-physical types of assets are patents, brands, trademarks and copyrights.

In most firms, fixed assets form a significant part of the total assets in the balance sheet, and therefore represent a large proportion of the owners' investment in the business. This large investment is undertaken to enable the organisation to be in a position to carry on profitable business transactions, and the benefits from holding fixed assets normally extend over **a number of accounting periods**.

Most fixed assets have a **finite life**: plant, machinery and motor vehicles, for example, simply wear out. Some fixed assets cease to have a use or value because **technological advances** make it cheaper or easier to produce the same output in a different way. The **legal right** which a business may have over some assets can **run out**, as with leases and patents. One asset which may not necessarily have a finite life is land; however, even here the specific **quality for which it is held may wear out** – overproduction of farming land can reduce its yields in the future, thereby reducing the benefits it can generate.

Assets are thus resources which wear out through usage or the lapse of time. In most instances, the use of a resource in an accounting period contributes to the **revenue produced** in that period, and diminishes the **future benefits** which can be derived from the asset. The wearing out or using up of assets is an **expense** in accounting terms, and the method used for measuring the expense and the remaining fixed assets can have a significant effect on the assessment of a firm's **value**, and therefore its **profit** in any given accounting period.

6.3 Recording and valuing fixed assets at acquisition

In general terms, the double-entry book-keeping procedures which result from the purchase of a fixed asset have been dealt with in Sect. 4.2 when the data in Ex.3.5, which included the purchase of a van, was processed. Ex.6.1 is a more detailed example which deals with a variety of different types of assets, as well as introducing some of the problems which can arise at acquisition over the valuation of long lived assets. This example will be used throughout the remainder of this chapter to demonstrate the measurement of fixed assets.

Example 6.1   Fred Flintstone Ltd

Fred Flintstone Ltd commenced business on 1 January 19X1, and the following transactions occurred during January.

Jan 1 Received £10 000 from owners, which is deposited in the business bank account.

    1 Purchased a delivery van for £3440 cash which included £120 for the road fund licence, £300 to have a towing bar fitted and £20 for a full tank of diesel; the van is second hand, and its expected useful life in the business is 3 years, at which time it should be possible to resell it for £300 scrap value.

    2 Purchased second hand machinery for £1000 on credit from Joe Smith, the expected useful life of which is 2 years with no perceived scrap value.

    3 Purchased a desk, chair and filing cabinet for £300 cash; these should last for 10 years.

    7 Acquired a lease on a shop for £5000 cash to cover a ten year period during which time the annual rent is fixed at £1000 p.a. payable at the end of each year; an additional £700 was paid for rewiring the premises.

Recording each of the above events involves using a day book (in this instance the journal) and posting an entry to the relevant asset accounts. First, we must identify the **categories** of fixed assets and determine their original cost or **acquisition values**. The acquisition value – the value entered into the accounts – is determined for a new asset by reference to the **costs incurred** in **making the asset fit for the purpose** for which it is being acquired. We shall now comment below on each of the company's transactions:

Delivery van

The sum of £3440 paid for the delivery van included the following:

(a) the price of the second hand van, £3000
(b) the towing bar, £300
(c) the road fund licence, £120
(d) the diesel, £20

At the time of purchase each item could be classified as an asset because each will provide future benefits for the business; however, some are **more short lived** than others. The diesel will soon be used up and will have to be continually replaced if the van is used during the accounting period. The £20 will thus be classified as an expense in the current accounting period (journal entry TR2 below). The road fund licence has a life expectancy of 1 year, and will have no value at the end of that time; its benefit will have been used up. It is, therefore, also an expense in the current accounting year (journal entry TR2). However, at the end of the first month of that accounting period it would still have **11 months of benefit remaining**, and this would need to be reflected in any accounts drawn up at that date.

The tow bar which had to be fitted to the van was a necessary part of making the van **useful to the business**; it forms an integral part of the basic asset, and should be included in the acquisition value of the asset (journal entry TR2)

Machinery, desk, chair and filing cabinet

These items all qualify as fixed assets as they will be used in the activities of the business for **more than one year**; they will be recorded at their respective **purchase costs** (journal entries TR3 and TR4).

Lease

The acquisition of the lease secures the benefit of using the premises for the 10 year period, and can thus be classified as a **fixed asset**[2] (journal entry TR5). The premises leased required adjustment to **make them useful to the business**; this involved an additional payment of £700 for rewiring. It is assumed that the benefits of the rewiring will be enjoyed over the duration of the lease and as such form an integral part of the cost of that asset (journal entry TR5). The annual rent will, by definition, have a life of 1 year, and will thus be classified as an **expense**.

The data from Ex.6.1 is presented below in journal form with the individual accounts affected identified.

Journal Entries

19X1	Journal No		Debit £	Credit £
Jan 1	TR1	Bank	10000	
		Capital		10000
Jan 1	TR2	Motor Vehicles	3300	
		Motor Expenses	140	
		Cash		3440
Jan 2	TR3	Plant and Machinery	1000	
		Creditor J. Smith		1000
Jan 3	TR4	Fixtures and Fittings	300	
		Cash		300
Jan 7	TR5	Premises	5700	
		Cash		5700

Relevant Ledger Accounts

Bank/Cash	
Jan 1 TR1 £10000	Jan 1 TR2 £3440
	Jan 3 TR4 £300
	Jan 7 TR5 £5700

Capital	
	Jan 1 TR1 10000

Motor Vehicles	
Jan 2 TR2 £3300	

Fixture and Fittings	
Jan 3 TR4 £300	

Plant and Machinery	
Jan 3 TR3	
£1000	

Shop Premises	
Jan 7 TR5 £5700	

J. Smith (creditor)	
	Jan 2 TR3 £1000

Motor Expenses	
Jan 2 TR2 £140	

In following the procedures which were identified in Chapter 4 we can now calculate the balances in the ledger accounts above and transfer these to a trial balance. Any adjustments necessary to make the information more useful should be undertaken – if, for example, financial statements were required at the end of the first month an adjustment should be made to record that there are still 11 months' worth of future benefit from the road fund licence; there would also be some reduction in the future benefits to be enjoyed from the other assets which have been acquired by the business. Sect. 6.5 discusses in detail the concept of **depreciation** which was previously used in respect of the van in ADJ 2 in Sect. 4.4.

6.4   Valuing fixed assets subsequent to acquisition

For many years an increase in a fixed assets value over its acquisition cost was excluded from the balance sheet by a restrictive interpretation of the realisation and prudence accounting principles. In recent years it has become common to recognise **increases in the value of fixed assets** in the balance sheet.[3] Until the asset is sold the increase represents an unrealised gain, and is therefore not recognised as revenue in the profit and loss account. It is instead recorded in a **revaluation reserve** in the owners' equity section of the balance sheet.[4]

The situation where a fixed asset value falls below acquisition cost because of depreciation is discussed in Sect. 6.5. Where, as a result of changing market conditions, there is a **permanent fall** in the value of a fixed asset, this fall should be recognised immediately: a typical example in recent years would be shipbuilding companies, who have faced a fall in demand for their services resulting in a reduction in the economic value of their property, plant and equipment. Applying the accounting concept of prudence suggests that the amount written off in this situation should be shown in the profit and loss account as a **reduction in profit**.[5]

6.5 Depreciation

Depreciation as a Change in Value

The wearing out or using up of an assets stock of benefits reduces its value, and this reduction in value is termed depreciation.[6]

In Chapter 2 the profit of an accounting period was defined as the **change in value during that period**. The use of assets usually means that their benefits are being **consumed**; this consumption will usually bring about a reduction in value as the total amount of future benefits has also fallen. The fall in value, or 'depreciation', reduces profit and will be an **expense** matched against the revenues in the profit and loss account (see Sect. 3.5). Depreciation here is the **difference between the opening and closing valuation of fixed assets**, and is depicted in Figure 6.1.

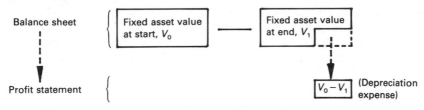

Figure 6.1

In circumstances such as these the calculation of depreciation would rely on the **annual valuation of assets**. If in any particular year a fixed asset does not decrease in value, or if it actually **appreciates**, then there appears to be no need for a depreciation expense. In the latter case, there appears to be a case for recognising additional revenue which is the result of **holding assets** rather than trading or business activities. In practice, as was shown in Sect. 6.4, the non-recognition of such gains as revenue is a function of the application of the relevant accounting concepts such as realisation and prudence.

Depreciation based on the difference between opening and closing values of assets assumes that these respective values are available. For the first accounting period of a fixed asset's life the opening value to be used in the calculation will be based on the **acquisition value**, or **original value**, as discussed in Sect. 6.3. The closing value, however, would depend on which of the four **value concepts** introduced in Chapter 2 are being used. These were original cost, replacement cost, realisable value and value to the owner. As we will see in Sect. 6.6, accountants have traditionally favoured the use of original cost as the basis of valuation and depreciation in financial statements, because it is a measure which is easy to corroborate – i.e., it is **objective**. Where original cost is used, the measurement of depreciation is essentially not a measure of change in value but is an **allocation of cost**.

As explained in Sect. 6.4, in recent years the use of concepts other than historic cost have become common because it is believed they provide a more relevant picture of the current position of the firm. The problems this causes for the depreciation process are discussed in Sect. 6.6.

Depreciation as a Reduction in Future Benefits

Depreciation was described above in terms of the changes in value of assets, and its measurement relied on knowing their opening and closing values. An alternative approach to the problem would be to measure the value of **benefits used up** in each accounting period, because, the use of the asset will reduce the **present value of its future benefits**. Since these benefits will have been used up to generate revenue for the firm it will be appropriate to match the value of the benefits used up against the revenue earned in each period. The initial value of the benefits to be derived from owning an asset will be reflected in its purchase price; the benefits used up in any one period can then be reflected as an **expense in that period**. We can relate this to Ex.6.1, where second hand machinery was purchased for £1000, by assuming that the machinery was purchased because of its capacity to produce 10 000 units of output. Each unit of output could thus be valued at 10p per unit. If 1000 units are produced in one accounting period then the value of benefits used up (i.e. depreciation) is £100. In the same example, a 10 year lease on shop premises was acquired for £5000 and some electrical work was carried out for £700. It will not be possible to recover the monies spent on the electrical work when the lease runs out, so in this instance the benefits to be derived are restricted to the **time period covered by the lease**. The asset will have no value at the end of the 10 year period; its benefits will have expired at the rate of £570 per annum and this sum can be treated as an **annual depreciation expense** which is being matched to the revenues that the premises have contributed towards during the 10 year period.

6.6 Depreciation methods used in practice

The methods of depreciation which are used in practice were developed for application with the original cost concept of asset valuation, since this is the traditional concept used in financial statements. The **residual value** (for example, any sale proceeds which can be obtained when the assets have no further use to the business) of most assets will be lower than their original cost; the use of the asset by the business, or the passage of time, or both, will have reduced its value by an amount which can be measured as the **difference between the original cost of the asset and its residual value**. This sum can be viewed as the cost of owning the asset, and therefore the expense which needs to be accounted for. Depreciation calculated in this way allocates the total fall in value, 'by a variety of methods' to accounting periods during the asset's life. This process of matching the depreciation expense based on original cost against the revenues arising in each accounting period as stated earlier is not one of annual valuation, but one of **cost allocation** to the relevant periods.

To examine the difficulties of allocating the cost,[7] of a fixed asset to the accounting periods during its life, we will consider three elements in the calculation – the life of the asset, its residual value, and the method of cost allocation.

The Life of an Asset

The life of some assets will be clearly defined in legal terms as with the lease discussed in Sect. 6.5. At the end of a 10 year period the premises revert back to their original owner and it will be necessary for Fred Flintstone Ltd to make alternative arrangements. Patents, licenses and copyrights may be subject to similar arrangements.

Other assets will have a physical life during which they will be able to function for their intended purposes; the duration of this physical life, however, may be very difficult to estimate accurately. Where an asset's life expectancy is tied to **usage** – e.g., the 10 000 unit machine mentioned in Sect. 6.5 – or is a function of **usage and time** – e.g., motor vehicles – estimates of future use, production and demand will be required. If sufficient resources are committed to the asset, its physical life may be **extended** – e.g., if repairs are continuously carried out without regard to cost a machine's production capacity or roadworthiness may be extended. However, an asset's usefulness will also be affected by **economic** factors, such as the demand for the products made using the fixed asset. In general, the fixed asset should be retained provided the additional revenue it generates **exceeds the cost of maintaining** it.

A firm will take a decision when it purchases a fixed asset about how long it expects to keep it; the firm will make an estimate of the asset's **useful economic life**. Any error in forecasts will have to be dealt with at a later date – for example, obsolescence may make it necessary to replace a machine earlier than expected. 'Obsolescence' is the term used when an asset falls in value due to factors other than its use or the passage of time – for example, changes in technology may result in alternative assets which can produce the output cheaper, or the demand for the product may have changed, making it uneconomical to continue its production.

The Residual Value of an Asset

To calculate the expense that has to be matched against the revenues arising over an asset's life the **estimated residual value must be deducted from the original cost**. In most cases this will be positive, but in certain circumstances the residual value could be **negative** (e.g., the disposal costs may exceed the final sale proceeds, and should, in this event, be added to the original cost).

The Method of Cost Allocation

The difference between original cost and the residual value has to be **allocated over the useful life of the asset**. The options open to the firm can be summarised in diagrammatic form as in Figure 6.2, which shows three alternative possibilities for cost allocation. The curves in the Figure 6.2 show the original costs *less* accumulated depreciation[8] at particular points in the life of the asset; all the curves start at the original cost and end at the residual value. Points on the curve represents **interim** valuations of the asset: curve *A* allocates more depreciation expense to the early years of the asset's life; curve *C* represents an increasing depreciation expense over the life of the asset; curve *B* is straight, representing an equal allocation each year.

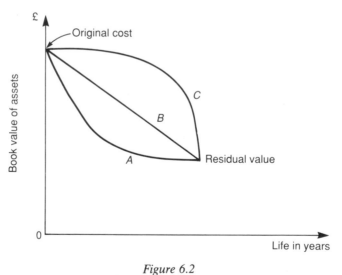

Figure 6.2

In practice, there are three types of allocation that are commonly used, and these are examined below:

The Straight-line Method
This allocates the difference between the original cost and residual value

(which can be called, the 'asset's total expense') **equally over each year of the asset's forecast life** (as in curve *B* in Figure 6.2). The formula is:

$$\text{Annual Depreciation Expense} = \frac{\text{Asset's Total Expense}}{\text{Forecast Life}}$$

The effect of this is to produce an **equal depreciation expense each year in the profit statement**, as in Figure 6.3.

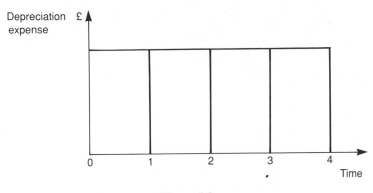

Figure 6.3

Example 6.2
Using the data relating to the purchase of the van in Ex.6.1 straight-line annual depreciation would be calculated as follows:

$$\frac{£3300 - £300}{3} = £1000$$

In the profit *and loss accounts* for 19X1, 19X2 and 19X3, there will be a depreciation expense of £1000. The balance sheet value of the Van at the end of each year will be shown as:–

	31/12/19X1	*31/12/19X2*	*31/12/19X3*
	£	£	£
Van at Cost	3300	3300	3300
Less			
Accumulated Depreciation	1000	2000	3000
Net Book Value	£2300	£1300	£ 300

The accumulated depreciation, sometimes termed a **depreciation provision**, is that part of the cost which has been treated as an **expense to date**.

Reducing-charge Method

This method, sometimes known as the reducing-balance method, produces a **decreasing annual depreciation expense during the asset's life** (as in curve Λ in Figure 6.2), with the largest expense in the first year and the smallest expense in the last year. One way of calculating the annual depreciation expense is to apply a **constant percentage** to the balance of the original cost *less* accumulated depreciation in each accounting period. The percentage should be such that the total amount of accumulated depreciation (the sum of the individual years' amounts) over the asset's expected useful life should be the same as the total amount under the straight-line method. The only difference is in the **distribution of depreciation between the years**. The appropriate constant percentage (Y) can be calculated from:

$$Y = 100 \left(1 - \sqrt[n]{\frac{RV}{C}} \right)$$

where n is the expected life, RV is the estimated residual value and C is the original cost.

Figure 6.4 shows the pattern of depreciation expense over the asset's life.

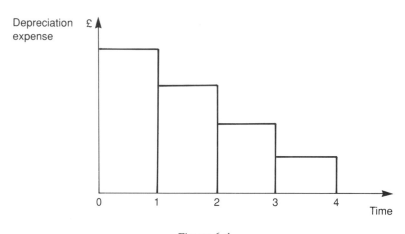

Figure 6.4

Example 6.3

Again using the data relating to the van from Ex.6.1, the constant percentage required will be 55% – i.e., $100 \left(1 - \sqrt[3]{\dfrac{300}{3300}} \right)$

The depreciation expense each year is:

Year					£
1	55%	×	(3300 − 0)	=	1815
2	55%	×	(3300 − 1815)	=	817
3	55%	×	(3300 − 2632)	=	368*

Total depreciation = 3000

£367.4 rounded to £368.

These amounts will appear as a depreciation expense in the profit and loss accounts each year and the end of year balance sheets will be:

	31/12/19X1	*31/12/19X2*	*31/12/19X3*
	£	£	£
Van at Cost	3300	3300	3300
Less			
Accumulated Depreciation	1815	2632	3000
Net book value	£1485	£ 668	£ 300

Usage Method

This method relates the depreciation expense in each year to the **use made of the asset**. 'Use' can be measured in many different ways: for a lorry it may be miles travelled; for a plane, hours of flying time; for a machine, hours or units of production. The depreciation expense is calculated as an amount **per unit of use**. The formula is:

$$\text{Depreciation Expense per Unit of Use} = \frac{\text{Asset's Total Expense}}{\text{Forecast Life Expressed in Units of Use}}$$

The depreciation expense each year will be the **rate** calculated in this way **multiplied by the actual use made of the asset in the period**. This could produce a curve similar to *A*, *B* or *C* in Figure 6.2, depending on the usage pattern.

Example 6.4

Using the data from Ex.6.1 as before, and additionally the knowledge that Fred Flinststone Ltd will use the van for approximately 15 000 miles over the

3 year period, it is possible to determine a **per mile depreciation rate** as follows:

£3000/15000 = £0.20

Each year's depreciation will be a function of that year's mileage: if the usage is 5000 miles per year, then the depreciation will be £1000 per annum, just as with straight-line depreciation. With any other mileage pattern the depreciation will differ.

Our examples above relate to three particular methods for depreciating fixed assets. However, one other method needs mentioning. This involves the treating of an asset as an **expense in the accounting period in which it is acquired**, and is used with assets whose value is immaterial in relation to the other numbers in the profit statement. An example of this would be a firm treating the purchase of small tools such as spanners as immediate expenses. Such items may be used for several years and thus qualify as fixed assets, but their relative small cost justifies their treatment as an expense.

In our example of the van, the use of different depreciation bases will lead to different annual depreciation figures, which in turn will lead to different annual profit amounts during the 3 year period, even though the other data about the firm on each occasion is the same. When original cost is the valuation basis in use the objective of depreciation is to allocate or spread the cost of the asset, *less* its residual value, over its expected economic (forecast) life. Each decision which the firm makes in relation to an asset – i.e., its expected life, its expected residual value and the method of depreciation to be used – will affect **current and future profit figures**.

Revision of the Expected Life of an Asset

The expected useful economic life of an asset is initially an estimate or forecast, and like any decision taken in respect of the future is **subject to error**. In the case of the van in Ex.6.1 the expected life was forecast as 3 years. This forecast may be based on company holding policy in respect of motor vehicles, it may be based on some average expected life for this model of van, or it may be a function of useful usage. A firm will normally review its forecast of an asset's life regularly, and in many instances the forecast will be **revised** and all future calculations will then be based on this revision.

Example 6.5
The Elf Co. Ltd purchases a machine for £12 000 and forecasts than its life will be 5 years. It is estimated that at the end of the fifth year the asset will be worthless. However, after only 3 years the firm finds demand conditions have changed and it cannot sell the goods produced. At this time the machine is scrapped and has no residual value.

During each of the 3 years, revenues are £10 000 and expenses are £5000. Three possible profit statements are shown for the third year below on the assumption that:

(a) the life is **5 years** (this was the original forecast);
(b) the life is **3 years** (this would have been the forecast life if the change in demand had been foreseen);
(c) the calculations have been **adjusted** in the third year from the initial forecast life of 5 years to 3 years.

Profit and Loss Account for the Third Year

	(a) 5 year forecast	(b) 3 year forecast	(c) 5 year forecast and adjustment
	£	£	£
Sales Revenues	10000	10000	10000
Less:			
Depreciation	2400	4000	4000
Other Expenses	5000	5000	5000
Additional Depreciation $(2 \times [4000 - 2400])$			3200
Net Profit	£2600	£1000	£2200 (loss)

In the case of profit and loss account (c) depreciation for the period is shown as £4000 (what it would have been annually if the details in respect of demand had been known earlier) and there is an adjustment for the under-depreciation in the first two years when depreciation had been provided at £2400. If the fall in demand had been known earlier, it would have been considered in the forecast, and annual depreciation would have been £4000 in each of the three years as in (b) above. In (b) and (c) the total depreciation for the three year period is the same: – in (b) 3 × £4000 and in (c) 2 × 2400 + 4000 + 3200, i.e. £12 000.

Changes in the Expected Residual Value of an Asset

The residual or scrap value estimated for an asset is a function of the assumption about **life expectancy and market conditions in the future**. Even if the life expectancy does not change, market conditions may change substantially between purchase and the end of an asset's useful life.

Example 6.6

The East Co. Ltd purchases a machine for £20 000 and estimates its residual value as £2000 if it retains it for 5 years. Over the 5 years it will thus match £18 000 of depreciation expense against the firm's revenues at the rate of £3600 p.a. At the end of the fifth year it sells the asset for £5000. Only £15 000 (20 000 − 5000) should have been matched against the revenues during the 5 year period. In matching £18 000 over 5 years (£3600 p.a.) depreciation was overstated each year by £600, and profits were understated by the same amount.

It is also possible that the residual value of an asset is **overestimated**: in the above example the East Co. Ltd might at the end of the 5 year period have to pay another organisation to come and remove its machine. Instead of receiving £2000 in payment an additional expense is thus incurred.

Selecting the Appropriate Method

Depreciation spreads the cost of the asset *less* its residual value over its expected life. If the residual value and expected life forecasts are correct, then the **total asset expense** which is depreciated will be the same irrespective of the depreciation method used; however, the **annual amount** will be altered depending on the method selected, as in our examples above. It is therefore necessary for the business to formulate some decision policy for selecting the depreciation method to use with any given asset. The relevant accounting standard[9] states that 'Depreciation should be allocated so as to charge a fair proportion of cost or valuation of the asset to each accounting period expected to benefit from its use'. This is an explanation of the accounting concept of **matching**. What constitutes a 'fair proportion' will depend on the type of asset, and on how the matching concept is interpreted. Consideration must also be given to the use of methods which are practical and which are not too costly to implement. Take as an example a company's motor vehicle fleet. Many firms have a standard policy whereby each vehicle is renewed, irrespective of use, every 2, 3 or 4 years. Company policy thus sets the expected life of all of the motor vehicles. However, usage and care will probably vary considerably between the different holders of the vehicles – a sales representative's milage would probably be far more than that of an office-bound member of staff. Choosing the appropriate depreciation method in this situation may be difficult if the objective is to find an appropriate matching of expenses and revenues. An alternative and popular approach is to attempt to ensure that the depreciation method used leads to an **annual book value** which is as close as possible to the market value of the asset itself. In the case of Motor Vehicles the reduction in value which arises from use is often more closely related to the passage of time in the first few years than to any specific usage characteristic – e.g., when selling a second hand car the price received is more closely associated with the age of the car than with its condition and mileage. The largest drop in value arises in the first year of ownership, and future reductions in value are smaller. This suggests that the **reducing-value** method is most appropriate if the external market value is an important criteria.

Where a firm owns machinery whose value is closely associated with use, then the **usage method** may be appropriate and where the asset life is related to a specific time period such as a lease the **straight-line method** becomes appropriate. In choosing a depreciation base the firm should select the most appropriate for their circumstances, and their skill in choosing will increase with experience. The firm's responsibility to shareholders and other users should lead to the provision of explanatory information in the event that they find an alternative or different base more appropriate than the one currently in use. In many situations, because a rigorous matching of cost and benefit is in practice difficult to achieve, the straight-line method is preferred, simply because of its ease of application.

6.7 Recording Depreciation

Example 6.7
The Eal Co. Ltd purchases a fixed asset for £20 000 cash on 1 January 19X0 (TR 1) and calculates the depreciation expense to be £2000 in 19X0 (ADJ 1) and £3000 in 19X1 (ADJ 2). Following the rules previously developed, the entries in the accounts will appear as follows:

Fixed Asset		*Accumulated Depreciation*	
TR 1 20000			2000 ADJ 1
			3000 ADJ 2

Cash		Depreciation Expense	
	20000 TR 1	ADJ 1 2000	2000 to P&L (19X0)
		ADJ 2 3000	3000 to P&L (19X1)

The cash purchase of the asset is recorded in the Fixed Asset and Cash accounts but the depreciation which accumulates in relation to that asset is recorded in a separate 'Accumulated Depreciation' account while the annual depreciation expense also has its own separate account (note that the accumulated depreciation account **reduces the balance sheet value of assets**, while the depreciation expense account is a **P & L expense**).

The balance sheet items in relation to this example will look as follows:

	31/12/19X0	*31/12/19X1*
Fixed Asset at Cost	£20000	£20000
Less Accumulated Depreciation	2000	5000
	£18000	£15000

6.8 Retirement and disposal of fixed assets

On disposal of a fixed asset an additional **disposal account** has to be created; this is used to eliminate the cost and accumulated depreciation in respect of the asset from the accounts, and bring these, together with the proceeds from the disposal into one account so that the final position in respect of the asset can be determined and a profit or loss on disposal can be calculated.

Example 6.8
Ex.6.7 continues on from Ex.6.6, with the additional information that the asset was sold for £14 000 cash (TR 2) on 2 January 19X2. The cost (ADJ 3) and the accumulated depreciation (ADJ 4) are eliminated from their respective accounts to the disposal account.

Fixed Assets				*Accumulated Depreciation*		
Bal	20000	20000	ADJ 3	ADJ 4 5000	5000	Bal

Cash		*Disposal of Fixed Assets*		
TR 2 14000		ADJ 3 20000	14000	TR 2
			5000	ADJ 4
			1000	ADJ 5
		£20000	£20000	

Profit (and Loss) Account 19X2	
ADJ 5 1000	

In this example, the asset which had originally cost £20 000 to purchase had been depreciated by £5000 at the time of sale leaving it with a net book value in the balance sheet value of £15 000. The sale proceeds of £14 000 did not correspond to the value of the asset in the balance sheet. The difference is regarded as a **loss** in the profit and loss account of 19X2. (ADJ 5) This concept of profit or loss can be very difficult to understand in relation to fixed assets: in this example, if the asset had been depreciated annually by £3000 instead of £2000 in the first year and £3000 the second year, then the balance sheet value would have been £14 000 and no loss would have arisen. Alternatively, if the annual depreciation had been £4000 the balance sheet value would have been (£20 000 − [2 × £4000]) £12 000 and the sale for £14 000 would have produced a profit of £2000. In this example we can assume that small differences between the selling price and balance sheet value of our asset arose because of the problems associated with estimating the residual value or appropriate depreciation basis to use. The effect of having made the incorrect calculation of depreciation in the profit and loss accounts of the years during which the asset was held may be immaterial; however in many instances the size of the difference may be **material**, and may need to be disclosed and treated separately in the accounts.

6.9 Depreciation and capital maintenance

Replacement of Assets

The purchase of an asset is generally accompanied by an **outflow of cash**. The effect on the balance sheet is that a **monetary** asset – cash – is replaced with a **physical** asset which is recorded at cost. Over time the physical asset's cost becomes a depreciation expense which to the extent that it reduces profits (and so reduces the amount which is available for distribution to the share-holders) will **conserve cash** within the business (see Chapter 12). Over time, the amount which is conserved by means of the depreciation process in relation to a specific asset will be equal to its original cost *less* its residual value and might, if it were held and set aside, be sufficient to **replace the asset** at the end of its useful life.

Example 6.9
On 1 January 19X0 the Smith Company purchases a van for £5000. Assume

> (a) either that the company depreciates the van on a straight-line basis for 2 years at £2500 a year; or
> (b) that no depreciation is charged.

In each of the years 19X0 and 19X1 the company's sales (all in cash) were £20 000 and its cash expenses were £7000. The company's policy is to pay a maximum dividend each year equal to all available profits.

Shown below is the profit and loss account for 19X0 under the two assumptions in (a) and (b). Alongside the profit and loss account is a statement of the cash flows in and out of the company in respect of the items in the profit and loss account.

	Profit and Loss Account 19X0		*Cash Flows*	
	(a) With depreciation	*(b) No depreciation*	*(a)*	*(b)*
Sales	£20000	£20000	+£20000	+£20000
Expenses	7000	7000	−7000	−7000
	13000	13000	+13000	+13000
Depreciation	2500	–	No direct effect	
Profit	10500	13000		
Dividends	10500	13000	−10500	−13000
Retained	–	–	£+2500	0

We can see from this example that in the case of the normal assumption (a) where depreciation is charged the potential profit is reduced by the £2500 depreciation expense, thus restricting the cash paid out in dividends to £10 500. Where no depreciation is charged the cash dividend paid out is £13 000. In effect, charging depreciation has forced the company to retain £2500 cash per year within the business.

In reality, the process of depreciating fixed assets does not necessarily mean that cash is available specifically to replace them because (1) the cash retained in the firm may have been used for other purposes, (2) the price of the replacement may be different, and (3) a decision not to replace may be taken.

Example 6.10

Using the information from Ex.6.9, the balance sheet immediately after the van is purchased and the year end balance sheets are as follows:

	1 Jan 19X0	31 December 19X0	31 December 19X1
Fixed Assets		£	£
Van at Cost	£5000	5000	5000
Less Accumulated			
Depreciation	—	2500	5000
	5000	2500	—
Current Assets			
Stock	9000	10000	16000
Cash	3000	4500	1000
	17000	17000	17000
Financed by			
Owners' Equity			
Capital	17000	17000	17000
	£17000	£17000	£17000

It can be seen from these balance sheets that instead of the initial cash balance of £3000 increasing to £8000 because of the cash retained as explained in Ex.6.9, the company only has £1000 cash at the end of 19X1. The cash has been used to purchase additional stock of £7000 (i.e., £5000 + £2000 from the original cash balance).

Even if there were £5000 cash retained within the business if the cost of replacing this asset has increased to say, £7000 then additional funds will be necessary if the asset is to be replaced.

Capital Maintenance

Sect. 5.4 explained that one of the ways in which company law seeks to protect investors is to prevent companies distributing resources which should properly be retained within the firm to ensure its future operations and to protect the investors' share of the firm's capital.

One of the ways in which accounting principles seek to implement this concept of capital maintenance is illustrated in Ex.6.9. It is also shown in Ex.6.10 where the balance sheets show that although the net book value of the van was reduced from £5000 to £2500 and then to zero the capital of the firm was maintained at £17 000. However, although the process of depreciating assets provides a **replacement fund based on the asset's original cost**, the **actual replacement cost** may differ substantially.

If the replacement asset costs more, it will become necessary to raise additional funds to replace it. These funds can be raised from shareholders so that their investment in the business will increase – but the profit generating ability of the business will not change since it will be using the same assets as before. The funds from shareholders can be generated by a direct injection of more capital – for example, by a new share issue. Alternatively the shareholders could leave more in the business by reducing their dividends and thus retaining more profit for use within the firm. In addition the firm could raise more funds by borrowing – but, as we will see in Chapter 10, this has further implications for the financial structure of the firm.

If the replacement asset **costs less** than the original asset, additional funds become available for distribution, or for investment in other assets. Acquiring additional assets will increase the firm's production capacity, which in theory should increase shareholders' profits in the future. Further consideration of the problem of interpreting the meaning of capital maintenance is given in Chapter 14.

6.10 Summary

To a large extent, our discussion of fixed assets and depreciation in Chapter 6 has been focused on the original cost concept. This is because it has traditionally been used to match the original cost of an asset with the revenues which the asset helps to generate. When used in the ways which have been described above no attempt is made to relate depreciation to the replacement cost of an asset. The practice of **regularly revaluing assets** has grown in popularity in recent times, and this has drawn attention to the shortfalls in the traditional approach: in times of inflation and changing prices, the replacement cost of assets can vary substantially from their original cost. It is possible to **reassess the depreciation figure** with each revaluation, and change the annual expense in the light of additional knowledge about the replacement cost of an asset. This question will be given further consideration in Chapter 14.

Notes and References

1. It has proved difficult in recent years to achieve a satisfactory accounting treatment of some intangible assets, notably research and development, goodwill and brands. Recognition of these items as assets is difficult because of the relative uncertainty often associated with their future benefit to the firm. Additional problems of measurement occur where the items are internally generated and are not acquired by an external transaction.
2. In practice whether a lease is classified as a fixed asset will depend on the nature of the **terms of the lease**. The Accounting Standards Committee have dealt with the issue in SSAP 21, 'Accounting for Leases and Hire Purchase Contracts'.
3. 'It has . . . become increasingly common for enterprises to revalue their fixed assets, in particular freehold and leasehold property and to incorporate these revalued assets in their financial statements' (SSAP 12, 'Accounting for Depreciation', 1987).
4. See Notes 12 and 23 to the annual statements of Marks and Spencer in Appendix B for an example of a revaluation reserve.
5. SSAP 12 'Accounting for Depreciation' states that where the fixed asset's net book value exceeds its 'recoverable amount', the asset should be written down to this **estimated recoverable amount**. It defines 'recoverable amount' as 'the greater of the net realisable value of the asset and where appropriate the amount recoverable from its future use'.
6. SSAP 12, 'Accounting for Depreciation' defines depreciation as: 'The measure of the wearing out, consumption or other reduction in the useful economic life of a fixed asset, whether arising from use, effluxion of time or obsolescence through technological or market changes'.
7. When the balance sheet value of a fixed asset is increased by revaluation, the result will be an increase in the amount to be depreciated over the remainder of its useful life.
8. Accumulated depreciation is the total amount of depreciation expense which has **already been allocated** in respect of an asset; the difference between the original cost of the asset and accumulated depreciation is termed the assets **Net book value**.
9. SSAP 12, 'Accounting for Depreciation'.

Questions and Problems

6.1 What do you understand by the following terminology:

Fixed asset   Intangible asset
Current asset   Tangible asset
Original cost   Forecast life
Depreciation   Physical life
Accumulated depreciation   Straight-line basis
Depreciation provision   Reducing-charge basis
Residual value   Usage basis
Net book value   Obsolescence

6.2 How would you prove that the following are assets of a firm:

(a) a ship;
(b) a lorry;
(c) an oil well;
(d) a good reputation;
(e) a patent;
(f) a well known brand;
(g) good employee relations.

6.3 The Ealing Company Ltd installs a new machine in its factory. The following are some of the costs incurred by the firm during the first year of operation of the machine. Should any of these be treated as part of the machine's original cost?

(a) The cash price was £100 000.
(b) An old machine was removed to make way for the new one and this removal cost was £2000.
(c) £155 was paid for delivery of the new machine.
(d) The firm's own labour force was used to install the machine; the relevant wages were £4000.
(e) A new air-conditioning unit (cost £7500) was installed because of extra heat generated by the new machine. It was estimated that the existing air-conditioning unit would have had to be renewed next year even if the machine had not been installed.
(f) The Managing Director, who is paid £18 per hour, spent two hours examining the new machine.
(g) The Chief Accountant is paid £15 per hour, and he spent 1 hour processing the new machine's invoice, as it contained some mistakes.
(h) Repair costs of £2000 were incurred in the first year.

6.4 Edgar purchased a car in kit form for £2000 and proceeded to assemble it himself. The following information was obtained:

(a) £1500 of special tools had to be purchased to construct the car.
(b) His garage was used for the work, and this was normally kept empty, but £200 per week rent could have been obtained for it if let.
(c) The construction time was 2 weeks, 1 week being Edgar's holiday, the other week a special unpaid week off work (he earns £400 per week).

(d) When constructed, the car could have been sold for £3000.
(e) The car will save Edgar £3250 over its life in travelling expenses, etc.
    What value would you assign to Edgar's car?

6.5 When measuring the depreciation of a fixed asset, what accounting
     concepts are important, and why?
6.6 What are the arguments for and against an organisation such as the
     government or the accounting profession specifying the depreciation
     basis to be used by all firms'.
6.7 MBA Incorporated, a firm of management consultants, acquire a
     four year lease on an office for £20 000.

(1) Should the lease be classified as an asset?
(2) Should the lease be depreciated over the four years?
(3) How will the lease appear in the balance sheet at the end of each
    year?

6.8 Elkington Traders Ltd purchases a machine for £2000 and estimates
     its optimal life to be five years and residual value to be £400. It is
     estimated that the sales, *less* expenses (other than depreciation)
     arising from the machine will be £3000 each year. Show the esti-
     mated profit over the five year period, using

(a) the straight-line base base;
(b) the reducing-charge base

6.9 Egg Eaters Ltd purchased a ship for £250 000 on 1 January 19X0 and
     decided to depreciate it at £25 000 each year. At the end of 19X3 it
     was sold for £180 000. Show the entries for these transactions in the
     accounts. How would the ship have been valued in the firm's balance
     sheet at the end of 19X2?
6.10 At 31.12.X1 Egg Eaters Ltd became aware that the market value of
     their ship had dropped to £175 000. What action should they take?
6.11 Two companies, Laurel Ltd and Hardy Ltd are in the same business
     and both regularly make profits before depreciation of £30 000 a
     year. Both companies acquire identical plant at a cost of £40 000.
     Laurel Ltd believes that the equipment could soon be outdated
     and proposes to write it off over three years, allow for a residual
     value of £5000 and use the reducing-balance method of depreciation.
     The rate applied is 50% the net book value each year. Hardy Ltd, on
     the other hand, expects the equipment to last for five years, with a
     residual value of £10 000. This company uses straight-line de-
     preciation. Show the effect of these proposals on the profit and loss
     account and balance sheet of each company.
6.12 A car rental firm is considering how long it should keep a car which
     cost £10 000. It constructs the following cash forecast for the first five
     years of the car's life:

	Possible life (in years)					
	0	1	2	3	4	5
	£	£	£	£	£	£
Rental income p.a.	–	15000	15000	10000	15000	10000
Repairs p.a.	–	–	2000	4000	8000	10000
Residual value	10000	6500	6000	5500	5000	4000

(a) Make whatever assumptions you consider necessary and explain the length of time you would recommend the firm to keep the car.

(b) Explain and justify the assumptions you have made.

6.13 MBS Inc. buys a car for £23 000 with an estimated life of four years. Residual value of £3000 is expected, and straight-line depreciation is used. After three years the car is sold for £12 000.

(a) Prepare a table showing how the car's cost is charged as an expense year by year.

(b) Calculate the profit or loss on disposal.

(c) What would the profit or loss be if there was no residual value?

6.14 Jim Clough starts a business with a capital of £1150. The business consists of buying automatic vending machines and selling confectionery through the machines.

Jim withdraws each year the whole of the profit shown by his accounts, but no more. His stock remains constant at £100 (at cost). He always pays cash for purchases. At the end of 5 years, his balance sheet is as follows:

J. Clough: Balance Sheet on 31 December 19X5

	£		£	£
Capital	1150	Machines at		
		cost	1000	
		depreciation	(500)	
				500
		Stock	100	
		Cash at bank	550	
				650
	£1150			£1150

Jim tells you he cannot understand why his cash balance is so high when he has withdrawn all his profit each year. Explain to him why this is so.

6.15 The Tahoe Co. has two fixed asset accounts, one for Buildings and one for Plant and Machinery. On 1 January 19X8 the relevant balances are:

	Cost	Accumulated Depreciation
Buildings	£220000	£30000
Plant and Machinery	140000	50000

During 19X8 the company purchased Buildings at a cost of £80 000 and sold Machinery for £15 000 which had cost £60 000 several years ago and had a net book value of £40 000.

The company's policy on assets bought or sold during the year is to take a full year's depreciation in the year of purchase and none in the year of sale.

The depreciation for 19X8 is to be made at 10% on the cost of Buildings and 20% on the reducing balance of Plant and Machinery.

Required:

(1) The relevant ledger accounts required to record the above information.
(2) The fixed asset section of the company's balance sheet at 31 December 19X8.
(3) Assume that the company have been told that the current value of its buildings at 31 December 19X8 is £400 000. What is the relevance of this information to the company? What adjustments (if any) should the company make to its accounts to reflect this information.

6.16 The Marin Co. purchased a building on 1 January 19X4 at a cost of £80 000. The building was to be depreciated over 10 years on a straight-line-basis with an estimated residual value of £20 000. On 1 January 19X8 the building is revalued to a figure of £120 000. At that time its remaining useful life is increased to 9 years and its residual value is increased to £30 000.

Required:

(1) Calculate the annual depreciation charge for 19X7 and for 19X8.
(2) Show the accounting journal entries required on 1 January 19X8 to reflect the revaluation.
(3) The managing director of the firm suggests that because the asset has increased in value from 19X4 to 19X8, there is no need to charge depreciation in 19X8. Comment on this suggestion.
(4) He also says that he has been told that while depreciation is said to provide resources for the firm's future it is also merely an end of year book-keeping entry. Explain the reason for this apparent confusion to the managing director.

6.17 ABC Ltd maintains its fixed assets at cost. Depreciation provision accounts are kept for each asset.
On 31 December 19X6, the following balances were held.

	Cost	Accumulated Depreciation
	£	£
Plant and Machinery	159600	78360
Motor Vehicles	58500	20340

Depreciation provision is made at 10% p.a. on cost for plant and machinery and at 25% p.a. on the net book value for motor vehicles. A full year's depreciation is provided on all assets owned by the company on the balance sheet date.
The following additional assets were purchased during 19X7:

	£
Plant and Machinery	30580
Motor Vehicles	23500

Motor vehicles bought in January 19X5 for £20 000 were sold for £8120 on 30 June 19X7.

Required:

(a)(i) The following accounts for the year ending 31 December 19X7:

Individual asset accounts, Accumulated Depreciation accounts, Motor vehicles disposal account

(ii) Show the fixed asset section of the balance sheet as at 31 December 19X7.

(b) Does the depreciation provision in the accounts of a company help the replacement of a fixed asset?

6.18 (a) The Cowie Company showed the following items under Fixed Assets for its balance sheet at 31 March 19X7:

	Cost £	Depreciation to Date	Net Book Value
Freehold Land	50000	–	50000
Buildings	200000	10000	190000
Plant and Machinery	100000	50000	50000
Vehicles	25000	10000	15000
			305000

The rates of depreciation used by the company are:

Buildings – 2% straight line
Plant and Machinery – 15% reducing balance
Vehicles – 25% reducing balance

During the year 19X7/X8 plant that had cost £50 000 (depreciation to date £40 000) was disposed of after transport, auction commissions and other expenses at a cost of £1000 to the company. New plant costing £60 000 was purchased. Assume that a full year's depreciation is taken in the year of purchase and none in the year of sale.

Required: The relevant entries for the balance sheet at 31.3.X8 and for the profit and loss account for the year to 31.3.X8.

(b) The Cowie Company's trading results for 19X7/X8 are disappointing, with profit down on previous years. The chairman has proposed that no depreciation of fixed assets should be made for 19X7/X8 on the grounds that their current market value is approximately equal to the net book value at the beginning of the year.

Required: A discussion of the chairman's proposal.

6.19 (a) Explain briefly the purpose of providing for the depreciation of fixed assets.
(b) Depreciation is often said to be a source of funds. Briefly comment on this statement.
(c) Mr Ventura set up in business on 1 January 19X5 by purchasing a taxi for £20 000. He expects to keep the taxi for four years at

which time he could sell it for £8000. During these four years he anticipates that his net cash flows (taxi fares less running costs) will be £32 000 each year. Each year Mr Ventura withdraws all the available profit as dividends. Assuming only the above transactions took place, show the firm's balance sheet at the end of four years:

(i) If they charge depreciation on the taxi on a straight-line basis.
(ii) If no depreciation is charged.

Comment briefly on the results in (a) and (b).
(d) Comment on the effect on the situation in (c) if there is an increase in the cost of new taxis from £20 000 to £28 000 over the four years.
6.20 Research and development, goodwill and brands are possible examples of intangible assets.

(a) Should they be classified as assets?
(b) If they are assets how should they be depreciated?
(c) What difference does it make if:

(i) They have been purchased from another company.
(ii) They have been internally generated.

(d) What accounting principles are relevant to this issue?

7
Stock and Cost of Goods Sold

7.1 Introduction

The terms 'stock' and 'cost of sales' have appeared frequently in preceding chapters. In many of the examples stock had been acquired by purchase and re-sold to provide sales revenue, stock remaining at the end of a period appeared under Current Assets in the balance sheet (Sect. 3.7). Cost of Sales (alternatively known as Cost of Goods Sold) is the term used in the profit and loss account to describe the **amount of stock used up or sold in the accounting period**. We have assumed to date that the value of closing stock and of cost of sales is known. We have not confronted the variety of problems which a business faces in measuring both the **quantity** and **value** of stock **used during a period**, and the **quantity** and **value** of stock **remaining at the end of a period**. The figures which form part of the annual financial statements are determined by a mix of physical characteristics, valuation assumptions and the application of accounting concepts and bases. Chapter 7 will introduce some of the measurement problems associated with stock and cost of sales, and Chapter 8 will extend the discussion.

7.2 Nature of stock in different organisations

In practice there are a large number of different types of business organisations, providing a vast range and variety of goods and services. **Service industries** – e.g., banking, accounting, law and insurance – do not generally hold physical stock for sale or use in production.

Retail organisations purchase goods for resale, and will usually not have to alter or adjust these goods significantly. Their stock at any point in time will be the **sum of the value of the individual unsold products**.

Other organisations acquire goods which require adjusting, manufacturing or assembling before they are ready for resale. It would be reasonable to suggest that adjusted stock has a higher value then unadjusted stock, and that the **value added** is partially explained by the labour cost associated with the adjusting, manufacture or assembly.

A bakery, for example, might hold a mixture of goods at different stages of completion – e.g., ingredients for making bread and cakes and bread and

121

cakes ready for sale. The stock of ingredients (raw material) can be measured, weighed or estimated and then valued using purchase prices; however the stock of cakes and bread (finished goods) is not as simple to value. The raw materials used can be measured in terms of their purchase price but additional resources such as power and labour have also been used, and it is reasonable to include these **transformation costs** as part of the finished cost of the cakes and bread produced. At this stage, the bakery stock of finished goods also has a **selling price** which may provide an additional potential valuation.

More complex organisations are subject to a wider range of stock measurement problems. Consider a tinned food processing factory producing a wide range of different tinned foods. At any time, it will hold large quantities and a wide variety of different **raw materials**, as well as a stock of **finished goods**. The process through which raw materials are passed to provide finished goods will also be at **varying stages of completion**. These partly finished goods (**work in progress**) also form part of the stock of the organisations, and have to be included in any measurement figure; there are often also problems in estimating the **level of completion**, which adds to the difficulties. Any processing, transformation or adjusting which is carried out on a raw material involves the use of **other resources**, such as labour and machinery, and these costs also have to be accounted for. No unique solution for dealing with these costs is available; however, in the interest of matching costs with the revenues they produce there is an argument in favour of treating any costs associated with bringing goods into saleable condition as **product (stock) or unit costs**. There are a number of different techniques and bases in use, and these will be discussed more fully in Chapter 8.

The balance sheet value for stock and the profit and loss figure for cost of sales can be based on a simple calculation, for example, in a retail organisation where it will be the purchase cost of items for resale. At the other extreme, where the production process is complex (such as in a refinery or a manufacturing firm), the calculation includes raw materials, work in progress and finished goods – whose valuation may be equally complex, being based on a calculation of the additional costs incurred in getting the goods to their current level of completeness. This is also dealt with in more detail in Chapter 8.

7.3 Physical stock data

Firms regularly have to assess their **physical quantities of stock** to measure profit, or to provide a check on the financial stock records. Figure 7.1 illustrates the connection between the physical quantities and the financial records.

Records of the physical quantities of the various stocks held normally form the basis of the financial records kept by the firm; this applies to raw

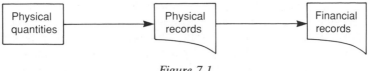

Figure 7.1

materials, work in progress and finished goods. When up-to-date physical and financial records are not kept, a physical count will need be taken when information about stock is required (e.g., at the year end). This figure is required so that closing stock can be calculated for use in the 'Cost of Sales' calculation, and the year end balance sheet. **Periodic physical stock counting** has traditionally been used in some industries instead of keeping detailed continuous records, (e.g., by firms with a large turnover of small items, such as in department stores and supermarkets, where it has proved more cost effective then keeping more complete records). However, computers have reduced the costs associated with stock records for most types of organisation, and it is thus now possible to maintain stock records which are **continually updated** when stock is bought and sold.

Some firms may keep continuous updated records on the physical levels of stock without including continuous up-dated financial records, while others will keep a complete (perpetual) record of physical and financial levels of stock updating with each physical change.

Physical records for each type of stock held will show quantities **received** and **used**. Financial records will be similar, but will record the **receipt and usage in financial terms**. A major benefit of continuous physical records is the control it gives over physical quantities, but this benefit has to be compared with the **cost of maintaining records**.

The benefits of continuous physical records can be summarised under **three** headings; they:

(1) provide up-to-date information about **stock levels** (quantity and type) which can be used to determine **reordering requirements**.

(2) provide useful information on **usage patterns** and so **highlight popular items**

(3) allow the **identification of reductions in stock which are not the result of sales** (e.g., losses arising through theft, deterioration and counting error) by comparing the physical count with the recorded levels (stock taking) at regular intervals.

7.4 Cost of sales

In Sect. 5.8 the concept of matching was described as an attempt to ensure that the revenues recorded in a period were matched with the expenses incurred in earning them. Organisations hold stock so that they are in a position to **make a sale**; this stock is an **asset** until it is sold, at which time there is a **reduction** in the value of assets. This reduction is an **expense**, and is usually called the 'cost of sales' or 'cost of goods sold' in the profit and loss account; the cost of a sale is matched with the **sales revenue** it produces. Taken literally, matching would involve an organisation identifying the specific purchase cost of each item of stock which is sold, and matching it with the sales revenue from that individual item. This may be possible when dealing with small quantities of items, and when complete physical and financial information regarding stock is maintained, however for organisations holding and selling a large number of different types of stock (e.g., department stores and supermarkets), without the benefit of computers, individual matching is costly and a simple alternative is usually used. The total cost of goods available for sale in an accounting period is found by measuring the **value of opening stock**, and adding to it the **total value of goods purchased**. A year end physical stock take is then used to determine the value (cost) of unsold stock for deduction from the total available to provide a figure for 'cost of sales', as in Ex.7.1.

Example 7.1
J. Smith & Co. Ltd had a closing stock figure of £10 700 at 31 December 19X0. Purchases during 19X1 amounted to £100 300 and the figure for closing stock at 31 December 19X1 has been calculated as £11 000.

Calculation for 'Cost of Sales'

Opening Stock at 1/1/19X0	10700
+ goods purchased during accounting period	100300
Total Available for Sale	111000
Less	
Closing Stock at 31/12/X0	£ 11000
'Cost of Sales'	£100000

This calculation provides a cost of sales expense figure for use in the profit and loss account. Because this method of calculation relies on an end of period physical count and valuation of stock it is often known as a **periodic system** of accounting for stock; it is often used by small retail organisations, who do not have the time or manpower to employ a more sophisticated system.

The more sophisticated system known as the **perpetual system** of accounting for stock was explained in Sect. 7.3 on physical stock data. It involves the **continuous updating** of stock records on both a **physical** and a **financial** basis.

This means that every time a sale is made, the related cost data for that sale must be retrieved. As was explained earlier, this is now much easier with the aid of computer controlled information systems. Assuming the cost data is identified, the recording entry will be:

Dr Cost of Sales
    Cr   Stock

If all purchases are debited to the stock account, it follows that at any time the stock account should record the 'correct' amount of stock held by the firm. This 'book' figure can be compared from time to time with the **actual stock figures**, in order to identify losses due to wastage, pilferage, etc.

In the alternative and simpler periodic system the stock account will be updated only by means of the periodic count of stock, and consequently the retailer using this system does not know what his stock 'should be'; it is therefore difficult to identify losses due to wastage, pilferage, etc. with this system.

Stock Obsolescence

Physical stock-taking either to determine the end of year level of stock in a periodic system, or to confirm an end of year level of stock in a perpetual system, should either directly or indirectly ensure that the **cost of stock lost through theft and breakage**, etc. is taken into account in calculating profit. Such losses will be identified separately in the accounts only if the amounts in question are material. It is possible, however, that the stock held includes items that cannot be sold at the normal selling price. This may need to be reflected in the valuation of stock if the revised expected selling price falls below original cost. This is the application of the accounting concept of **conservatism**. In practice, the concept is interpreted by valuing stock at the **'lower of cost or net realisable value'**.[1] 'Obsolescence' is as we know a fall in selling value caused by **physical factors**, or a change in **demand conditions**. The selling value could fall to zero, in which case the stock is completely obsolete. The effect of obsolescence on profit measurement is illustrated in Ex.7.2.

Example 7.2
The Freedom Co. commences business as a wholesaler on 1 January 19X0. During 19X0 it purchases £40 000 of stock and sells half of this for £80 000. It incurs £30 000 administrative overhead costs. At the end of 19X0 it ascertains the physical quantity of stock, and finds stock that cost £5000 is worthless because of deterioration due to bad storage. The profit and loss account will thus be:

Profit and loss account for the Year Ended 31 December 19X0

	£
Sales Revenue	80000
Less: Cost of Goods Sold	20000
Gross Profit	£60000
Less: Expenses	
Administration Overhead Costs	30000
Obsolete Stock	5000
Profit	£25000

The profit has been reduced here by £5000, demonstrating the effect of obsolete stock. The valuation of stock carried forward will be £15 000 rather than £20 000, reflecting the fact that the **net realisable value** of part of the stock which originally cost £5000 is now **zero**.

7.5   Stock valuation

It is common for firms to find that the purchase price of materials change over time, so that its stock at any point in time may be made up of a collection of identical goods acquired at different costs. This creates additional problems in determining the value of stock held at any point in time. We examine here three bases for dealing with these variations, so that profit can be determined and stock can be valued.

First in First Out (FIFO)

This basis assumes that the **first goods purchased** are the **first goods sold**, irrespective of the actual physical flow of goods. Figure 7.2 illustrates this using the data in Ex.7.3.

Example 7.3

Fearless Plc purchases and sells the following goods in 19X0;

		Cost £	Sales £
1 Jan. 19X0	100 units at £100	10000	
31 Mar. 19X0	200 units at £120	24000	
30th June 19X0	200 units at £140	28000	
31st Dec. 19X0	400 units at £200		80000

Figure 7.2

The firm assumes a FIFO flow of costs irrespective of the actual pattern of usage:

Profit and loss account for the Year Ended 31 December 19X0

	£	£
Sales Revenue		80000
Less: Cost of Goods Sold		
100 @ £100	10000	
200 @ £120	24000	
100 @ £140	14000	48000
Gross Profit		32000

The stock valuation at 31 December 19X0 will be £14 000 (100 units at £140).

Last in First Out (LIFO)

This assumption is that the **last goods acquired** are the **first goods sold**, again irrespective of the actual pattern of usage. Figure 7.3 illustrates this using the data in Ex.7.3.

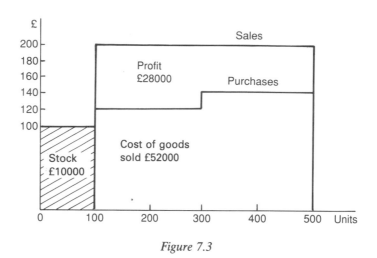

Figure 7.3

Example 7.4
Assume the same facts as in Ex.7.3, but that the firm assumes a LIFO flow of costs.

Profit and loss account for the Year Ended 31 December 19X0

	£	£
Sales Revenue		80000
Less: Cost of Goods Sold		
200 @ £140	28000	
200 @ £120	24000	48000
Gross Profit		28000

The stock valuation at 31 December 19X0 will be £10 000 (100 units at £100).

Average Cost

A compromise between LIFO and FIFO is the average cost basis. The cost of goods sold and the year end stock are calculated at the **average cost during the accounting period**. The average cost is found by adding the cost of a purchase to the existing stock and dividing by the number of units involved.

Example 7.5
Assume the same facts as in Ex.7.3, but that the firm uses average cost for its calculations.

Profit and loss account for the Year Ended 31 December 19X0

	£
Sales Revenue	80000
Less: Cost of Goods Sold	
400 @ £124	49600
Gross Profit	30400

The stock valuation at 31 December 19X0 will be £12 400 (100 units at £124). The average cost per unit is £124.00:

$$\text{i.e.,} \quad \frac{\text{Total Cost}}{\text{No. of Units}} = \frac{10000 + 24000 + 28000}{100 + 200 + 200} = \frac{62000}{500} = £124.00$$

Implications of LIFO, FIFO and Average Cost Bases

A **different measure of profit** was produced with the same information using each of these bases. In addition, they each produced a **different valuation for closing stock**:

	FIFO	LIFO	Average
	£	£	£
Profit in 19X0	32000	28000	30400
Stock Valuation @ 31/12/X0	14000	10000	12400

The cost of materials was rising in 19X0, and thus FIFO gives a higher profit than LIFO, with the average basis figure being in between them. The LIFO profit would have been greater than FIFO if costs had gone down in 19X0.

If the concept of matching were applied literally, then none of the above bases would be acceptable because they all ignore the **physical flow of goods**. However, each of the above methods are acceptable if they are deemed to give a reasonable approximation of the 'actual cost'. Whatever basis a firm chooses, they should apply it **consistently** each year.

Comparison of These Valuation Bases

The stock valuation which appears in a firm's financial statements is the result of combining physical and financial data relating to that stock. When a firm chooses a basis for applying financial values to its physical stock it should be aware of the **implications** of that choice.

The LIFO method calculates the cost of sales by assuming that the **most recent purchases are used first**. This may provide a better surrogate for replacement cost than the use of FIFO or average cost, because the cost of sales figure is more up to date. The profit of any selling transaction can be divided into **two parts**:

(a) Selling price *less* current replacement cost;
(b) Current replacement cost *less* original cost (also known as a holding gain).

Conventional historic cost profit is measured by using selling price *less* original cost, and during a period of unchanging prices LIFO, FIFO and average cost would produce the same profit number. However, in recent years many prices have tended to rise and because the firm usually has to replace its stock it may be considered that (a) above is a better measure of profit. LIFO is a better approximation to (a) than FIFO although FIFO and average cost are more commonly used in the UK. The use of replacement cost (or a good approximation) for cost of sales ensures that an organisation will retain sufficient resources to be able to **replace the same quantity of stock over time**; the effect of non-use of replacement costs in times of rising prices is considered in Sect. 7.6.

7.6 Cost of sales measurement and capital maintenance

The measurement of the cost of sales is necessary to enable a **gross profit** to be calculated in the profit and loss account, by deducting the cost of sales from the sales revenue. This deduction, as well as calculating gross profit, restricts the amount of resources (which have been generated by sales) available as profit for distribution to the owners. In so doing the cost of sales deduction creates a **reservoir of resources** which can be used to replace the products sold. Ex.7.6 provides an illustration of this, and of the problems of using historical instead of replacement cost.

Example 7.6
Powerless Plc starts business on 1 January 19X0 with £100 000 in cash. The company's transactions (all in cash) are as follows:

		Cost £	Sales £
1 Jan. X0	100 units purchased at £100	10000	
31 Mar. X0	100 units purchased at £100	10000	
30 Jun. X0	200 units purchased at £400	80000	
31 Dec. X0	400 units sold at £600		240000

The profit and loss account based on historical cost principles and a FIFO assumption will be:

Profit and Loss Account for the Year Ended 31 December 19X0

	£	£
Sales Revenue		240000
Less: Cost of sales		100000
Profit		140000
Dividend		140000
Retained profit		–

All profits are assumed to be distributed and at 1 Jan 19X1 there is again £100 000 in cash available, to buy more stock for 19X1.

Transactions during 19X1 are as follows:

		Cost £	Sales £
1 Jan. X0	100 units at £400	40000	
31 Mar. X0	100 units at £400	40000	
30 Jun. X0	50 units at £400	20000	
31 Dec. X0	250 units at £600		150000

Profit and loss account for the Year Ended 31 December 19X1

	£	£
Sales Revenue		150000
Less: Cost of sales		100000
Profit		£ 50000

When the profit for 19X0 of £140 000 is distributed as dividend the £100 000 available to buy units of stock for use in 19X1 will purchase only 250 units at the replacement cost of £400. The size of the business operations has thus decreased and this is reflected in the reduced profit in 19X1.

The original financial sum of £100 000 provided by shareholders is not sufficient to maintain the operating capacity[2] of the organisation in times of rising prices. It becomes necessary either to make an additional adjustment to costs to reflect the increase[3] and therefore reduce distributable profits or ensure that only a proportion of the apparently distributable profits are actually distributed to shareholders.

7.7 Summary

Chapter 7 has been concerned with accounting for stock and its inclusion in the profit and loss account as cost of sales. The distinction between physical quantities, physical records and financial records was explained together with the related issue of the adoption of the alternative approaches of periodic and perpetual stock valuation systems. The problem of matching stock costs with appropriate revenues when costs fluctuate was considered with a discussion of FIFO, LIFO and average cost systems. The issue of matching and capital maintenance when prices are fluctuating was also introduced.

Notes and References

1. SSAP 9 'Stocks and Long-Term Contracts'.
2. In this example capital maintenance has been explained in terms of operating capacity. For a further discussion of the meaning of capital maintenance see section 14.2.
3. As we saw in section 7.5 this can be partially achieved by the use of LIFO.

Questions and Problems

7.1 What do you understand by the following terminology?

Stock	Raw materials
Finished goods	FIFO
Specific cost	Net realisable value
Average cost	Obsolescence
Cost of sales	Capital maintenance
Work in progress	Periodic cost system
LIFO	Perpetual cost system
Replacement cost	

7.2 Provide examples of organisations which might use

(a) the continuous or perpetual method of recording stock;
(b) the periodic system.

7.3 Why is it often difficult to value work in progress?

7.4 What constitutes the 'original cost' of stock?

7.5 A company starts year 19X0 with stock valued at £12 000. During the year it makes two purchases, one costing £30 000 and the other £34 000. It makes two sales, one for £40 000 and one for £75 000. At the end of 19X0 closing stock is valued at £7200.

Required: Show the journal entries and ledger accounts to record this information, using:

(a) a periodic stock system;
(b) a perpetual system, where the cost of the two sales has been identified as £22 000 and £46 000.

7.6 A firm commences business on 1 January 19X0. It buys and sells silver pots. The following information is available about its purchases and sales in 19X0:

		Purchases £	Sales £
1/1/X0	100 units at £30.00	3000	
1/2/X0	200 units at £35.00	7000	
1/6/X0	200 units at £100.00		20000
8/6/X0	300 units at £40.00	12000	
30/9/X0	200 units at £105.00		21000

The only other costs incurred by the firm in 19X0 are £5000 of administrative non-product costs.

Calculate alternative measures of profit for 19X0. Choose the one you think gives the best measure and justify your choice

7.7 J. Dune started in business on 1 January 19X5 with capital of £1000. He bought and sold a single product and by the end of 19X5 his transactions in this product were as follows:

	Purchases		Sales	
	Units	Unit Price £	Units	Unit Price £
January	50	6	20	8
March	40	7	20	8
May	–		30	9
August	30	8	40	10
October	40	9	20	10
December	20	10	10	11
	180		140	

Assume that Dune uses a perpetual recording system, and that purchases are made at the beginning of the month and sales at the end of the month.

Required:

(1) Calculate J. Dune's gross profit for the year, assuming that:

(a) stock is valued on a LIFO basis;
(b) stock is valued on a FIFO basis.

(2) Assuming that all transactions are made for cash and that there are no other transactions for the year, prepare balance sheets as at 31 December 19X5, assuming that:

(a) stock is valued on a LIFO basis;
(b) stock is valued on a FIFO basis.

(3) Comment on the results shown in (1) and (2) above.
(4) What difference would it make to the calculations in (1) if J. Dune had used a periodic recording system?

7.8 John and Bill Briggs were each left £12 000 in the will of their aunt.
They each set up in business on 1 April 19X6, John trading in widgets and Bill in sprockets.
The following were their transactions during the year ended 31 March 19X7 (all transactions were for cash):

John Briggs			£
Purchases	1 Apr.	500 widgets at	8.00 each
	14 Jul.	200 widgets at	10.00 each
	31 Dec.	400 widgets at	15.00 each
Sales	1 Mar.	600 widgets at	18.00 each

Bill Briggs			£
Purchases	3 May	400 sprockets at	11.00 each
	2 Aug.	400 sprockets at	10.00 each
	30 Nov.	400 sprockets at	9.00 each
Sales	28 Feb.	1000 sprockets at	12.00 each

Required:

(i) At the end of the first year both John and Bill wish to withdraw all their profits. How much would each withdraw:

(a) Calculating profit on FIFO basis?
(b) Calculating profit on LIFO basis?

(ii) Comment on the relative profit figures.
(iii) After withdrawing the profits in cash, what ability has each of them to replenish his stock of goods? What assumption do you need to make in answering this question?

7.9 A boutique stocks leather coats, which it sells at £60 each. In a month when there was no opening balance, the records show the following:

		Leather Coats
May 1	Purchases	50 coats at £30 per coat
6	Sales	40 coats
8	Purchases	40 coats at £35 per coat
13	Sales	20 coats
15	Purchases	70 coats at £42 per coat
20	Sales	80 coats
22	Purchases	60 coats at £28 per coat
27	Sales	70 coats
29	Purchases	30 coats at £32 per coat

The boutique owner has heard that there are different methods of pricing stock, and has asked you to write up his records on a perpetual basis for the above items using the following three methods as alternatives: (1) FIFO; (2) LIFO; (3) Weighted average.

Required:

(i) Relevant stores records for each method.
(ii) Calculate the gross profit under each of the three alternatives.
(iii) Comment on the advantage and disadvantages of each of the above methods.

7.10 The Acme Co. has four different product lines A, B, C, and D. The following information is provided for the most recent year:

	A £	B £	C £	D £
Stock at start of year	2000	4000	3000	8000
Purchases	45000	50000	28000	36000
Stock at end of year (cost)	3200	6400	3300	7400
Estimated net realisable value of stock held at the end of the year	3500	5800	2900	7600

Required:

(i) Calculate the cost of goods sold figure for the company for the year in question. Explain your calculations.
(ii) Explain the principles underlying the calculations in (i).

7.11 The San Ramon Company buys and sells a single product. Its stock on 1 January 19X8 consists of 100 units at £6 each. The company's transactions during 19X8 are:

	Purchases		Sales	
	Units	Price	Units	Price
Jan. 10	150	£7		
Feb. 5			70	£10
Mar. 15	100	£8		
May 6			120	£10
Jul. 20	60	£9		
Aug. 25			50	£12
Oct. 9	40	£9		
Nov. 12			110	£12
Dec. 14	80	£10		

Required:

(i) Assuming the company uses a perpetual recording system, calculate the gross profit for 19X8 based on:

(a) A FIFO basis.
(b) A LIFO basis.

(ii) Explain the problems of accounting for cost of sales and stock in times of changing prices, including an analysis of the usefulness of FIFO and LIFO in these circumstances.

7.12 The stock records for the Carter and Gurney partnership reveal the following information for the year ending 30 April 19X8:

	Purchases (Quantity)	Cost per unit £
May	200	12
August	200	13
November	300	16
February	350	20

Sales for the year were 800 units at £25 each. Total expenses for the year were £4000 and there was no opening stock. Mr Carter has calculated profits for the year at £4200 but his partner Mr Gurney disagrees, and calculates profits as £2250.

To resolve the difference, they consult a firm of accountants, who advise them that the profit for the year is £3200.

Required:

(i) Explain the reasons for the difference in the three computations of profit, and show how each figure has been calculated.
(ii) 'In the long run, different computations such as those in part (i) will have no lasting effect on the firms' overall profit.'
   Comment on this statement.

7.13
(1) Explain what you understand by the idea of 'capital maintenance' in the context of measuring a firm's profit.
(2) A firm starts its operation by purchasing a fixed asset for £6000. The asset is expected to last for three years and have no residual value. In each of the three years the firm earns a net cash flow (i.e., sales *less* expenses other than depreciation) of £3500. The firm has a policy of distributing all available profits as dividends. The firm intends to continue in business after three years by replacing the asset.

Assume the firm has no other transactions apart from those mentioned above.

Required:

(i) What would be the firm's balance sheet at the end of three years:
(a) If depreciation was charged each year on a straight-line basis?
(b) If no depreciation was charged?
(ii) Comment on the relative position in (a) and (b).
(iii) Comment on the firm's position if the asset to be bought to replace the original asset at the end of three years is expected to cost £7500. Should the firm adopt any particular policy in respect of its accounting during the first three years to meet this situation.
(3) During 19X4 a firm purchases 1000 units of a product at £20 per unit. It sells all the units at £30 each. For the purposes of this exercise assume there are no other expenses. The firm wishes to pay a maximum dividend of all available profits.

Required:

(i) What profit has the firm made?
(ii) Explain the cost of sales figures in relation to the idea of capital maintenance.

(iii) Assume that the cost of the product has risen at the end of the year to £25. Should this effect the accounting measurements for 19X4?

7.14 A friend of yours runs a part-time business, spending one day a week in it. She has drawn up a draft trial balance at 31 December 19X2, covering the second year of trading. The trial balance is as follows:

	£	£
Sales		6100
Purchases	3100	
Expenses	1700	
Equipment – Cost	3400	
– Depreciation		340
Stock 1 Jan. 19X2	1100	
Debtors	900	
Bank		200
Creditors		1560
Capital		2000
	10200	10200

On enquiry, you discover the following additional facts. You may assume that they are the only facts relevant to the situation.

1. Stock was counted on 31 December 19X2. At cost prices, the total amounted to £1240.
2. The stock is in good condition except for two items: one cost £200 and is worthless because of a burst water pipe; the other which cost £100 is less severely damaged and will be sold for £115 – less than one-third the normal profit margin.
3. An invoice for purchases arrived on 3 January 19X3 – it had been delayed in the Christmas post. The amount of the invoice is £500. It is not included in the trial balance although the stock arrived before Christmas.
4. A piece of equipment which cost £140 on the very first day of trading (i.e., 1 January 19X1) was sold on credit for £30 during 19X2. No entries have been made in the ledger.
5. No depreciation has been charged for the year. Depreciation policy is to write 10% off the cost of each asset each year (except in the year of disposal of an asset).

   Required: Prepare a profit and loss account for the year ended 31 December 19X2, and a balance sheet on that date.

7.15
(1) Recalculate the data in example 7.6 using a LIFO assumption of stock valuation.
(2) Compare your LIFO solution with the FIFO figures in example 7.6.
(3) Discuss the meaning of capital maintenance in the context of accounting for stock. Suggest other aspects of accounting for companies where the idea of capital maintenance might be relevant.

8
Costing Methods

8.1 Introduction

In Chapter 7 some of the problems associated with valuing a firm's resources used during an accounting period, or held at the end of the period, were introduced. The discussion concentrated mainly on the **alternative bases** which can be used in the valuation of identical goods which are purchased at different prices. The main difference between the bases – such as FIFO, LIFO and average cost – related to the **time period** in which a specific purchase cost is expensed as cost of sales. The assumption was made that no processes were involved in holding and/or preparing the goods for sale – i.e., we were using the retail industry as a basis for our discussion. In Chapter 8 we drop that assumption and extend the discussion to cover the additional measurement problems which arise in organisations which incur a range of different costs in making goods ready for sale – e.g., manufacturing organisations which have to value the full range of stock introduced in Chapter 7 (i.e., raw material, work in progress and finished goods).

The valuation objective is the same irrespective of the organisation – that of **matching** the cost of resource used in producing sales revenue. This involves identifying the **relevant costs** associated with the manufacture of goods across the different stages of production, and then assigning these to provide a valuation for stock in its varying stages. Figure 8.1, illustrates a typical flow of resources in an organisation. Within each category, there may be several different items, with varying costs.

The production process referred to in Figure 8.1, may be complex and thus requires carefully designed **accounting systems** to record its activity and provide accounting information which can be used to measure the efficiency of the operation, as well as to provide information to measure cost of sales and profit. In order to meet these requirements, **costing systems** have been developed for identifying and classifying the information into useful categories. The classification systems selected, and the number of different categories used, will be a function of the specific organisation and the nature of its activities, as well as the potential use to which that information will be put.

Before we consider (in Sect. 8.3) costing systems which might be used to ascertain a firm's cost of production, we will consider an example of a complex costing problem which illustrates some of the difficulties that may

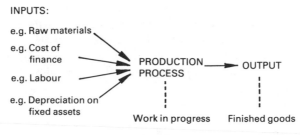

Figure 8.1

arise. An oil company may wish to know the cost of producing North Sea oil; this information may be used for valuing unsold oil, for determining a selling price, or to see whether it costs more or less than oil from another field. Examples of some of the possible costs to be considered are:

Wages of oil rig operators
Maintenance of oil rigs
Cost of raising finance (including interest)
Exploration licences
Research into better exploration methods
Office administration
Exploration of non-productive wells
Pipelines and refining

This list of possible costs should make it clear that the calculation of, for example, a cost per barrel of oil or cost per oil well, is likely to be very difficult to ascertain, yet the oil company will have to find some way of putting all the relevant cost information together in an organised and consistent fashion in order to determine, for example (a) the cost of production, (b) an appropriate selling price for oil, and (c) profitability of a particular oil well. The discussion of cost classifications and cost systems that follows is designed to help in the analysis of this and other problems while at the same time introducing some of the technical terminology which is associated with costing.

8.2   Cost classification

Cost data is collected by organisations through accounting systems. The collection process will be organised in a way which will produce information useful for decision-making within that particular organisation. The information collected has a number of possible applications, as we saw in the example of the oil well in Sect. 8.1. Increases in a firm's costs reduces its level of profits, thus making cost control an essential part of management's task, and the **collection of cost information** is the first step in this process. We have indicated already that the potentially large number of costs which organisations incur will render cost information useless unless it is organised in a meaningful way; this is achieved by **grouping** and **classifying costs** together within a **formal costing system** which has clear objectives. In this section we will consider direct and indirect costs, fixed and variable costs, product and period costs, and will include in the latter the principles of absorption and variable costing.

Direct and Indirect Costs

Costs which can be **identified with a unit of a firm's activities** are termed 'direct'; all others are termed '**indirect**' costs. This latter group of indirect costs are also termed '**overheads**'. All expenses incurred by a business are **costs**, and when related to the firm as a whole they are all **direct**; however, when a firm is divided up into subdivisions (e.g., the individual stores of Marks and Spencer Plc, the departments within a store, or a product line within a department) some costs which are **direct** at the level of the department will be **indirect** at the level of the individual product line. To be meaningful, the use of the term 'direct' or 'indirect' in association with a cost should be qualified by the existence of some **relationship to the subdivision (or unit) of the firm's activity** with which the costs are to be identified.

The label of 'direct' or 'indirect' is often arbitrary, because there are many costs which can be identified with a unit of activity but doing so would be inconvenient or costly. An illustration of a classification of costs into 'direct' and 'indirect' is shown below, using wage costs as an example. A similar analysis could be applied to any other costs arising in the firm.

Subdivisions of Firm	*Direct Wages*	*Indirect Wages*
Firm	Central administrators Factory supervisors Production department supervisors Production operatives	None
Factory	Factory supervisors Production department supervisors Production operatives	Central administrators
Production Department	Production department supervisors Production operatives	Central administrators Factory supervisors
Individual units of production	Production operatives	Central administrators Factory supervisors Production department supervisors

A manufacturing organisation will generally incur a wide range of different costs in the process of producing its output. It will have to select a number of departments, subdepartments or units of output around which costs can be collected. These costing subdivisions are often termed '**cost centres**', and the actual organisation and selection of appropriate costs centres will be a function of the **use** to which the relevant information collected at these points **will be put**. Information about costs has a potential use in a wide variety of different decision-making situations; as well as providing information for **stock valuation**, cost data may also be used in **pricing**. The collection of information about costs can also form part of a formal planning and control system in which an acceptable level of costs for a given period, product or process is determined (planned). **Actual** costs are then collected and **compared with expectations** (controlled). If control is to be successful, individual costs should be collected at cost centres for which individual managers have responsibility: a common saying is that you cannot achieve control without first identifying responsibility; it follows that managers can exert control only over costs for which they are **responsible**. In relation to a particular cost centre it will generally be possible to exert control over its **direct** costs, but not over its **indirect** costs. This is one of the major reasons for the use of such a classification in costing systems. The size and location of a cost centre will therefore be a function of management's need to reflect its **cost system's objectives**.

Fixed and Variable Costs

The distinction between fixed and variable costs relates to the change in total costs which arises as a result of **changes in the level of activity** – e.g., units produced. When a cost changes directly in relation to changes in the level of activity it is termed a **variable cost**, while a cost which is unchanged is termed a **fixed cost**. Making assumptions about how costs vary over a particular relevant range of activity – e.g., the range between 1000 and 2000 units of production – will often simplify the decision-making process. If the **relevant range** defined is large enough, most costs will vary, but within a restricted range some costs will vary whilst others remain fixed. For most firms, the rate of change of variable costs will not be constant over a wide range of activity; in practice, however, the rate of change is often assumed to be constant because this facilitates the costing of production. Unit costs are usually calculated by assuming that the unit variable costs are the same over all levels of activity, and the cost of **alternative levels of production** can thus be predicted.

As with direct and indirect costs, the distinction between 'fixed' and 'variable' is often arbitrary and if, for example, the variation of change over a range of activity is sufficiently small the cost may be assumed to be fixed. In Figure 8.2, which illustrates this pragmatic approach, two wages costs (X and Y) are ascertained for each level of activity and plotted on a graph as a series

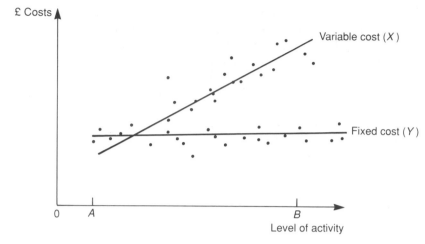

Figure 8.2

of dots. The series is then joined by the best fitting line. The costs (X) would be assumed to be variable within the range considered (from output of A units to output of B units) – i.e., the relevant range. The cost (Y) would be assumed to be fixed.

There may be costs that do not fall easily into either classification, and these are often termed '**semi-variable**' – electricity costs are an example. In this case some element of the cost is fixed and some variable. Figure 8.3 illustrates the fixed, variable and semi-variable classifications:

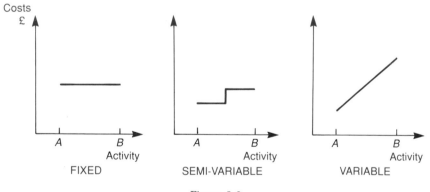

Figure 8.3

All three groups show the cost in relation to a particular range (A to B) of activity of the firm, and the assumptions about classifications are made within that range; they may not hold outside this particular (relevant) range, but may change as the level of output changes. During the course of this chapter some costs will be described in accordance with common practice as variable overheads. It may seem incorrect to classify overhead costs (i.e., indirect costs) as 'variable' because variable costs will normally be traceable to the unit of production and therefore be direct. However, some variable costs may be classified as indirect (e.g., electricity in a machine shop). They could be traced to the product because they are variable, but the identification with the units of production may take too much time and effort.

Product and Period Costs

Those items of expenditure defined as part of the cost of a unit of production are termed 'product costs'. These costs are classified as **expenses** in the accounting period in which the relevant product is **sold**. All other costs are treated as period costs, and are usually classified as **expenses** in the accounting period in which they are **incurred**.

The **cost of production** can be defined as that expenditure which has been incurred in **producing the product or service**. Most of the items of expenditure incurred by a firm could come within this definition, with the exception of costs incurred **after production**, such as salesmen's salaries. However, in practice not all items of expenditure are treated as costs of production.

Figure 8.4 illustrates the flow of costs through a firm, and the different treatment of product and period costs. It shows the payments and accruals (i.e., costs of a firm) being treated in one of the three ways. First as a period cost (*A*) (e.g., office salaries, when they are treated as an expense immediately). Secondly, as a cost of fixed asset (e.g., machinery, from which the related depreciation could be either a period expense (B^1) or a product cost (B^2). Thirdly, as a product cost (*C*) (e.g., raw materials, flowing through work in progress and finished goods, being treated as an expense (cost of goods sold) when sold). The product costs that relate to unsold production will represent the value of the stock of the firm.

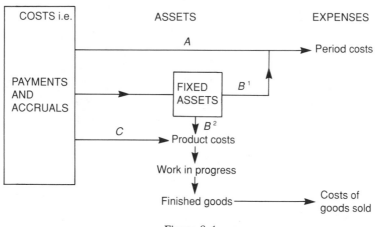

Figure 8.4

Absorption Costing and Variable Costing

The definition of what constitutes a 'product cost' as opposed to a 'period cost' is not in practice precise, and will vary from firm to firm and from industry to industry. However, there are two approaches, known as **absorption costing** and **variable costing**, which can be identified, and these are explained below. For *internal* reporting purposes a firm can choose the method which it considers provides it with the best information; however for **external** reporting they are required by the relevant accounting standard (SSAP 9) to use **absorption costing**.

Where a firm calculates its product costs using variable (or direct) costing only the variable production costs are classified as product costs. Where all the variable production costs and the fixed production costs are classified as product costs this is known as absorption costing. Figure 8.5, illustrates the distinction between the two methods.

Costs	Absorption costing	Variable costing
Direct materials (variable)		
Direct labour (variable)	Product	Product
Variable indirect production costs		
Fixed indirect production costs		Period
Fixed indirect administrative costs	Period	Period
Variable indirect selling costs		

Figure 8.5

The effect of the two types of costing on profit measurement and valuation is illustrated in Ex.8.1

Example 8.1
The Fifty Co. Ltd has the following balances extracted from its trial balance at 31 December 19X0:

Extract From Trial Balance at 31 December 19X0

	£	£
Sales revenue		50000
Raw materials, 1 January 19X0	5000	
Raw materials, purchases	10000	
Work in progress, 1 January 19X0	–	
Finished goods, 1 January 19X0	–	
Direct labour	15000	
Power	4000	
Depreciation of machinery	6000	
Factory rent and rates, etc.	8000	
Supervision of production	1000	

	£	£
General administration expenses	2000	
Selling expenses	9000	

During 19X0 two-thirds of the completed production was sold. The stock details at 31 December 19X0 were:

Raw materials, £7000
Work in progress (this has been assumed to be nil for simplicity)
Finished goods (1/3 of goods completed in year remain unsold)

To calculate the profit or loss from the relevant trial balance information we need to prepare

> (a) a statement of the cost of completed production (sometimes termed a 'manufacturing account');
> (b) a profit and loss account

(a) *Cost of Completed Production, Year Ended 31 December 19X0*

	Variable		Absorption	
	£	£	£	£
Raw Materials at 1.1.19X0	5000		5000	
Purchases	10000		10000	
	15000		15000	
Less: Raw Materials at 31.12.19X0	7000		7000	
Cost of Raw Material Used		8000		8000
Direct Labour		15000		15000
Power		4000		4000
Depreciation of Machinery		–	6000	
Factory Rent and Rates, etc.		–	8000	
Supervision of Production		–	1000	15000
		27000		42000
Add: Work in Progress 1.1.X0		–		–
		27000		42000
Less: Work in Progress 31.12.X0		–		–
		£27000		£42000

(b) *Profit and loss account for the Year Ended 31 December 19X0*

	Variable		Absorption	
	£	£	£	£
Sales revenue		50000		50000
Less: Cost of Sales:				
Finished Goods 1.1.19X0	–		–	
Cost of Completed Production	27000		42000	
	27000		42000	
Finished Goods 31.12.19X0	9000		14000	
(1/3 of production)		18000		28000
Gross Profit		32000		22000
Less: Other Expenses				
Depreciation of Machinery	6000		–	
Factory Rent, Rates, etc.	8000		–	
Supervision of Production	1000	15000	–	
General Administration expense		2000		2000
Selling Expenses		9000		9000
Net Profit		6000		11000
Stock Valuation at				
31 December 19X0				
Raw Materials		7000		7000
Work in Progress		–		–
Finished Goods		9000		14000
		£16000		£21000

The difference in profit of £5000 under the two systems is created by one-third of the fixed costs of £15 000 being included in the balance sheet as stock using absorption costing, but as a period expense using variable costing. In this example we have assumed that depreciation, rent, and supervision are fixed costs.

For internal production planning purposes the gross profit using variable costing might be considered to give more useful information because it will vary in **direct proportion to alternative levels of sales**. Gross profit using absorption costing will not vary directly with changes in the level of sales because of the inclusion of fixed costs in the calculation of cost of sales. However, where product costs are being used as a basis for pricing decisions the absorption cost figures may be a better approximation of the production costs which have to be recovered from the customer. This will be especially true in a firm which employs expensive machinery to produce its products and where the main product cost may be the fixed cost of depreciation.

8.3 Cost systems

In Chapter 4 we saw that financial information emerged from an information system which was designed for the preparation of financial statements. It had three components: data collection, data processing and data communication. We have been discussing so far in Chapter 8 the collection of financial information relating to costs for use in management decision-making and for control purposes. It is possible for data to be collected separately for financial and costing purposes, but in practice most firms use one system to provide **both types of information**. Costs will initially be collected in order that management are provided with timely information for control purposes, and then reclassified to produce costing information. In the case of direct product costs the firm will normally deal with them initially by allocating them to the product; this gives information for costing and control purposes and thus no reclassification is necessary. The actual information system through which the costs flow will be designed so that indirect costs of the products are initially identified and collected at points where individual managers can be given responsibility for them. As a consequence, a cost centre may be very large (e.g., a whole factory), or very small, (e.g., the maintenance team for a factory). Cost information is also used in determining the **selling price** or products, and for this purpose an absorption costing system (full cost) is normally used.

Figure 8.6 gives an illustration of a typical flow of cost components. In costing the product, the indirect costs (i.e., overheads) collected at the different cost centres are **absorbed to the product**. Some cost centres are not directly related to the production of a product (e.g., a factory canteen) and these are known as 'service cost centres'; costs collected at these service cost centres will be **apportioned out between cost centres which are directly involved in production**. The apportionment will be made on some suitable basis (i.e., with a canteen it could be done on the basis of the number of employees using the canteen from each of the other cost centres).

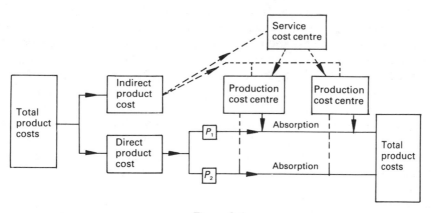

Figure 8.6

Figure 8.6 shows the direct costs allocated to the product, while overheads are allocated first to cost centres and then identified with the product. The dashed lines show, first, the process of apportioning overheads among cost centres on some suitable base, secondly the reapportionment of the service cost centre to production cost centres, and thirdly the absorption of costs to the product. From the production cost centres the costs are absorbed to the products (P_1 and P_2) flowing through the production process; indirect costs are those which **cannot be directly identified with the unit of production**. The process of absorption uses some relatively arbitrary assumptions about the indirect costs' association with the production of a particular unit; a common assumption is to identify the **level of indirect costs** with the **level of production activity**. This can be done using a number of bases:

Direct labour hours
Machine hours
Units of production
Direct labour costs
Cost of material used

At the beginning of an accounting period the indirect product costs (or overheads) and level of production activity will be estimated (i.e. budgeted). From this an **overhead absorption rate** can be calculated:

$$\text{Rate} = \frac{\text{Estimated Overhead Cost}}{\text{Estimated level of production activity}}$$

During the year the overhead costs will be absorbed to the product by measuring the level of activity for each product (e.g., direct labour hours, machine hours, etc. per product) and multiplying by the overhead rate. At the end of the year it is likely that there will be an under- or over-absorbed overhead cost because the rate is based on **estimates**; the under- or over-absorbed indirect cost can be treated as a **period cost** if not material or, it is if material, all the products can be **recosted** based on the actual production data.

The choice of the level of production activity can be determined by looking at the production process and finding what contributes the largest element in the overhead cost – e.g., the indirect costs of a department with mainly machinery costs could be absorbed on the basis of **machine hours**.

Example 8.2
A component manufacturer wishes to calculate its product costs. It makes two products (components *1* and *2*) both of which use the paint-spraying department (cost centre *A*) and the assembly department (cost centre *B*). The manufacturer wishes to calculate its product costs from the data below:

(1) Unit Cost and Hours

	Component 1	Component 2
Direct cost per unit of product	£	£
Material	40.00	30.00
Labour (£10 per hour)		
cost centre *A*	40.00	10.00
cost centre *B*	50.00	5.00
	£130.00	£45.00
	Hours	*Hours*
Machine Hours – cost centre *A*	1	5
– cost centre *B*	2	3
Labour Hours – cost centre *A*	4	1
– cost centre *B*	5	0.5

(2) Fixed Overhead Cost and Hours

	Cost Centre A	Cost Centre B
Fixed Overheads	£	£
Depreciation	80000	10000
Indirect Labour	20000	70000
	£100000	£80000

Note: The paint-spraying department (*A*) uses automatic machinery, which it estimates will be in operation for 10 000 labour hours, with little labour input, while in the assembly department (*B*) the work is mainly done by hand (16 000 labour hours). Hence machine hours are used for (*A*) and labour hours for (*B*).

Basis of Absorption:	*Machine Hours*	*Labour Hours*
Total Hours of:		
Machines	10000	
Labour		16000

(3) Fixed Overhead Rates Calculation
The overhead rates can be calculated as follows:

	Cost Centre A		Cost Centre B	
Fixed Overhead Rate	$\dfrac{£100000}{10000}$	= £10.00 per machine hour	$\dfrac{£80000}{16000}$	= £5.00 per labour hour

(4) Product Cost Calculated Per Unit

The total product cost per unit can be calculated by combining the information in (1) and (3) as follows:

	Component 1 £	Component 2 £
Direct Material	40.00	30.00
Direct Labour – cost centre *A*	40.00	10.00
– cost centre *B*	50.00	5.00
Fixed Overhead – *A* (machine hours × £10)	10.00	50.00
– *B* (labour hours × £5)	25.00	2.50
Total Product Cost	£165.00	£97.50

Component *1* uses less of cost centre *A*'s machines than component *2* and therefore absorbs less fixed overhead costs from cost centre *A* than component *2*. In cost centre *B* component *1* requires more labour and therefore it absorbs more fixed overhead costs here than component *2*.

Levels of production can vary from period to period while indirect product costs may remain constant. This will lead to different absorption rates for different periods and may produce different selling prices. To avoid this, a firm may use the **same normal level of activity in each period** to calculate the rate. The level selected will be based on an estimate of normal production, such as what happened in the past or on expectations for the future. The basis will usually remain static over a number of years once the assumption has been made.

In Ex.8.2 the indirect costs absorbed were all associated with the production of the two components. There may be additional costs which need to be considered before a selling price can be determined – for instance, it may be necessary to allocate the costs from service cost centres and additionally some firms may choose to allocate the overhead costs associated with administration, selling and distribution costs to the product cost, thus arriving at a full unit cost of sales.

8.4   Summary

Our initial concern in Chapter 8 was with the valuation of the resources used by a firm in its operations, together with valuing the units of production remaining unsold at the end of an accounting period, in order that profit measurement could take place. Cost data is also used in pricing decisions and can form part of a formal planning and control system. We have identified a variety of different ways in which an organisation might collect and allocate costs, which can result in different measures of profit. For this reason, it is essential for a firm to select an **appropriate costing system**, and then use it **consistently**.

Questions and Problems

8.1 What do you understand by the following terminology?

Costing systems   Absorption costing
Direct and indirect costs   Overheads
Fixed and variable costs   Cost control
Product and period costs   Allocation of costs
Variable costing   Apportionment of costs
Direct costing   Absorption of costs
Overhead absorption rate

8.2 Discuss the relevant issues in determining the cost of the following products:

(a) a dress included in a retailer's stock;
(b) the same dress when it was in the manufacturer's stock;
(c) a barrel of crude oil;
(d) a barrel of refined aviation fuel;
(e) a motor vehicle.

8.3 Discuss the relationship between 'control' and responsibility in accounting for costs.

8.4 What is the difference, if any, between:

(a) direct and variable costs;
(b) fixed and indirect costs.

8.5 What is the significance of the distinction between 'product' and 'period' costs'.

8.6 Explain the differences between 'absorption costing' and 'variable costing'.

8.7 Describe the process of allocation, apportionment and absorption of costs, explaining the difference between each of the three methods.

8.8 Design a product costing system similar to that in Figure 8.6 for:

(a) a car manufacturer;
(b) a chemical refinery;
(c) a manufacturer of china, crockery and vases.

8.9 Describe the process of overhead absorption. What objectives is it trying to achieve? What are the main problems in achieving such objectives?

8.10 The following is a summary of the trading results of the Acme Razor Co. for the year ended 31 May 19X1, during which 8000 electric shavers were sold:

	£	£
Sales		64000
Costs:		
Material	24000	
Labour: Direct	10000	
Indirect	4000	
Other Costs	12000	
		50000
Profit		£14000

Required: Prepare a summary of the expected results for the following year, taking into consideration the matters listed below:

(a) the selling price of the shaver is to be reduced by 50p;
(b) sales volume is expected to increase by 40%;
(c) owing to larger quantities of material being purchased, suppliers have agreed to grant a discount of 5% on all purchases;
(d) operatives whose wages are classified as 'direct' are to be paid an incentive bonus of 2½% in order to stimulate production; indirect labour is not expected to increase during the forthcoming year.
(e) 'other costs' vary directly with production except to the extent of £2000 which is considered 'fixed', and a further £500 which will arise in the forthcoming year, due to additional rent payable in respect of an extension to the factory;
(f) you are to assume there is no stock or work in progress at 31 May 19X1.

8.11 The following summarised information was extracted from the records of the Up and Over Garage Door Co. Plc, for the last two years:

Sales: £200 per unit, this price remained constant during the two years.
Number of units sold Year I 8000
II 9000

Production was:
Year I 9000 units
Year II 11000 units

Costs:	YEAR I	YEAR II
Fixed Factory	£	£
overheads	150000	160000
Direct labour cost		
per unit	50	60
Variable overheads		
per unit	40	40
Direct materials		
per unit	30	40
Administration and other		
non-production period costs	150000	180000

Other Information
There was no opening stock at the commencement of Year I.

Required:

(a) Management is interested in comparing the profits using (1) variable costing principles and (2) absorption costing principles. Draw up alternative financial statements, showing the difference between variable costing and absorption costing for each of the two years.
(b) Comment on the most important features which distinguish variable costing from absorption costing.

8.12

(a) Explain briefly the meaning of:

(i) direct costs and overheads;
(ii) the three stages of calculating overheads known as cost allocation, cost apportionment and overhead absorption.

(b) The Green Bay Company has three cost centres, machining, assembly, and stores.

Costs incurred during January 19X7 were as follows:

1 Costs already allocated

	Total £	Machining £	Assembly £	Stores £
Indirect Materials	2000	500	1500	–
Indirect Wages	24000	8000	12000	4000
Power	2000	1400	600	
Maintenance	3000	2000	1000	

2 Other costs

Rent	3000
Heating	600
Depreciation (Plant and Equipment)	10000
Factory Administration	4000

3 General information

	Machining	Assembly	Stores
Area Occupied (square metre)	2000	3000	1000
Plant and Equipment at Cost (£000)	6000	3500	500
Number of Employees	800	1150	50
Direct Labour Hours	100000	150000	6000
Number of Stores Requisitions	500	1500	–

Required: An analysis of overhead for each cost centre, and a calculation of an overhead absorption rate based on direct labour hours for the machining and assembly cost centres.

8.13 P. C. Gray and Company Ltd has prepared the following budget figures for the current year.

	Units	£	£
Sales	10000 @	20	200000
Direct Materials	10000 @	1	10000
Direct Labour	10000 @	2	20000
Variable Factory Overhead	10000 @	1	10000
Fixed Production costs			50000
Selling and Distribution Variable Costs	10000 units at	£1	10000
Fixed Selling, Distribution and administration costs			40000
Net Profit			£60000

An area sales manager has asked the sales director for permission to sell 5000 additional units for £7 each. The sales director has refused on the grounds that the price offered is below full cost.

Required: Determine whether the correct decision has been made, assuming the following conditions.

(a) The normal operating capacity of the firm is 15 000 units and there are no other opportunities to increase sales above the budgeted 10 000 units.
(b) The firm is operating at full capacity and the order will need to be worked on overtime. Production workers are paid time-and-a-half on overtime and it is estimated the order will add £5500 to the fixed selling, distribution and administration costs.

Justify your answer in each case, and comment on the basis on which your decision has been made.

8.14 Roker Plc manufactures three products in two production departments, a machine shop and a fitting section; it also has two service departments, a canteen and a machine maintenance section. Shown below are next year's budgeted production data and manufacturing costs for the company.

Product	X	Y	Z
Production	4200 units	6900 units	1700 units
Prime cost:			
Direct Materials	£11 per unit	£14 per unit	£17 per unit
Direct Labour –			
Machine Shop	£6 per unit	£4 per unit	£2 per unit
Fitting Section	£12 per unit	£3 per unit	£21 per unit
Machine Hours,			
per unit	6 hr per unit	3 hr per unit	4 hr per unit

Budgeted Overheads:	Machine Shop	Fitting Section	Canteen	Machine Maintenance Section	Total
	£	£	£	£	£
Allocated Overheads	27660	19470	16600	26640	90370
Rent, Rates, Heat and Light					20000
Depreciation and Insurance of Equipment					30000

Additional data:				
Gross Book Value of Equipment	£150000	£60000	£30000	£60000
Number of Employees	20	16	4	4
Floor Space Occupied – square metres	5000	2000	2000	1000

It has been estimated that approximately 70% of the Machine Maintenance Section's costs are incurred servicing the Machine Shop and the remainder incurred servicing the Fitting Section.

Required:

(i) Calculate the following budgeted overhead absorption rates:

- A machine hour rate for the Machine Shop.
- A rate expressed as a percentage of direct wages for the Fitting Section.

All workings and assumptions should be clearly shown.

(ii) Using the rates calculated in (i) above, calculate the budgeted manufacturing cost per unit of Product *X*.
(iii) Evaluate the usefulness of a unit absorption cost calculation, such as that in part (ii) above.

9
Sales and Purchases, Debtors and Creditors

9.1   Introduction

Chapter 6 was concerned with accounting for the fixed assets which a firm needs to carry out its operations. Chapters 7 and 8 were concerned with various aspects of accounting for stock. The acquisition of a firm's assets and stock are necessary to enable the firm to generate sales. The purpose of Chapter 9 is to explain the accounting issues related to sales, and to deal with some aspects of accounting for purchases.

The activity of buying and selling requires and generates resources just as the purchase of a firm's assets requires resources. The cycle of the application and generation of these resources is depicted in Figure 9.1.

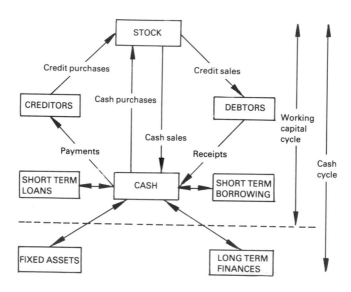

Figure 9.1

9.2   Working capital

Figure 9.1 shows how resources flow in and out of a business. In the final analysis the success of a business rests on its ability to generate sufficient cash to finance all its activities, and Figure 9.1 also shows the **overall flow of the cash cycle**. Chapter 10 is concerned with the methods adopted by firms to raise both long term and short term finance for their operations; Chapter 9 deals with the sales and debtors, purchases and creditors which, together with stock, are the constituent parts of the working capital cycle as shown by Figure 9.1.

'Working capital' is normally defined as **current assets less current liabilities**. It therefore refers to the short term resources available to the business. **Current assets** are typically stock, debtors, short term investment and cash. **Current liabilities** are usually amounts owed by the business in respect of credit purchases or unpaid expenses, taxation or dividends. The significance of working capital in the efficient operation of a business is discussed further in Chapters 10, 12 and 13. In the remainder of Chapter 9 we deal with the accounting procedures necessary to **record the cash and credit purchases and sales** depicted in Figure 9.1.

9.3   Accounting for sales and purchases

The accounting procedures for dealing with purchases are in many ways similar to those for dealing with sales. In the explanations which follow, to avoid duplication, we have concentrated on the sales transactions and referred in parenthesis to purchases where appropriate.

From an accounting viewpoint sales (and purchases) can be classified into **cash** or **credit** transactions:

(a) *Cash sales* occur when goods or services are exchanged for an **immediate payment**; many retail transactions take the form of cash sales 'over the counter'.

(b) *Credit sales* occur when ownership of the goods and services passes from the firm to the customer, but **no immediate payment** is made. For the purpose of accounting (as opposed to a strict legal definition) the timing of the sale is normally dependent on the **date of the invoice** related to the sale or the **date the goods are physically delivered** to the customer.

The different characteristics of cash and credit sales (or purchases) results in the need for different accounting treatment. In a **cash** sale, the customer fulfils his responsibility to the retailer **when the payment is made**; the seller does not consequently usually need to keep a record of the customer's name. The book-keeping record for a sale of £100 is simply:

	£	£
Dr Cash	100	
Cr Sales		100

Or for cash purchases

	£	£
Dr Purchases	100	
Cr Cash		100

In a **credit** sale, however, the customer **has not paid for the goods or services at the time of the sale**; the seller therefore needs to keep a record of the name of the customer and the details of the sale to show how much is owed to the seller. A credit sale of £100 will be recorded as:

Dr Customer (by name)	£100	
Cr Sales		£100

Or for a credit purchase

Dr Purchases	£100	
Cr Supplier (by name)		£100

We have seen from earlier chapters that the collective term used for credit customers who owe money in respect of sales is **debtors** and for amounts owed to suppliers for purchases is **creditors**. It is possible that a firm may have a large number of credit customers (or suppliers); this requires the use of additional accounting records, and these are explained further in Sect. 9.4. A further practical problem which may occur when dealing with credit sales (and purchases) is that the amounts eventually received from the customer may be different from the original sales price of the goods or services. This can be the result of an agreed discount, or the result of unforeseen bad debts. Discounts are dealt with further in Sect. 9.5 and bad debts in Sect. 9.6.

9.4   Sales and purchases day books, ledgers and control accounts

As in Section 9.3, the explanations in Sect. 9.4 concentrate on the sales transactions; only where the requirements for purchases differ is a separate explanation given. The three **elements** of accounting for credit sales discussed in this section are:

(1) Sales Day Books
(2) Sales Ledger
(3) Debtors Control Account

Sales Day Books

We saw in Sect. 4.4 that the first step in the accounting recording process was to **identify** transactions and **record** them in books of prime entry. In the case of credit sales transactions the source document will be the **invoice** sent to the credit customer which confirms the detail of the sale. Sales invoices are recorded in the **Sales Day Book** which constitutes a record of each sale made. Invoices are often listed daily, hence the name 'Day Book'. However, the term is still used even if the firm prepares and lists its invoices at less frequent intervals (e.g., weekly or monthly). A typical extract from a Sales Day Book is shown in Ex.9.1.

Example 9.1
Sales Day Book of the Tetron Co. for the Month of February 19X2

		Sales Day Book		*SDB 15*
Date	*Invoice Number*	*Customer*	*Sales Ledger Reference*	*Amount Invoiced*
19X2				£
Feb. 8	166	T. Smith	SL356	86.00
12	167	Jones Ltd	SL182	124.18
17	168	Harvey Co.	SL158	166.24
25	169	Brown & Co.	SL16	78.00
				£454.42

The SDB15 reference shows the page number in the Sales Day Book and can be used to trace the invoice number for a particular transaction, and thus provide a **trail to the actual invoice**. The Sales Ledger reference is the customer's account number in the Sales Ledger, which is explained below.

The Day Book, as well as providing a record of each customer invoiced, also constitutes the source document for accounting entries in respect of **overall sales**. In Chapter 4 it was emphasised that the book-keeping rule for recording each transaction is that there must be an **equal debit and credit**; for each credit sale transaction the appropriate entry will be (using the data from Ex.9.1):

Feb. 8	Dr Customer (T Smith)	£86.00	
	Cr Sales		£86.00
Feb. 12	Dr Customer (Jones Ltd)	£124.18	
	Cr Sales		£124.18
Feb. 17	Dr Customer (Harvey Ltd)	£166.24	
	Cr Sales		£166.24

Feb. 25   Dr Customer (Brown & Co.)   £78.00
           Cr Sales   £78.00

In practice, a firm may have many such transactions each day rather than the four in one month in our example. Each of the above accounting entries **debits the customer** and **credits sales**. It is therefore clear that a single entry to record all the February transactions can be made as follows:

Dr Debtors   £454.42
    Cr Sales   £454.42

The use of Day Books for Purchases. Cash Receipts and Cash Payments as well as Sales provides an efficient and economical means of summarising data for entry into the double-entry book-keeping system.

Sales Ledger

Where a firm makes sales on credit it is necessary to keep records of **how much is owed by each individual customer**; this is usually achieved by maintaining a Sales Ledger, which contain separate accounts for each credit customer. In Ex.9.1, each of the four customers would have an account in the Sales Ledger; these accounts would record the debit entries in respect of the February sales. When payments are received from these customers they would initially be entered in the Cash Receipts Day Book and then posted to the credit of the individual customer accounts in the Sales Ledger. A balance on a customer's account will normally be a **debit balance**, and signify that some invoices for goods or services received by that customer remain unpaid.

Control Accounts

We saw above that the individual sales invoices in Ex.9.1 were posted to the customer's personal accounts in the Sales Ledger. However, the Sales Ledger does not usually form part of the double-entry system described in Chapter 4. The entry for the double-entry system is that described earlier.

Dr Debtors (Control) Account   £454.42
    Cr Sales   £454.42

The entries in the Sales Ledger account are said to be for **memorandum purposes only**, and as they are merely a detailed version of the above entry they would result in duplication if they were included in the double-entry system. The Debtors Account contains a summary of all the entries in the detailed customers' accounts in the Sales Ledger, and is known as a Control

Account for reasons which will be explained below. The relationship of the Debtors (Control) Account and the Sales Ledger is illustrated in Figure 9.2.

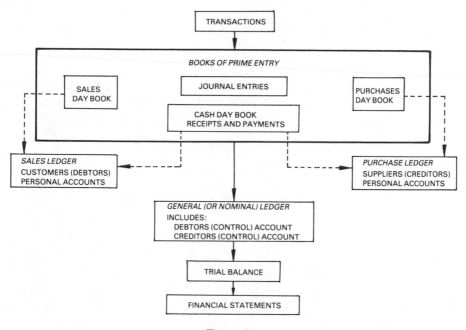

Figure 9.2

Note: Dotted lines denote entries outside the double entry system

Because the information from the Books of prime entry (day books) are entered **in detail** in the Sales and Purchase Ledgers and **in summary** in the Debtors (Control) Account and the Creditors (Control) Account in the General Ledger, it follows that at any one time the **balance on the Debtors (Control) Account** should be **equal to the sum of the balances on the individual customers' accounts in the Sales Ledger**. The same should be true of the Creditors (Control) Account and the individual suppliers' accounts in the Purchase Ledger. A worked example will help to make this clear.

Example 9.2
In addition to the information from Example 9.1, assume that during March the Tetron Co. had the following transactions:

Mar. 2 Invoiced (No. 170) T. Smith for a credit sale of £72
      5 Invoiced (No. 171) Harvey Co. for a credit sale of £120.50
      12 Received payment from T. Smith of £86 for Invoice No. 166

14   Received payment from Jones Ltd of £50, being part payment of
     Invoice No. 167
20   Invoiced (No. 172) Jones Ltd for a credit sale of £135.86
28   Received payment from Brown & Co. of £78 for Invoice No. 169

Assuming there are no other transactions for March the information would be
recorded as:

	Sales Day Book			*SDB 16*
Date	*Invoice Number*	*Customer*	*Sales Ledger Reference*	*Amount Invoiced*
19X2				£
Mar. 2	170	T Smith	SL356	72.00
5	171	Harvey Co.	SL158	120.50
20	172	Jones Ltd	SL182	135.86
				£328.36

	Cash Receipts Book		*CB 27*
Date	*Details*	*Reference*	*Amount Received*
19X2			£
Mar. 12	T Smith	SL356	86.00
14	Jones Ltd	SL182	50.00
28	Brown & Co.	SL16	78.00
			£214.00

The summary entries for the double-entry system resulting from the Sales
Day Book and the Cash Receipt Book for March 19X2 will be:

Dr Debtors (Control) Account	£328.36	
Cr Sales		£328.36
Dr Cash	£214.00	
Cr Debtors (Control) Account		£214.00

In addition, and outside the double-entry system the customers' personal
accounts in the sales ledger would be posted to record the February transactions from Ex.9.1. and the March transactions from Ex.9.2:

Brown & Co.   *Acc No. SL 16*

19X2				*19X2*			
Feb. 25 Sales	SDB 15	£78.00		Mar. 28 Cash	CB17	£78.00	
		£78.00				£78.00	
Apr. 1 Balance		–					

Harvey Co.   *Acc No. SL 158*

Feb. 17 Sales	SDB 15	£166.24
Mar. 5 Sales	SDB 16	120.50
		£286.74
Apr. 1 Balance		£286.74

Jones Ltd   *Acc No. SL 182*

Feb. 12 Sales	SDB 15	£124.18		Mar. 14 Cash	CB 27	£50.00
Mar. 20 Sales	SDB 20	135.86				
		£260.04				£50.00
Apr. 1 Balance		£210.04				

T Smith   *Acc No. SL 356*

Feb. 8 Sales	SDB 15	£86.00		Mar. 12 Cash	CB 27	£86.00
Mar. 2 Sales	SDB 16	72.00				
		£158.00				£86.00
Apr. 1 Balance		£72.00				

The list of customers' debtor balances taken from the Sales Ledger at April 1 would therefore be:

	Balance
	£
SL 16 Brown & Co.	–
SL 158 Harvey Co.	286.74
SL 182 Jones Ltd	210.04
SL 356 T Smith	72.00
	£568.78

The figure of £568.78 represents the total amount owing to the company at April 1, as shown by the information in its Sales Ledger. From the above information, we can also show details of the Debtors (Control) account from the general ledger for the same period:

Debtors (Control) Account				*Acc No. GL 86*
19X2				
Feb. 28 Sales	SDB 15	454.42	Mar. 31 Cash CB 27	214.00
Mar. 31 Sales	SDB 16	328.36		
		£782.78		£214.00
Apr. 1 Balance		568.78		

The balance of £568.78 on the Debtors (Control) Account agrees with the total of the list of balances from the Sales Ledger shown above. It is to be expected that they should agree as they are different ways of presenting the results of the same transactions. However, we will see that the knowledge that these two totals **should agree** is an important feature of the use of control accounts.

Advantages of Having Control Accounts

We saw in Ex.9.2 that the sales and cash receipts transactions were recorded in detail in the Sales Ledger and in summary in the Debtors Control Account and the Cash Account in the General Ledger. It is therefore, clear, that it is not essential to have control accounts; instead, the personal accounts in the Sales Ledger could be used as part of the double-entry system rather then as merely memorandum accounts. However, the apparent duplication of effort implied by the use of control accounts is widely adopted, for the following three reasons:

(1) A large company may have thousands of credit customers and deal with several thousand invoices each week, and with similar volumes of amounts of cash received. The maintenance of accurate up-to-date customer records in these circumstances is obviously important but it is also clear that with this volume of transactions it is easy for errors to be made. As can be seen from Ex.9.2, the control account balances provide a check on what the aggregate of the balances on the sales ledger accounts **should be**; a comparison of these totals may thus reveal that errors have been made.

(2) The total debtors figure is required as part of the process of producing a trial balance. The availability of a debtors control account enables this to be done quickly and easily; otherwise it would be necessary to add up all the individual customer account balances every time a trial balance was required.

(3) The areas of a firm's activity which deals with sales invoices, cash receipts, purchases and cash payments, if not properly controlled, are a potential source of the deliberate or accidental **misappropriation of resources**. The use of control accounts is an important part of a firm's **internal control system** which attempts to avoid, or detect, such occurrences. If the activities of raising invoices, posting the sales ledger, receiving cash and posting the control account are performed, for example, by four different employees it is much more difficult to cover up attempts to change invoices or cash payments or to misappropriate cash receipts.

As explained earlier the content of Sect. 9.4 has been largely concerned with the Sales Day Book, Sales Ledger and Debtors (Control) Account. The principles involved can, however, be applied equally to the Purchase Day Book, Purchase Ledger and Creditors (Control) Account.

9.5 Discounts

Discounts occur when the price actually paid for goods or services is **less than their normal price**, and it is usual to distinguish between **trade** discounts and **cash** discounts. **Trade** discounts are those granted to dealers or wholesalers who can negotiate special prices because of the volume of goods they purchase; this reduction in price is normally deducted before arriving at the invoiced amount. As the accounting for sales and purchases is usually based on the **invoiced amount**, trade discounts do not need to be recorded separately.

Cash discounts, however, are inducements to customers to pay for their purchases promptly. If the ABC Co. buys goods for £1000 from the Exes Co. on 1 June, for example it might be offered a cash discount of 5% if the account is settled within 30 days. The accounting treatment of cash discounts differs from that of trade discounts, because whereas the trade discount is **fixed at the time of sale**, the existence of a cash discount is **uncertain**, as it is dependent on whether the invoice is paid within the specified time period.

In the above example the Exes Co. will record a sale on 1 June at the invoice price of £1000 and the ABC Co. will similarly record in its own records a purchase of £1000. If the ABC Co. does not pay within the specified 30 days then no entry in respect of a discount need be made. If the ABC Co. does pay within the 30 days, say on 20 June, then the entries (shown as journal entries) for the whole transaction will be:

In *Exes Co.'s Books*	£	£
June 1 Dr Debtors (ABC Co.)	1000	
Cr Sales		1000
June 20 Dr Cash	950	
Dr Discounts allowed	50	
Cr Debtors (ABC Co.)		1000

In *ABC Co.'s Books*	£	£
June 1 Dr Purchases	1000	
Cr Creditors (Exes Co.)		1000
June 20 Dr Creditors (Exes Co.)	1000	
Cr Cash		950
Cr Discounts Received		50

The decision to offer a discount and to take advantage of the offer is related to how the two companies organise their cash flows, and is essentially a **financing decision**. It is therefore usual to show discounts allowed as an **expense** and discount received as a **revenue** in the profit and loss account, rather than to deduct them from sales or purchases.

9.6   Bad and doubtful debts

When goods or services are sold on credit there is the possibility that, for a variety of reasons, the payment may not be subsequently received from the customer. This may be the result of deliberate dishonesty, or more likely because the customer is unable to pay because of financial circumstances. The firm to whom the debt is owed will, of course, make every effort to collect the debt but there will be occasions when they decide to give up the fight and write it off as a **bad debt**. The accounting treatment of bad and doubtful debts must be viewed in the context of the treatment of the **original sale**. It is normal to recognise sales revenue at the time the credit sale takes place; this is based on the assumption that there is a reasonable probability that cash will be eventually received from the customer. In the case of a bad debt, of course, this assumption is subsequently seen to be invalid.

Assume that the Harvey Co. in Ex.9.2 goes into liquidation and is unable to pay any of its creditors. The Tetron Co. would lose £286.74 owed to it by the Harvey Co. The sum was included in the sales for February and March, and is part of the total debtor figure at the end of March. In recognising and accounting for the bad debt the two sales of £166.24 and £120. 50 would not normally be deducted from the sales total for February and March. They remain as sales, even though the customer does not pay for the goods purchased. Instead, the sum of £286.74 which has been lost is treated as a

financial expense (i.e., a bad debt expense). The appropriate accounting entry would be:

Dr Bad Debt (Expense)   £286.74
   Cr Debtors (Harvey Co.)   £286.74

The credit to debtors reduces the value of this asset; this acknowledges that the firm's accounts are worth less once it is realised that this debt will not result in a cash receipt. In addition to this credit to the Debtors Control Account, the customer's account should also be credited with £286.74 in the Sales Ledger.

The bad debt figure is treated as an expense in the profit and loss account **for the period in which the bad debt is written off**. It will be appreciated that a firm will write off a bad debt only after it has exhausted all the legal processes open to it. This may take months, or even years. The bad debt expense may consequently be recognised in a different (later) period from that in which the original sale was recognised; this means that the profit for the earlier period was 'overstated', and it could be argued that the principle of 'matching' has not been followed.

It should however be realised that the profit and loss account for each accounting period includes many figures which are based on assumptions and estimates; it is inevitable that some of these assumptions and estimates will prove to be inaccurate, and credit sales which eventually result in bad debts are a typical example. The issue of principle is that with the inclusion of such assumptions and estimates, do the accounts give a 'true and fair view'? In most situations, the assumption is that the treatment of bad debts by the method described above is within the scope of generally accepted accounting principles.

Doubtful Debts

The bad debts described above refer to those debtor balances which have been identified as **definitely irrecoverable**. In addition, there will be a proportion of the debtor balances whose eventual recovery is **uncertain**. The principles of conservatism states that debtors can be classed as assets only if there is a reasonable probability of the amounts being paid; if some debts are doubtful some sort of provision must be made for the possibility of these eventually turning into bad debts. The estimate of doubtful debts can be made in two ways:

(1) *Specific estimate* By inspecting each outstanding Debtors Account in the Sales Ledger, to identify those customers who may not be able to pay.

(2) *General estimate* By estimating what percentage of the debtors' total may be doubtful, using for example an analysis of available statistical evidence on bad debts in the industry in recent years or by using past experience of bad debts for the firm.

Example 9.3

The Watson Co., after writing off bad debts of £750, still has debtors totalling £25 000. The company estimates that 5% of this debtors' total is doubtful. The appropriate book-keeping entry to record the doubtful debts would be:

    Dr Profit and Loss Account (increase in the
        provision for doubtful debts)   £1250
           Cr Provision for Doubtful Debts   £1250

If the Watson Co. already have a provision brought forward from the previous accounting period of (say) £600, then the above entry would be for £560, which would be the amount by which the **existing provision needs to be increased to bring it to the required level**. It is possible that the firm's existing provision is already sufficient; for example if the Watson Co. had brought forward a provision of (say) £1400 then the appropriate entry would be:

    Dr Provision for Doubtful Debts   £150
        Cr Profit and Loss Account (decrease in the
           provision for doubtful debts)   £150

In effect, the last entry is 'writing back' to the profit and loss account a part of the expense which had been debited to the profit and loss account in a previous period, but which is no longer needed given the current size of the firm's debtors. The size of the percentage required will vary between firms, and also between different accounting periods. In times of economic depression, with many more firms going out of business, it is likely that the volume of bad debts will be higher compared with periods of prosperity. Also firms in industries which have a stable history are likely to have fewer bad debts than firms in a risky sector of the economy.

    The provision for doubtful debts is a way of revaluing the debtors' total which will appear in the balance sheet. It is normal, therefore, to show the provision as a **deduction** from the related debtors' figure. Using the data from Ex.9.3:

Debtors	£25000
Less provision for doubtful debts	1250
	£23750

9.7 Summary

Chapter 9 has dealt with the accounting problems created by sales and purchases and with their associated accounting records. Cash sales and purchases respectively **generate** and **use up cash**; credit transactions **generate debtors and creditors**. These current assets and current liabilities, together with unsold purchases (stock), constitute working capital which is considered further in Chapters 10 and 12. Credit transactions also generate the need to maintain individual customers' and suppliers' account and the related control accounts. Some credit transactions will also result in the need for accounting procedures to deal with discounts and bad and doubtful debts.

Questions and Problems

9.1 What do you understand by the following terminology?

Working capital cycle	Discount allowed
Day books	Discount received
Sales ledger	Trade discount
Purchase ledger	Cash discount
Control accounts	Bad debts
Personal accounts	Doubtful debts
	Provision for doubtful debts

9.2 What does 'capital' mean in the context of the expression 'working capital'? Explain other possible uses of the word 'capital' in accounting.

9.3 Explain the significant differences between 'cash' and 'credit' sales. Why is this difference important from an accounting recording viewpoint?

9.4 What accounting principles are important in the recording of sales and purchases?

9.5 Explain how the system of control accounts operates. What are the advantages of having such a system?

9.6 The Orter Co.'s normal level of operation results, on average, in the following:

- 1000 separate cheques are received daily from customers
- 400 cheque payments are made each week to suppliers
- 1200 invoices are sent daily to customers
- 500 invoices are received weekly from suppliers

Suggest what accounting records need to be maintained to record this information. What particular problems arise from dealing with such a volume of operations?

9.7 On 1 October the Oxford Transport and Trading Co. had no debtors. During October, the following transactions occurred:

(a) Oct. 2 Invoiced Arnold Motors for credit sale of £2500
(b)   4 Invoiced Baker Transport for credit sale of £1200
(c)   5 Invoiced Cleveland Taxis for credit sale of £800
(d)   7 Invoiced Derby China for credit sale of £1400
(e)   14 Received £2250 from Arnold Motors who had taken a discount of 10% for paying within 14 days
(f)   16 Received £360 from Cleveland Taxis who had also taken a discount of 10%
(g)   24 Received £1100 from Derby China who were unable to claim a discount.
(h)   26 Baker Transport returned faulty goods which had cost £400

> *Required*: Write up the Sales Day Book, Cash Book, Sales Ledger Accounts and the Debtors Control Account for October. Reconcile the Control Account with the Sales Ledger.

9.8 Staines Trailers has a large number of credit customers. When preparing the accounts for the year to 31 December the accountant discovered that the total of all the personal accounts in the sales ledger amounts to £12 380 but the balance on the debtors control account is £12 550. Upon further investigation, the following errors were discovered:

1. One week's sales in June amounting to £850 had been omitted from the Control Account
2. A Sales Ledger Account balance of £800 had not been included in the list of balances.
3. Cash received of £750 had been entered in a personal account as £570
4. Discounts allowed of £100 had not been entered in the Control Account
5. A personal account balance had been undercast by £200
6. A contra item of £400 with the Purchase Ledger had not been entered in the Control Account
7. A bad debt of £500 had not been entered in the Control Account or the personal account
8. Cash received of £250 had been debited to a personal account
9. Returns inward of £200 had not been included in the Control Account
10. A cheque for £300 received from a customer had been subsequently dishonoured by the bank, but no adjustment had been made in any of the company records

> *Required*:
>
> (a) Prepare a corrected Debtors Control Account.
> (b) Prepare a statement showing the necessary adjustments to the list of the personal account balances, so that it reconciles with the corrected balance in (a).

9.9 The following balances appear in the ledger of the Needles Company as at 1 January 19X9.

	£
Debtors control account	40000
Creditors control account	28000
Provision for doubtful debt	1500

The following transactions took place during 19X9:

	£
Credit sales	285000
Cash received on cash sales	25000
Cash received from debtors	165000
Goods returned (from credit customers)	21000
Credit purchases	142000
Discounts allowed	4200
Cash paid to creditors	122000
Discount received	3100
Bad debts written off	3600
Return of goods (to credit suppliers)	16800
Debtor balances set off against creditor balance (contra entries)	7400
Cash received in respect of a bad debt written off last year	9200

The provision for doubtful debts is to be 10% of the outstanding debtors at 31 December 19X9

Required: Prepare the following accounts for 19X9:

(1) Debtors control account
(2) Creditors control account
(3) Provision for doubtful debts accounts

9.10 Albert Wilson, who is a sole trader, extracted the following trial balance from the accounts of his business the Wilson Fresh Fruit Company on 31 December 19X9

	£	£
Sales		230000
A Wilson – Capital 1/1/X9		18000
Drawings in 19X9	6000	
Freehold premises – at Cost	25000	
Debtors and Creditors	20500	15000
Salary Expenses	10000	
Postage and Telephone	3000	
Packing and Carriage	4000	
Rent and Insurance	2800	
Fixtures and Fittings – at Cost	14000	
Fixtures and fittings – Accumulated Depreciation		4500
Motor Vehicle – at Cost	8000	
Motor Vehicle – Accumulated Depreciation		2000
8% loan (repayable in 8 years)		20000

Motor Expenses	1600	
Purchases	180000	
Repairs and Maintenance	1900	
Stock 1/1/19X9	13000	
Bank Account		2500
Interest Charges	2200	
	£292 000	£292 000

You discover that the following information has not been included in the above accounts:

(1) Stock was valued at £15 000 on 31 December 19X9
(2) On 31 December 19X9, unpaid salaries amounted to £1500 and unpaid telephone bills to £1200
(3) The rent and insurance expenses included an insurance premium of £1200 for the year beginning 1 October 19X9
(4) The repairs and maintenance expenses include £400 for storm damage repairs to Mr Wilson's own house
(5) Depreciation of fixtures and fittings at 10% of cost for the year, depreciation of motor vehicles at 25% of reducing balance for the year
(6) It has been decided to revalue the freehold premises as at 31 December 19X9 to £35 000
(7) The company wish to set up a provision for doubtful debts of 5% of debtors

> *Required*: Prepare a profit and loss account for the company for 19X9 and a balance sheet as at 31 December 19X9.
> *Note*: Show clearly the basis for any adjustments or calculations you find necessary to answer the question.

10
Owners' Equity, Debt and Working Capital

10.1 Introduction

Chapter 10 continues the analysis of the balance sheet by analysing the **financing of the firm**. We consider how firms obtain their finances through the use of owners' equity, by incurring long term liabilities and by organising and controlling their working capital. A firm will require resources to cover its short term requirements – for example, to finance its holding of stock and debtors and to make payments to its creditors. These issues are analysed in Sects 10.8 and 10.11. It will also require finance to procure its long term investment in fixed assets such as land, buildings and machinery. We examine the major factors which contribute to the firm's **financing decisions**, and provide a framework for the analysis of **financing problems**. Long term and short term finance and the concepts of equity and debt are analysed and the importance of liquidity is examined in Sect. 10.10 as a special problem in the financing of the limited company. We begin with an explanation of different **forms of ownership** of an organisation, and illustrate how the method of financing a business may be related to the type of organisation involved.

10.2 Forms of ownership

The three forms of ownership introduced in Sect. 1.5 and discussed further in this Sect. 10.2 are the sole trader, the partnership and the limited liability company. These constitute the great majority of the businesses operating in the UK. The impact of these forms of ownership on the **preparation of financial statements** is dealt with in Sect. 11.2.

Sole Trader

This refers to a business which is owned, and usually managed, by a **single proprietor**. There may, of course, be more than one person working in the

173

business – the reference to 'sole' is concerned only with **ownership**. Sole traders have the simplest form of financial structure. The single owner provides the **capital** for the business, is entitled to any **profit earned**, but also incurs **all the risks**; one of these risks is that the owner is **personally liable for any debts** incurred by the business. As we shall see below when dealing with companies this is one of the major disadvantages of operating as an **unincorporated sole trader**. The law does not distinguish between the owner and the business, and contracts are in effect made by the owner, not the business. If the owner wishes to **share the risk** and create **alternative sources of capital**, he may wish to form a partnership.

Partnerships

Similar in many ways to a sole trader, a partnership is formed where additional owners are admitted to the business. This creates additional sources of capital and the risks are shared, as each partner is **jointly and severally liable for the debts** of the partnership. The partners, however, still have unlimited liability, and therefore are **personally liable** for these debts. The accounting implication of operating as a partnership are dealt with in Sect. 11.3.

Limited Liability Companies

A business which is not a company will usually be restricted in size because of the characteristics of unincorporated types of organisations – i.e., sole traders and partnerships. The benefits arising from incorporation, set out below, explain why it is possible to raise the amounts of capital necessary to enable a business to grow. 'Incorporation' means **registering a business as a company** under the rules and regulations of the UK Companies Acts. Perhaps the most significant effect of the move to company status is that the law recognises the company as a **separate legal entity**, distinct from its owners. This enables the company – as opposed to the owners of the company – to **make contracts** and **incur debts**. The company is taxed as a separate entity under the special taxation rules applying to companies (corporation tax); in sole traders and partnerships the owners are subject to personal taxation on their share of the profits of the business. The creation of a business as a separate legal entity entails three further important characteristics.

Limited Liability
The company is liable for **any debts incurred in its name**. Where a company is incorporated with limited liability, however, the members (or owners) are **not personally responsible**, and cannot be sued by a creditor if the company does not have the resources to repay their debts. A company will normally be

incorporated with limited liability and this must be disclosed in the company's official name – (e.g., John Smith Limited[1] or Marks and Spencer Plc (Public Limited Company).

The significance of limited liability is that it enables individuals to buy shares in an organisation knowing that their **maximum commitment** is the **amount contributed when buying the shares**. However badly the company performs, their maximum loss is known at the time of becoming a shareholder. Even if the company goes into liquidation and its assets are insufficient to cover its liabilities, the owners are not required to make up the deficit. Without limited liability, few people would be prepared to make an investment in shares, which could lead to their being responsible for all the debts of the company. As we shall see below, this implies that anyone lending to a limited liability company may be taking more risk than when lending to a partnership (or even a sole trader) where they could have recourse to the private resources of the partners in the event of the business defaulting on its debts.

Transferable Shares

In a sole trader or a partnership, if one of the owners wishes to withdraw his or her capital from the business it may be necessary to **dissolve** the existing business and **restart** under the new ownership. This is because, as we have seen, the business is not legally separate from the owners. A company, however, as a separate legal entity can issue shares in the business which constitutes partial ownership certificates and which, more importantly, can be **transferred to another person without affecting the organisation of the company**. This possibility, like limited liability, makes share ownership more attractive, because it enables people to invest in a company's capital knowing that it may be possible to end their investment by selling their shares to someone else. The ultimate expression of this is where the shares are quoted on a recognised stock exchange and such investments can be bought and sold with ease.

The combination of limited liability and ease of transferring share ownership has led to an expansion in the number of people who are prepared to become involved in providing capital for companies. This has enabled companies to expand by raising large amounts of capital from a wide range of investors and has led to the next characteristic to be discussed.

Separation of Ownership and Management

In sole traders and partnerships it is usual for the owners to operate the business as **managers**. This can also be true of some companies. However, the phenomena discussed in the previous paragraph has resulted in many owners who have bought shares in a business but have no intention of being involved in its management. The company may thus also have managers who have no share in the ownership. This is an important development for accounting, because it has increased the need for means of **communication between the company and its owners**. The Companies Acts recognise this by requiring regular reports of the managers' stewardship of the owners' investment. This is one of the main reasons for the company's **annual report of its financial statements**.

Capital and Capital Maintenance

It was explained earlier that because of limited liability a company's debts must be met by the company itself, without recourse to the owners. This means that the only security a lender to a company has are the **assets owned by the company**. Some of these assets have been acquired with the capital provided by the owners of the company, so when lending to a company it is always prudent to examine the company's balance sheet to see how much **capital** it has, and what **assets** it owns, which might act as security for a loan. It would clearly be unfair in this situation if the company decided to sell its assets and distribute the proceeds to the owners. Company legislation recognises this possibility, and seeks to prevent it happening in order to protect the creditors (and also other potential investors). The Companies Acts state that a company is in normal circumstances **not allowed to distribute the company's capital to the owners**; it must be retained as a fund to meet the company's debts. In accounting measurement this is sometimes referred to as 'capital maintenance', and has been discussed several times already in this book. It is discussed at length in Sect. 14.2 in connection with maintaining capital in times of changing prices.

10.3   Company finance and financial structure

Sect. 10.2 analysed three different forms of business ownership. The financial structure of sole traders and partnerships is relatively simple, and for the rest of this chapter we shall concentrate on the financial arrangements of companies.

The pattern of a firm's finances is termed its 'financial structure' (sometimes termed 'capital structure'). An extract from the balance sheet of Greenwich Ltd, which illustrates its financial structure, is shown below. This example will serve as the basis for much of the analysis in the later sections of this chapter.

Greenwich Ltd, Extract from Balance Sheet at 31 December 19X1

	£000	£000
Owners' Equity		
Ordinary Shares 200 000 £1 nominal value	200	
Share Premium	20	
Retained Profit	40	260
8% Preference Shares 40 000 £1 nominal value		40
		300
Long-term Liabilities		
6% Debentures (1994/1999)		90
Current Liabilities		
Trade Creditors	20	
Bank Overdrafts	15	
Dividends Payable	25	60
		£450

A firm will require finance to enable it to undertake economic activity which necessitates the purchase of assets, the returns from which are not immediate. This finance can be provided by owners or lenders. Before examining the way in which the choice between these sources is made, consideration must be given to the type of returns they will require to persuade them to give up their resources for the firm's use.

Providers of finance to a firm require returns to compensate them for the **loss of alternative opportunities for their cash**. The loss of opportunities is normally referred to as an **opportunity cost** imposed on the provider of finance. It arises from:

(1) Loss of **consumption** because the cash provided to the firm is no longer available for the provider's expenditure.

(2) Loss of **returns** caused by the loss of opportunities to invest the cash elsewhere.

(3) Increase in **payments**, such as interest, which may be required to restore consumption and investment possibilities in (1) and (2) (e.g., by personal borrowing).

In an uncertain world providers of finance will also assess the amount of returns they require in relation to the **possible uncertainty of those returns**. 'Uncertainty' can be measured by potential variability in the future returns (e.g., by their standard deviation): providers of finance may be prepared to accept low returns if the possibility of variability is small, whereas high returns may be required if the possibility of variability is high; this will depend on their attitudes towards uncertainty. In a firm's financial structure it may thus be necessary to arrange the finances in a way to satisfy the varying objectives of the providers of finance. Consideration of the **security of the repayment** may also influence the returns required.

As there will be many possible outcomes from a firm's use of finances in business activities the firm will give consideration in decisions about its financial structure to:

(1) The **permanency** of finance and the **requirement to repay** at some time the amount of finance obtained, along with the penalties associated with non-compliance.
(2) The ability to provide the providers of finance with the **periodic returns** they require.
(3) The possibility of **repaying at short notice** any finances which the firm finds are in excess of requirements, or providing for unforeseen requirements.
(4) Minimising the **cost of finance** in the context of an optimal financial structure.

The problems of finance are those of determining which is the optimal financial structure consistent with the objectives of the firm and its owners. The pattern ultimately chosen will depend on the firm's assessment of the relative importance of the factors listed above. The firm must produce an appropriate financial structure with long term and short term finances, and a mixed ownership and lender interest in the firm. Much of this chapter is concerned with this problem.

Long term finances are characterised by arrangements which are considered as perhaps almost permanent, or at very least not rearrangeable at short notice (e.g., ordinary shares and debentures). Finance is considered as 'long term' when neither the firm nor the source can demand that the arrangement is terminated at short notice without mutual agreement. Where these characteristics are absent finance is 'short term', and is normally classified under current liabilities (e.g., trade creditors).

It may be appealing to suggest that the firm uses its long term finances to provide fixed assets, and uses its short term finances to provide current (short term) assets. If we analyse a firm's activities we will find that the provision of current assets, such as inventory or debtors, is as important to the success of a firm as are its fixed (long lived) assets; although individual items within current assets are continuously changing, a firm will require a minimum level of current assets (e.g., cash) on a permanent basis. We may also find that many firms use finances such as bank overdrafts which are classified as current liabilities to acquire fixed assets; they may effectively be a long term source of finance because the bank allows the time for termination of the agreement to be continuously moved forward. In Sect. 10.8 we examine the reasons behind the need for short term finance. We will now examine two concepts, the concept of **equity** and the concept of **debt**, which are central in the analysis of financial structure.

10.4 The concepts of equity and debt

The concepts of equity and debt identify the relationship between the firm, its owners and lenders.

Concept of Equity

The shareholders of a company are in an ownership relationship, as are the partners in a partnership, but the partners are also more likely to be concerned in a partnership's management, as discussed in Sect. 10.3. In a company the owners are likely to be different persons from the managers.

Equity financing has the following important characteristics.

(1) *Relationship with the firm* The interests of owners in the firm can cease **only with cessation of the firm**, although ownership of a part of a firm can be transferred through the sale of the specific interest to another party (e.g., when a shareholder in a company sells his shares). Owners of a firm can, of course, have other relationships with the firm and could be, for example, managers, lenders, customers or employees.

(2) *Participation in profits* If the firm earns a profit the owners have a **right to all of the profits**, and the size of an individual owner's share depends on the extent of his ownership. The owner's share includes profits distributed as dividends (termed 'drawings' in a sole trader and partnership) and those retained within the firm. The firm's management may decide on its owners' behalf to retain some of the dividends for use within the firm (e.g., for providing new assets), with the expectation of paying higher future dividends.

(3) *Participation in residual assets* In the event of cessation of the firm, normally termed its **liquidation**, any assets that exist, after all liabilities of the firm have been repaid, **belong to the owners**.

(4) *Control* The owners have rights to **control the policies of the firm** through the appointment of managers or directors; the particular type of arrangement will depend on the type of firm (e.g., a partnership or a company).

(5) *Duration of relationship* As stated in Sect. 10.3, the owner's capital cannot normally be returned to the owners except in liquidation. Retained profits, though part of the owners' equity, can be returned to the owners as **dividends**.

Concept of Debt

Debt finance is distinct from equity finance, and has the following important characteristics:

(1) *Relationship with the firm* The relationship between the firm and the source is of **borrower** and **lender**; there is no owner-ship relationship.

(2) *Participation in profits* The lender will be entitled to receive **periodic interest payments**, which are expenses of the firm, independent of the level of profit; these would be contrac-tually determined. This requirement is, of course, ultimately subject to the power of the lender to **enforce** the claim, if necessary, in the courts as a creditor.

(3) *Participation in residual assets* As a lender, the claim against the firm in the event of cessation is limited to the **full amount of the loan**. It is normal for the lender to have a **prior claim** to the assets over that of the owners.

(4) *Control* Provided that the firm satisfies its contractual obli-gations to lenders with respect to interest payments and return of the amount borrowed, the lenders **do not usually participate in the management** of the firm. A lender may, of course, also be a shareholder. The firm will recognise, however, that if it is unable to satisfy these obligations, the firm may then go into liquidation, or alternatively control may be passed to the lenders. The possibility of control imposed by debt finance may thus be an indirect influence on the **policy of the firm**, so as to avoid these events.

(5) *Duration of relationship* The firm must repay the amount borrowed when it is due, and thus it is not considered as a **permanent source**. The arrangements are usually for a fixed duration, but in practice many firms will merely arrange a further loan to replace the former loan as it comes to maturity.

10.5   Equity finance

We will now examine how we can apply the concept of equity in the analysis of sources of finance. In Greenwich Ltd, the equity finance is classified as owners' equity. We can see that a distinction is made between the ordinary shareholders' interests, which are pure equity, and preference shares, which are a hybrid form of finance.

Once the company has decided the total finances required to begin oper-ations and also the mix between debt and equity, it will issue sufficient shares to raise the amount of equity finance that it requires. The shares that it issues will have a face or 'nominal' value, but they may be issued **at a premium** by requiring more cash from the purchaser of the share than their face value. Thus, if Greenwich Ltd wishes to raised £200 000 it might issue any combination of number of shares and nominal value as necessary (e.g., 40 000 shares of £5 nominal value, or 200 000 of £1 nominal value). If 200 000 shares of £1 nominal value were issued, but the prospective owners were required to subscribe £1.10 per share, a premium of £0.10 per share would be created. The company would sell its shares at a price determined by market forces (i.e., the supply of shares and the related demand). This example is based on the information in the balance sheet of Greenwich Ltd. The value to the shareholder of the shares after issue will not necessarily bear any relationship to the nominal value and share premium; this is the value at the time of issue. To avoid confusion for the shareholder, it has been suggested that firms should be allowed to issue shares which have no nominal value, so as not to suggest that the nominal value is an indicator of value. However, a company is not allowed by the Companies Acts to issue shares of no nominal value, though this is legitimate in other countries (e.g., the USA). In the course of its operations, the firm may decide to obtain further new equity share finance. It can effect this in two ways, either by issuing further shares to its current shareholders (termed a 'rights issue'), or otherwise to new shareholders.

As the 'share capital' of a company is not returnable it is thus long term finance. Retained profits can be considered as either long or short term equity as they could be distributed as dividends, but in practice a large part of retained profits are effectively permanent finance.[2] Apart from retained profits, there is no other form of short term equity finance in the UK.

The firm's management, on behalf of the shareholders, can retain all or part of the profit that has been earned in the past; Sect. 3.4 showed how retained profits became part of the owner's equity. A useful distinction can be made between equity financing through the new issues of shares and the internal generation of resources by retention of profits. The process of profit retention is identical in its effect to a dividend payment, followed by a rights issue to obtain from the shareholder the amount just received in dividend. Profit retention is thus a pre-emptive rights issue, but with none of the expenses associated with such an issue.

Assuming that cash is available, the maximum dividend distribution in a year is limited to the **amount of retained profits carried forward from previous years, plus the profit from the current year**. It is thus not necessary for a company to earn a profit in a particular year for it to pay a dividend in that year. A dividend can always be proposed provided that the total value of the owner's equity does not fall below the value of the firm's capital (i.e., share capital and share premium). This requirement is another aspect of the idea of 'capital maintenance' as discussed in Sect. 10.2.

Distribution of profits as dividends need not necessarily use the firm's cash resources: there may be circumstances where a firm has insufficient cash resources to pay a cash dividend, or where perhaps for shareholders' personal taxation reasons shareholders do not wish to receive a cash dividend. A dividend of shares in place of cash is termed a **bonus issue**, and will involve the 'capitalisation of retained profits'; this is a reclassification of its retained profits as issued share capital. This reclassification and further issue of bonus shares (sometimes termed a 'scrip issue') has no associated cash flow, but results in the shareholder having more shares to represent his interest in the company than he had before the bonus issue. It also has the effect of converting the amount of retained profit into **permanent owners' equity**, and it is no longer available for distribution. The total market value of a shareholding should be unaffected by the changes, though it is argued in favour of bonus issues that the more shares that are issued, and hence the lower the market price of each share, the more marketable the share is. This increased marketability arises as less must be invested in a company by a prospective shareholder to acquire the same number of shares, and with more shares being available, the greater is the size of the potential market. This may lead to a rise in the total market value of the company's shares after the capitalisation of retained profits.

Using the data from Geenwich Ltd, if we assume that the ordinary shares have a market value of £2.40, the overall market value of the ordinary shares will be £480 000. If all the retained profits are then capitalised the company will make a bonus issue of 40 ordinary shares for every 200 ordinary shares formerly held. After the capitalisation, the relevant section of the owner's equity in the balance sheet of Greenwich Ltd would would be:

	£000	£000
Owner's Equity		
Ordinary Shares 240 000 £1 nominal value	240	
Share Premium	20	
Retained Profit	–	
		£260

The shareholders will have received 40 000 £1 ordinary shares in proportion to their original holdings. Subject to the assumptions outlined above the total market value of the ordinary shares will still be £480 000; the new market value per share should thus be £2.00 compared to £2.40 previously.

Preference shares are a special category of share. The dividend entitlement is fixed at a predetermined level (i.e., they have a fixed rate of return like debt, but the returns are classed as dividends). Their security, in the event of a liquidation, is one of participating in any residual assets (i.e., similar to equity, though usually preference shareholders have a claim prior to ordinary shareholders). As shareholders, there is **no entitlement** to a dividend, but if dividends are to be paid, the claim of the preference shareholders dividend is prior to that of the ordinary shareholders. Most preference shares have an **accumulative dividend entitlement**, and no ordinary dividend can be paid until arrears of preference dividends are paid. They do not fall conveniently into our equity/debt classification, but are normally shown as part of owners' equity in the balance sheet.

10.6　Debt finance

Debt finance has many possible variations, as we can see by inspection of the balance sheet of Greenwich Ltd or the Marks and Spencer's balance sheet in Appendix B. Debt finance covers all kinds of borrowing including fixed interest long term loans, and formally arranged short term borrowing such as bank overdrafts. It will also include incidental borrowing or liabilities to trade creditors or to shareholders for dividends which have been declared, but not paid.

Fixed interest long term loans are normally termed '**debentures**' and the conditions of debentures represent a contract between the borrower and the lender. In the Greenwich Ltd balance sheet we can see that the interest rate, which was fixed at the time of borrowing, was 6%, and that the repayment date at the company's discretion is between 1994 and 1999.

The safety of a loan and interest for a lender arises from the legal obligation of the firm to **return the amount borrowed and any associated interest** in accordance with the debt contract. If the firm is unable to discharge this obligation the lenders can make a claim against the assets of the firm through the courts, and the lenders' claim against the assets in liquidation takes precedence over the claims of equity. Lenders can improve their safety by increasing their priority through converting an unsecured loan into a loan secured against the potential proceeds from the sale of particular assets. A prior claim established against the firm's assets in general is termed a '**floating charge**'; when secured against a specific asset it is a **fixed charge** – often termed a 'mortgage' – such that the firm cannot dispose of the asset without the lenders' consent. If a firm is forced to sell charged assets any surplus after the secured creditors have been repaid belongs to the firm, though if the proceeds are insufficient the remainder of the outstanding loan reverts to an unsecured loan. As an alternative, lenders may seek personal guarantees from owners or directors as a means of securing their loan against persons with unlimited liability.

In deciding on its financing policy the firm will consider whether it can offer additional safety to its lenders, as the rate of return required may be less for secured than unsecured loans. The ability of a firm to offer loan security will depend on the range of its economic activities. A firm such as a property company, with fixed assets about which a selling price valuation can be reasonably established, will be able to offer substantial loan security. On the other hand, a firm engaged in research activities, or perhaps prospecting for minerals, may have few assets which could be sold in the event of an enforced liquidation. In this case, little loan security can be offered, and debt financing may be less possible.

While a firm which falls into arrears with its interest payments to lenders will normally have what is effectively an additional loan secured in the same way as the initial loan, the security of periodic interest receipts by lenders is determined by the firm's profitability. Lenders' interest security also arises from their claim, prior to that of shareholders, against the firm's profits, which ensures that shareholders receive the residue of profits **only after all other claims have been satisfied**.

10.7   Financial risk

The most important implication for the firm – and hence the owners of the firm – through the use of debt financing is that with the introduction of debt into the financial structure, the firm undertakes an additional form of risk, which is termed '**financial risk**'. This arises from the possibility that the firm may be unable to satisfy the conditions attached to the borrowing. It can be distinguished from '**business risk**', which relates to the possible variability of returns on the use of finance in the firm, and which arises from uncertainties **inherent in business**.

The payment of interest to lenders is an **expense** that the firm must meet and allow for in the calculation of profit. Debt financing introduces a claim prior to dividends against the profits of the firm and a claim against the assets. If the interest or the loan itself is not repaid when due, the lenders may use their legal powers against the firm, perhaps through an enforced liquidation – equity, it should be recalled, has no similar rights.

Once debt financing is undertaken, the policies of a firm must always recognise that a **new set of obligations exists**, and the decisions about its future activities will necessarily be influenced by these new obligations.

If a firm does not earn a profit in any one year (or a series of years), this will not necessarily lead to a firm's inability to make interest payments, any more than it would be unable to make other payments such as wages. Interest payments use cash resources; it is neither necessary nor sufficient that a firm earns a profit for it to be able to satisfy its creditors for interest payments. However, over a period of years recurrent losses will mean that the shareholders will no longer receive their dividends; and they or other prospective shareholders may be unwilling to provide further finance. The cash resources of the firm will decline until no further cash is available to make interest payments, and the firm may be unable to repay any of its loans. On the other hand profitability will not necessarily ensure in the short term a sufficiency of cash, and the introduction of debt financing will increase the monetary claims against the firm's cash resources.

It is argued that debt financing can benefit the owners of a firm. The idea on which this proposition is based is that the firm may be able to borrow at a known, certain rate of interest from those who consider that security of loan and security of periodic payment is important, and use these finances to generate a series of profit flows that are greater than the additional interest payments required. This is normally termed **'gearing'** or **'leverage'**. Section 13.3 includes the impact of gearing on the assssment of a firms performance and Chapter 14 examines the possible benefits from borrowing during periods of changing price levels. Ex.10.1 provides an illustration of the use of gearing; in this example the effect of company or personal taxation is ignored, as are the effects of changing price levels.

Example 10.1
Goat Ltd has 5000 £1 shares issued and earns £8000 per annum in profits which are all distributed as dividends. The shareholders expect that the firm will continue to earn that level of profits and pay the same dividends in the foreseeable future. Goat Ltd has an opportunity to undertake expenditure of £5000 which it is forecast will return £450 p.a. in cash for twenty years, and a further £5000 in cash in twenty years' time when the project finishes. The firm can borrow money on a long term basis at an interest rate of 8% per annum.

Assuming that Goat Ltd borrows £5000 repayable in twenty years' time at 8% interest p.a., the forecast annual profit for Goat Ltd after it has undertaken this project would be:

Goat Ltd – Forecast Annual Profits for Next Twenty Years

	£
From current activities	£8000
From proposed project	450
Profit before interest	8450
Less	
Interest payments	400
Profit available for distribution	£8050

£8050 is available for distribution to shareholders, whereas only £8000 was available previously, increasing the prospective dividends per share from £1.60 to £1.61. This has been achieved by **using finance with an expense less than the associated anticipated revenue**. This additional return or profit is attributable to the shareholders alone.

In Ex.10.1 it can be seen that the ordinary shareholders take most of the risks related to the new project, and should the project fail the interest payments will continue to be borne by the firm as a whole. The issue of a long term loan gives the lenders a claim against profits which were formerly solely available as dividends for the ordinary shareholders. The liability to repay £5000 is a further claim against the assets of Goat Ltd as a whole.

It may appear that this projected increase in dividends is an improvement for the shareholders, assuming that the firm continues to distribute all its profits as dividends. Alternatively, it can be argued that this increase in the potential dividends of the shareholders does not necessarily mean an increase in their wellbeing. Associated with this projected increase in their dividends is the possibility that the project may not come to fruition and that the firm may become insolvent, or that dividends per share may fall if the project fails to return its projected profits. If we could say with certainty that the project would yield the forecast returns we could say with confidence that the shareholders were better off. Whether in practice the potential extra dividend compensates them for their increased risk depends on the attitudes of the individual shareholders towards risk.

Measurement of Financial Risk – Using Balance Sheet Data

It will be clear that the degree of financial risk will relate to the amount of debt in the financial structure – and, of course, the terms of the contracts relating to the borrowing.

It will be useful for the firm, shareholders and the current or potential lenders to be able to make an assessment of the extent of a firm's financial risk. For the firm and the shareholders the importance lies in attaining the **maximum benefits from gearing** (i.e., minimising the overall cost of finance to the firm, consistent with the attitudes of current and potential shareholders to the increased risk). For the potential and existing shareholders and lenders an assessment of financial risk will be important in assessing their **own personal financial risks**.

It is possible to comment fully on financial risk only by examining a firm's **future plans**; these will show its future cash availability, its future projects and expectations. With less precise information, a conventional measurement of financial risk is the **debt/equity ratio**. Problems arise in deciding which data is appropriate for this purpose. To gauge financial risk at a particular point in time we could use the ratio of all debt to equity, but as the amount of short term debt may fluctuate we may prefer to use a ratio of **long term debt to equity**. The classification of preference shares and convertible debentures may also be open to question, and as the balance sheet is likely to reflect historical rather than current values we could use either book value or market values.

Using the data from the Greenwich Ltd balance sheet, as shown in Section 10.2 we can compute two ratios:

$$\text{All debt/equity ratio} \qquad \frac{\text{All debt}}{\text{Debt} + \text{Equity}} = \frac{150}{450} = \qquad 0.33$$

$$\text{Long term debt/equity ratio} \quad \frac{\text{Long Term Debt}}{\text{Long Term Debt} + \text{Equity}} = \frac{90}{390} = 0.23$$

But if we reclassify preference shares as long term debt we can compute two more:

All debt/equity ratio $\quad\dfrac{\text{All debt}}{\text{All Debt + Equity}} = \dfrac{190}{450} = \quad 0.42$

Long term debt/equity ratio $\quad\dfrac{\text{Long Term Debt}}{\text{Long Term Debt + Equity}} = \dfrac{130}{390} = 0.33$

These ratios show the proportion of debt in the overall financing of the firm.

As can be seen from these ratios, the measurement of the degree of financial risk depends on the ratios that are chosen. They may be useful for comparison of financial risk for the same firm through time, or in comparison between firms which have similar assets and business risks. The ratios are also useful as relative measures for inter- or intra-firm comparison in ranking the relative extent of gearing, but as absolute measures they mean little.

The notion of a **gearing limit**, measured in terms of a maximum debt/equity ratio, is a traditional approach to the problem of determining the maximum gearing possible. The extent to which a firm can gear itself to increase the returns of the shareholder will, however, depend on the types of economic activities in which it is involved, the attitudes of management and investors to financial risk and the institutional financial environment.

Another measure of financial risk and security of loans could be to examine the extent to which the **total debts** of the firm can be covered by its **realisable assets**. The notion of 'cover' is based on the relationship between **claims** and the **size of the pool** from which they are to be satisfied. This form of analysis will not be so easily applicable where assets are charged as security for a loan, as the secured loan is not competing for repayment with other unsecured loans.

A suitable measure for loan safety is **debt cover**:

$$\dfrac{\text{Realisation (Selling Price) Value of Assets}}{\text{Total Liabilities}}$$

If the realisation value of assets covers the total liabilities the ratio will be greater than 1, and show that the firm would, if necessary, be able to satisfy all its lenders. Using the data from Greenwich Ltd the net book value of assets would be £450 000 as a going concern. However, assume that the realisation value, if assets are sold individually in a forced sale, is estimated as £90 000. The relevant data is the **realisation value**, giving a ratio of:

$$\dfrac{£90000}{£150000} = 0.60$$

This shows that if Greenwich Ltd tried to repay all its liabilities they would receive 60p per £ owing. But, as many of the liabilities are not current liabilities and are thus not due for repayment now, the company may be in a position to repay in the future. However, as seen in previous chapters, realisation values do not necessarily have any relationship with the book values shown in balance sheets.

As a further surrogate for the measurement of financial risk we could analyse the **security of interest and dividend payments**, by examining the extent to which the **revenues** of a period cover its **expenses** and **dividends**. It must be recalled that expenses and dividends are paid from cash, not revenues, but that if a firm is to be able to continue in existence it must ultimately cover its interest expenses and pay dividends to satisfy the shareholders.

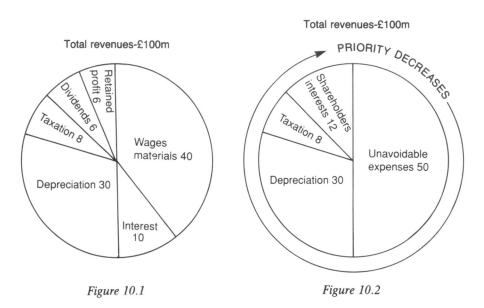

Figure 10.1   Figure 10.2

Figure 10.1 analyses the claims against the revenue of a hypothetical firm with revenue of £100m.

The data of Figure 10.1 can be reclassified as in Figure 10.2, to give an indication of the possible **type** and **priority** of claims against revenues. In Figure 10.2 we can see that some of the firm's expenses are unavoidable commitments, such as wages, salaries and interest. The expenses that could be classified as 'unavoidable' depend on the **time scale** (e.g., debenture interest has a long term commitment and wages could be avoided by reducing the labour force). While depreciation does not use up a firm's revenues, if over many periods there are insufficient revenues to cover both unavoidable expenses and depreciation there may be insufficient resources to enable the firm to replace the assets it is using up, or to repay the finances it used to acquire the assets. Taxation claims against a firm's revenues occur only when a firm's revenues exceed all its expenses. In Figure 10.2 we can see that if revenues fall by 20%, there will be no tax liability, but all expenses are covered. Figure 10.2 also illustrates the residual claim of equity.

This kind of analysis is useful in gauging security and financial risk as it can give an indication of the effect of **variability in a firm's revenues** on its ability to meet its expenses and pay dividends. We could calculate the extent to which revenues would have to fall to effect dividends, expenses, etc. A complementary exercise is to calculate the **cover for various claims** against revenues and profit. We will do this using the data in Figures 10.1 and 10.2. The unavoidable expenses cover ratio is:

$$\frac{\text{Revenues From Operations}}{\text{Unavoidable Expenses}} = \frac{£100\text{m}}{£50\text{m}} = 2 \text{ times}$$

As this data is difficult to obtain from published company statements, many financial analysts use what is known as **interest cover**:

$$\frac{\text{Net Profit Before Tax and Interest}}{\text{Interest Payments}} = \frac{£12\text{m} + £8\text{m} + £10\text{m}}{£10\text{m}} = \frac{30}{10} = 3 \text{ times}$$

The former calculation indicates that all the unavoidable expenses are covered twice, and the latter that interest is covered three times. The latter calculation is not very satisfactory as the coverage does not arise from net profits before tax and interest but from revenues, and even if the net profits before tax and interest were zero, interest would be covered.

The application of 'coverage' can be applied further:

Preference dividend cover:

$$\frac{\text{Net Profit After Tax}}{\text{Total Preference Dividends}}$$

Ordinary dividend cover:

$$\frac{\text{Net Profit After Tax and Preference Dividends}}{\text{Total Ordinary Dividends}}$$

To illustrate the calculation of coverage ratios, we can consider Ex.10.2

Example 10.2
The following is an extract from the profit statement from Gorgon Ltd:

		£000
Net Profit Before Tax and Interest		20
Interest Expense (on Debentures)		4
Net Profit Before Tax		16
Corporation Tax		4
Net Profit After Tax		12
Preference Share Dividend	4	
Ordinary Share Dividend	6	
		10
Retained Profits		£2

The cover for the sources of finance:

Interest cover $\dfrac{20}{4} = $ 5 times

Preference dividend cover $\dfrac{12}{4} = $ 3 times

Ordinary dividend cover $\dfrac{12 - 4}{6} = \dfrac{8}{6} = 1.33$ times

Corporation tax is simplified in this example for ease of explanation, and personal taxation is ignored.

10.8   Short and long term finances

In the process of budgeting cash requirements a firm will need to select a combination of long term and short term finances for its financial structure. This combination is required because the total amount of assets (and hence finances that a firm may require) will probably **fluctuate over time**. In Figure 10.3 we show the cumulative amount of cash that a firm might require from debt or equity sources from its inception, over a period of time – say one year. Cash could be required to acquire fixed assets, current assets such as stock, or to repay liabilities. Large increases in the cash requirement may perhaps be associated with the acquisition of fixed assets, and decreases with the re-duction of current assets (e.g., stock or debtors). The cumulative cash requirements of firms with cyclical or seasonal activities will be variable, with both increases and decreases over time.

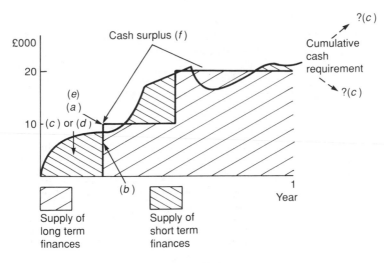

Figure 10.3

We have illustrated in Figure 10.3 a possible pattern of financing which uses both short and long term finances; it shows the selection of a particular financial structure which changes through time. Initially it is all short term, and it later changes to various mixes of short and long term. The long term finance is raised in two stages with £10 000 raised each time. The letters in brackets can be related to the **optimality considerations** explained in (a)–(f) below. Whilst an extensive discussion of the procedures is outside the scope of this book the following are the major considerations:

(a) The **relative returns** required by providers of short and long term finances.

(b) The **greater reliability** of supply of long term as opposed to short-term finances for the firm.

(c) Uncertainty about the future because of **potential variability in future returns**, and cost of finance may not justify the entering into a fixed long-term commitment.

(d) The **availability** (or **non-availability**) of both long and short term finances (e.g., small firms may not have long term finances available to them due to the imperfections of the capital markets);

(e) **Indivisibilities**: the firm may be able to borrow long term in large fixed amounts which are not divisible (e.g., £10 000 units, as shown in Figure 10.3).

(f) **Variability in cash requirements**: a firm with variable cash requirements through time may find that it will have excess cash if it has obtained its maximum requirement through the use of long term sources. Unless the firm has use for this excess, such as short term lending or purchase of marketable securities, it will be incurring costs of finance of cash it is not using.

10.9   Cost of finance

The firm should be able to measure its cost of finance because it is important in its choice of financial structure and in making decisions about its use. By choosing between possible financial structures, the firm may be able to **reduce its overall cost of finance**: as explained in Sect. 10.3 the cost of finance to the firm is the opportunity cost arising from the alternative use of cash.

The cost of equity finance is the rate of return required by owners to compensate them for their opportunity costs (see Sect. 10.3). As compensation they receive returns in dividends and the proceeds from disposal of their shares.

The cost of debt is the rate of return required by lenders, which could be expressed in terms of a required interest rate. In some cases the original rate of interest may not be a true indication of the cost of debt: if the amount borrowed is different (excluding interest) from the amount to be paid back (e.g., debentures issued at a discount), or if interest rates change and the firm still pays the original rate. Although the firm still pays the original cost in most cases, the opportunity cost of finance becomes the amount the firm **could get by lending at the new rate of interest**.

The opportunity costs for both equity shareholders and lenders of long term debt will depend on the prevailing market rates for similar types of finance. However, the **individual firm's level of gearing** will also affect the rates of return required by both equity and debt. As the gearing of a firm increases, the financial risk increases for both types of finance; the required rates of return will also increase, thus increasing the **overall cost of finance for the firm**.

10.10   Liquidity and solvency

A firm will require cash to enable it to commence (or continue) its business activities. The ability of a firm to provide sufficient cash for its activities is termed its '**liquidity**'. The concept of 'liquidity' relates to the balance between the **demands for** and **supply of cash resources over a period of time in the future**. We can develop a notion of short term and long term liquidity according to our horizon in time: for example, a firm may be unable to pay a creditor on demand because it has insufficient cash in the bank. The firm would be illiquid in the very short term if it was, for example, unable to borrow the necessary cash from the bank, and it would be illiquid in the long term if it was unable to obtain further cash from any source at that time, or at any time in the future. A firm must **plan its sources and applications of cash** if it is to attain its objectives and maintain an appropriate level of liquidity.

The concept of 'solvency' is closely related to that of liquidity. A firm would be considered solvent if at a moment in time **its assets if realised would exceed its liabilities**. This is related to debt cover discussed in Sect. 10.7. However, a short term illiquid firm may be forced to sell its assets quickly (i.e., not as a going concern) and may become insolvent, although if it had been allowed to continue as a going concern it might have been long term liquid and thus solvent. It is possible to comment on a firm's long-term liquidity only by analysing the demand and supply for cash in the firm's future plans. A guide to short term liquidity can be obtained from its working capital position.

10.11 Working capital

The cash flowing around the firm in the cash cycle is illustrated in Figure 10.4, which we met earlier as Figure 9.1. The **working capital cycle** is a flow within the overall cash cycle of the firm. The importance of working capital is that it identifies a relationship between **current assets** and **current liabilities**. Current liabilities are closely related to the financing of current assets, and an increase in current liabilities can often be thought of as a source of finance – for example, a firm may acquire its stock on credit and hence is effectively

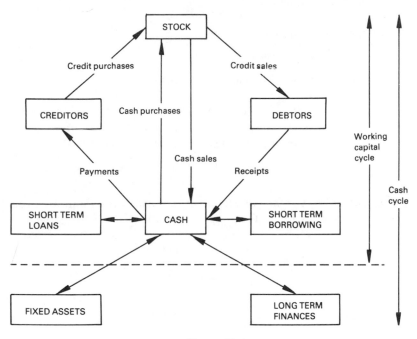

Figure 10.4

financing its current assets through current liabilities. However, fixed assets may be acquired using credit, which would also be classified as current liabilities.

The overall rate at which current assets and current liabilities change is termed the '**rate of working capital turnover**'.

We can now analyse the rate of turnover of individual current assets and current liabilities:

- **Cash turnover** depends on the amount of cash the firm holds on average per day in relation to its daily usage.
- **Creditors' turnover** depends on the time between the purchase of resources on credit, payment to creditors and the amount of creditors.
- **Stock turnover** depends on the time between the purchase and use of stock and the amount of stock held.
- **Debtors' turnover** depends on the time between the credit sale and the collection of cash, and the amount of credit allowed.

Turnover can be measured as the number of times per year an item of working capital changes. It can be calculated as:

$$\frac{\text{Average amount of } z \text{ held}}{\text{Average daily usage of } z} = \text{Average number of days } z \text{ held}$$

$$\frac{\text{Number of working days in a year}}{\text{Average number of days } z \text{ held}} = \text{turnover of } z \text{ per annum}$$

where z is an item of working capital.

Limitations in using this analysis arise from the reliance on **averages** in our calculations, especially when published data is being used. If an average is being calculated from the balance sheet it must be **representative**.

Example 10.3
Glasgow Ltd holds £20 000 of stock on average throughout the year. Its average daily usage is £500. There are 240 working days[3] in the year.

$$\text{The number of days stock held is } \frac{£20000}{£500} = 40 \text{ days}$$

$$\text{The stock turnover is } \frac{240}{40} = 6 \text{ times p.a.}$$

We can measure the rate of the working capital turnover by adding the number of days we hold current assets and deducting the number of days we hold current liabilities.

Example 10.4
Glasgow Ltd holds its stock for 40 days before it is sold on credit, it obtains 60 days' credit on its purchases and gives 50 days' credit on its sales. Therefore the total time that the company's cash is tied up is

$$40 + 50 - 60 = 30 \text{ days}$$

This can be shown as in Figure 10.5.

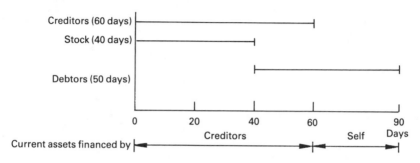

Figure 10.5

The working capital cycle of 90 days is financed by the creditors for the first 60 days, and by the firm's cash for the last 30 days.

The importance of the analysis of the working capital cycle is that a firm can **control the amount of working capital**, and hence the finance required by increasing net current asset turnover (e.g., holding less stock or the same stock for less time) and by increasing its short term finance (e.g., current liabilities); it can also influence its liquidity by speeding up the conversion of debtors into cash.

The choice of an appropriate level of working capital depends on an evaluation of the **cost of finance**, and the **costs of not having sufficient working capital** (e.g., shortage of short term liquidity or stock when required).

Comparison of rates of working capital turnover between industries becomes difficult because of different technologies and norms. As with the use of debt/equity ratios they may be useful as comparative rather than absolute measures.

Working Capital and Liquidity

Ex.10.5 illustrates how we can analyse the changes in working capital and use data to measure liquidity.

Example 10.5
Gloucester Ltd wants to analyse the change in working capital during 19X1 and examine its liquidity position. It has prepared a statement of its working capital position extracted from its balance sheets at the end of 19X0 and 19X1.

Working Capital Summary: Gloucester Ltd
(Extract From Balance Sheets) at:

	31 December 19X0		31 December 19X1	
Current Assets	£	£	£	£
Stock	3500		7000	
Debtors	7500		8000	
Marketable securities (see note 1)	2500		500	
Cash	1500		1000	
		15000		16500
Current Liabilities				
Trade creditors	5000		3000	
Interest payable			500	
Dividends payable	2000		1000	
		7000		4500
Working Capital		£8000		£12000

Note:

        1. Short-term investments.

From this data the following statement can be prepared to explain the change in working capital from £8000 to £12 000 during 19X1.

Statement of Changes in Working Capital During 19X1:
Gloucester Ltd

	£	£
Increases in working capital		
Increases in current assets		
Stock	3500	
Debtors	500	
Decreases in current liabilities		
Trade creditors	2000	
Dividends payable	1000	7000
Less: Decreases in working capital		
Decreases in current assets		
Marketable securities	2000	
Cash	500	
Increases in current liabilities		
Interest Payable	500	3000
Net increase in working capital		£4000

Before we can comment meaningfully about the **significance** and **relevance** of this change, we will have to obtain information about how the changes relate to the **size** and **activities** of the company.

A change of working capital is clearly important for a firm's **liquidity**. Changes in particular items, such as cash, will influence a firm's very short term liquidity; although a firm's working capital could rise, its very short term liquidity could decrease. When examining the time scale we must be careful to define it in terms of the **firm's life** and not in terms of the working capital cycle only.

We will analyse liquidity in **comparative** rather than absolute terms, using the data in Ex.10.5:

	19X0	*19X1*

Very short term liquidity (known as quick ratio)

$$\frac{\text{Very liquid assets}^4 \ (\text{cash} + \text{marketable securities})}{\text{Current liabilities}} \qquad \frac{4}{7} = 0.57 \qquad \frac{1.5}{4.5} = 0.33$$

Short term liquidity (known as current ratio)

$$\frac{\text{Current assets}}{\text{Current liabilities}} \qquad \frac{15}{7} = 2.14 \qquad \frac{16.5}{4.5} = 3.66$$

As we can see, the very short term liquidity of the company has deteriorated, whilst the short term liquidity is much improved. It is normal to consider a firm's short term liquidity as satisfactory if the quick ratio is more than 1, and the current ratio is more than 2. However, this will depend on the **industry**, and the **management's policies**.

The use of this form of analysis of liquidity is limited by the data we use. Balance sheets do not provide all the relevant data (e.g., an unused overdraft arrangement would normally be excluded), and they provide valuations based on the **original cost** rather than **selling price** bases. They do not provide information about rates of working capital turnover – with this information added we could make predictions of cash flows in and out of the firm for future periods in the very short and short run; this would provide a more sophisticated liquidity analysis. The analysis also assumes that the factors determining the ratios will **remain constant** in the future. However, if these limitations are recognised the ratios may provide crude approximations. Discussion of these ratios is also included in Chapter 13, and a further analysis of changes in working capital in included in Chapter 12.

10.12 Summary

Chapter 10 initially discussed the effect that forms of ownership can have on the provision of finance for a business. The chapter then examined the dimensions of a firm's decisions about financing its activities. A firm will need to provide returns to compensate providers of finance for their opportunity costs, and for the risks they undertake. It will wish to select an optimal financial structure which may consist of a combination of debt and equity finance, and long and short term finance. One of the major objectives of financing decisions is to attain optimal financial structures in the context of financial risk, cost of finance and liquidity considerations. As well as financing fixed assets a firm must maintain its liquidity and provide sufficient working capital.

Notes and References

1. The term 'limited' after a company's name denotes that it is a private limited company and Plc that it is a public limited company. A private limited company is one which can restrict the rights of its owners to transfer their shares to other potential owners. It can not, however, make an issue of its shares to the general public. A public limited company cannot have limitations on the transfer of its shares but can issue its shares to the public. As a consequence, it has access to a wide ownership and greater sources of finance. A public limited company may also be a 'quoted' company. This means that its shares are quoted on a recognised stock exchange, and this creates **greater ease of transferability** and makes the company's shares more **readily marketable**.
2. Reference to the Marks and Spencer Plc balance sheet in Appendix B shows that retained profit provides around 40% of the company's owners' equity (i.e. Capital and Reserves).
3. The basis for this calculation varies. Some analysts use working days as in this example. Some use the actual days (i.e. 365) as in the example in Section 13.3.
4. Very liquid assets may in some situations include **debtors**.

Questions and Problems

10.1 What do you understand by the following terminology?

Incorporation	Limited liability
Public limited company	Capital maintenance
Stewardship	Quoted companies
Financial structure	Equity finance
Capital structure	Debt finance
Share premium	Bonus issue
Nomimal value	Floating and fixed charges
Ordinary share	Financial risk

Preference share   Gearing
Debenture   Liquidity
Opportunity cost of finance   Solvency
Provisions   Working capital turnover
Cash cycles

10.2 Discuss the advantages and disadvantages of operating a business without incorporation.

10.3 Explain clearly the benefits from incorporation as a limited liability company.

10.4 What difficulties arise for those lending to a company which has limited liability? What protection do such lenders have?

10.5 Gault Ltd obtains the following finance during 19X4:

(a) it borrows £1000 to be repaid in two years time with annual interest of 10%;
(b) it borrows £5000 with £5832 to be repaid in two years time, with no annual interest payment.

What is the annual cost of finance in (a) and (b)?
What valuation would be shown in the balance sheet at the time of the borrowing, and after one year?

10.6 How would you calculate your personal opportunity cost of finance if you are deciding whether to buy:

(a) a sweepstake ticket for an event in one year's time;
(b) a season ticket on British Railways;
(c) a car;
(d) a house.

Explain the differences, if any, between the costs you calculate.

10.7 The market value of the ordinary shares of Gallic Ltd is £80 000. The shareholders expect to receive £10 000 per year in dividends in the future. What discount rate are the shareholders applying to their expected dividend stream to arrive at this valuation?

10.8 The following details relate to Blackmore Engineering Plc, a quoted public company, for the year ended December 31 19X2:

Extract from balance sheet

	£
Ordinary shares of 50p	140000
12% cumulative preference shares of £1	80000
Share premium account	40000
Revaluation reserve	30000
General reserve	50000
Profit and loss account	70000
	£410000
10% debenture stock 1994/99 (secured on freehold property)	300000
	£710000

Extract from profit and loss account
    Net profit (before tax and debenture interest)   £120000

A client is considering purchasing some ordinary shares in the company but his understanding of accounting is limited and he has raised the following questions:

(1) What would be his rights as an ordinary shareholder, and what sort of risk is he taking in buying the shares?
(2) Which of the various amounts in the balance sheet are available for distribution to the ordinary shareholders as dividends?
(3) What is the difference between the Preference Shares and the Debentures?
(4) He has been told that 'gearing' is important. What is gearing, and how does it affect his situation?

Required: Brief answers to the above questions.

10.9 Below are listed details from the Balance Sheets of Hurley Ltd and Baxter Ltd for the financial year ended 31 May 19X0:

	Hurley Ltd £000	Baxter Ltd £000
Authorised Share Capital		
£1 ordinary shares	400	250
5% £1 preference shares	250	–
Issued Share Capital		
£1 ordinary shares	300	200
5% £1 preference shares	250	–
Loan capital		
8% debentures 19X5	400	–
Bank loan @ 10% p.a. repayable 19X2	–	70
Reserves		
Share premium account	70	50
Retained profits	130	80
Revaluation reserve	100	–

Required:

(a) Using the information above to illustrate your answer, describe what is meant by the term 'gearing' and discuss the factors a company will take into account when deciding upon the most appropriate sources of long term funds to finance its business.
(b) Explain what is meant by the term 'reserve', and describe the purpose of the three types of reserve listed above. Why may a company decide to issue new shares at a premium?

10.10 The following three companies are the same size and operate in the same industry. Their financial structures are as follows:

	A £	B £	C £
Ordinary £1 shares	100000	50000	20000
10% Preference shares	–	–	40000
8% debentures	–	50000	40000
	£100000	£100000	£100000

A range of estimates of future profits for the three companies is as follows:

Pessimistic forecast	£8000 net profit (before interest and dividends)
Middle of the road forecast	£10000
Optimistic forecast	£12000

Assume the three forecasts are relevant to all three companies.

A client has asked your advice on whether, **in general**, he should invest in ordinary shares, preference shares or debentures and, **in particular**, whether he should invest in company A, B or C.

Required: Advise your client as requested. (Ignore taxation)

10.11 The following are the balance sheet and profit and loss account of Geranium Ltd:

Balance Sheet at 31 December		*19X1* £000		*19X2* £000	
Fixed Assets					
Machinery at cost		52		80	
Less: accumulated depreciation		20		35	
			32		45
Current Assets					
Stock		7		2	
Debtors		3		1	
Cash		2		7	
		12		10	
Current Liabilities					
Creditors		3		5	
Dividends payable		1		2	
		4		7	
Net Current Assets			8		3
			£40		£48
Financed by					
Owners' Equity					
Ordinary £1 shares		26		26	
Retained profit		6		10	
			32		36
8% preference shares £1			---		4
			32		40
Long-term Liabilities					
12% debentures 19X6/X9			8		8
			£40		£48

Profit and loss account for 19X2		£000
Sales revenue		80
Less: cost of goods sold		49
Gross profit		31
Less: other expenses		
depreciation	18	
interest – debentures	1	
administration	10	
profit on sale of machinery	(4)	
		25
Net profit		6
Dividends – ordinary and preference		2
Increase in retained profit		£4

Using the above data and any assumptions you think necessary answer the following questions:

(a) Has the financial risk of the firm changed during 19X2?
(b) What factors would determine whether the optimal financial structure had been achieved?
(c) Has the liquidity of the firm improved or deteriorated during 19X2?
(d) To what extent can the debtors and stock be considered as available to pay off creditors?

10.12 If you are considering investing £10 000 what criteria would you use in choosing between an investment in ordinary shares, preference shares and debentures?

10.13 When analysing the accounts of Gen Ltd you discover that the following information has not been considered:

(a) Only 90% of the debtors included in the balance sheet at £25 000 are expected to pay even after £500 is spent on legal fees.
(b) Included in the creditors is £600 owing to an unknown supplier.
(c) The firm is being sued for £50 000 damages from a road accident.

How would this information affect the accounts?

10.14 At a meeting to discuss the liquidity problems of a firm, the following proposals are made:

(a) An increase in the depreciation expense to conserve more cash in the firm.
(b) A reduction in the credit given on sales from 60 days to 30 days.
(c) An increase in the credit taken on purchases from 60 days to 90 days.
(d) An increase in the working capital cycle from 40 days to 50 days.
(e) An issue of 1000 shares as a scrip issue.

Comment on these proposals.

11
Preparation and Presentation of Financial Statements

11.1 Introduction

It was established in Chapter 1 that financial statements should be designed to meet the needs of the users of the statements. It follows that their preparation and presentation will be influenced by the **context** in which they are prepared – the type of organisation will be a significant factor, for example. The accounts of a small business operating as a sole trader may be prepared for use by only the owner of the business, whereas the accounts of a Plc with a stock exchange quotation will be made available to a wide variety of users (as discussed in Sect. 1.6).

Sect. 5.2 introduced the distinction between 'internal' and 'external' reporting. **Internal** reporting refers to the use of accounting information **within the organisation** – management accounting reports, for example, would come into this category. For this type of report the preparation and presentation will be determined by the needs of the organisation and the individuals within the organisation using the information, and will not usually be subject to external constraints. However, if the financial statements are for **external** consumption – say, for presentation to a bank manager, to the inland revenue or for publication according to the requirements of the Companies Acts – then they are subject to external constraints as described in Sects 5.2–5.5 and in Sect. 11.6.

A further influence on the preparation of financial statements will be the extent and level of sophistication of the **underlying accounting records** available to the preparer. The preparation of a profit and loss account and balance sheet is relatively straightforward if they are based on a properly maintained system of double-entry book-keeping records. If, on the other hand, proper records are not available, or are incomplete, for one of the reasons described in Sect. 11.4, then (as can be seen from that section) the financial statements may be much more difficult to prepare.

Before we go on to a detailed consideration of the preparation and presentation of financial statements, we will discuss further the issues raised in this introduction. In Sects 11.2 and 11.3 we deal with the impact of the form of organisation and in Sect. 11.4 the preparation of financial statements from incomplete records is explained. The preparation and presentation from full accounting records is then dealt with in Sects 11.5 and 11.6.

11.2   Influence of forms and ownership

Chapter 10 explained the significant differences between sole traders, partnerships and limited liability companies. In Section 11.2 we consider the impact of these differences on the **content of financial statements**.

In the basic accounting equation:

Assets = Liabilities + Owners' Equity

introduced in Chapter 1, the meaning of Owners' Equity was defined as 'the residual interest of the owner of the organisation'. It is in the area of owners' equity that the different forms of ownership have an impact. Otherwise the accounting treatment of assets and liabilities is usually unaffected by the type of organisation and their presentation is dealt with in later sections. The owners' equity under different forms of ownership can now be considered.

Sole Trader

The sole proprietor (or owner) provides the business with its **initial capital** and may, from time to time, introduce further amounts. The owner is entitled to any profits earned by the business and when profits are withdrawn they are usually referred to as 'drawings'. A typical owners' equity section of the balance sheet of a sole trader would be:

Owners' Capital	£	£
Capital at the beginning of the year		XXX
Capital introduced during the year		XXX
Profit for the year	XXX	
Less drawings	XXX	
Retained profit		XXX
Capital at the end of the year		£XXX

Partnerships

A partnership arises where there is more than one owner of a firm. This requires special arrangements to deal with each partner's **capital contribution**, and with the way in which **profits are shared**. The impact of these arrangements are explained more fully in Sect. 11.3.

Limited Liability Companies

The owners' equity of a limited company consists of **share capital and reserves**; the details of these were explained in Chapter 10. In principle there is little difference between the content of a sole trader's capital described above and that of the limited liability company. In the latter, capital is represented by the details of the various types of **share capital issued**. The withdrawal of profits by means of dividends is similar to the sole trader's 'drawings'. An example of a limited company's financial statements is shown in Sect. 11.5.

11.3 Partnerships

Partnerships are commonly used as a form of organisation in Britain for professional groups such as accountants and solicitors where in the past limited liability has been prohibited. However, it is possible to organise most types of business activity as a partnership. The Partnership Act 1890 defined a partnership as 'the relationship which subsists between persons carrying on a business in common with a view to profit'. In the absence of a partnership agreement specifically designed for a particular organisation, the rules of the Partnership Act 1890 are assumed to apply. A partnership agreement will normally deal with the following matters which are relevant from an accounting view point:

(1) *Capital*
The agreement shows **how much capital** each partner should contribute to the partnership.
(2) *Share of profit*
With a sole trader, all the profit each year is added to the owner's capital. In a partnership, the division of profit between the partners is determined by the partnership agreement. The proportions of profit for each partner may be influenced by the amount of capital contributed or by the level of expertise or experience provided by an individual partner. It is common for this appropriation of profit to include elements referred to as salary, interest on capital and division of residual profit, but it should be emphasised that the method and formula for the **appropriation of profit** is usually agreed by the partners and is likely to differ from partnership to partnership. A typical situation would be: as in Ex.11.1.

Example 11.1

Dan Smith and Tom Jones form a new partnership on 1 January 19X0 with
capital of £40 000 contributed by Smith, and £10 000 by Jones. The partnership agreement includes the information that interest on capital of 10% is to
be paid. A salary of £4000 is to be paid to Smith and £6000 to Jones. Residual
profits are to be shared 2/5 by Smith and 3/5 by Jones.

During 19X0 the net profit of the partnership is £40 000 and during the year
drawings by the partners amounted to £13 000 by Smith and £16 000 by
Jones.

A typical statement showing the appropriation of the partnership profit
would be:

Appropriation of Net Profit for 19X0

Net Profit			£40000
Salaries: Smith	4000		
Jones	6000		
			£10000
			£30000
Interest on Capital:			
Smith (10% on £40000)		4000	
Jones (10% on £10000)		1000	5000
			25000
Residual Profit:			
Smith 2/5		10000	
Jones 3/5		15000	
			£25000
			–

This statement would normally be shown as part of the presentation of the
profit and loss account, after net profit where the details of dividends would
be shown in a limited company's profit and loss account. Note that no figure is
shown separately for retained profit because all the net profit has been
allocated to the partners and will appear in their accounts as shown below.

It is usually necessary to segregate the partners' **capital contributions** from
their **share of profits**. This is achieved by maintaining a **Capital Account** and a
Current Account for each partner. They may also maintain a separate account
to record details of **drawings** made by the partners. In Ex.11.1 it is assumed
that drawings are debited direct to the current accounts as shown below:

Partners' Capital Accounts

	Smith		Jones
	19X0 Jan. 1 Cash £40000		19X0 Jan. 1 Cash £10000

Partners' Current Accounts

Smith			Jones		
19X0	19X0		19X0	19X0	
−Drawings(1) 13000	−Salary(2)	4000	−Drawings(1)16000	−Salary(2)	6000
	−Interest(2)	4000		−Interest(2)	1000
	Dec. 31 Profit	10000		Dec. 31 Profit	15000
£13000		£18000	£16000		£22000
	19X1 Jan 1 Balance 5000			19X1 Jan 1 Balance 6000	

Notes:

(1) Drawings may have been made on several dates during the year. Shown here are the totals for the year.

(2) The dates on which the salary and interest are credited will depend on the partnership agreement.

The partnership balance sheet as far as assets and liabilities are concerned will be same as if it were a sole trader or a limited company. The capital and reserves section, however, is represented by the **partners' share of the owners' equity**, and will be presented as:

Balance Sheet of Smith and Jones as at 31 December 19X0

	£	£
Capital Accounts		
Smith	40000	
Jones	10000	
		50000
Current Accounts		
Smith	5000	
Jones	6000	11000
Total partners' funds		£61000

If the firm in Ex.11.1 had been a sole trader, the equivalent section of the balance sheet would have been:

	£	£
Capital – 1 Jan. 19X0		50000
Profit for 19X0	40000	
Drawings	29000	
Retained profit		11000
Capital – 31 Dec. 19X0		£61000

11.4 Preparation of financial statements from incomplete records

Chapter 4 described the components of a double-entry book-keeping system. The preparation of financial statements from such a system is described further in Sect. 11.5. In some circumstances, however, a complete set of accounting records will not be available. This could be because the basic system is inadequate or non-existent, or it could be that it has been inefficiently operated. Other circumstances which give rise to incomplete records occur where some or all of the accounting records have been accidentally lost (for example, in a fire), or where they have been lost as a result of a burglary.

Preparation of a set of financial statements from incomplete records may be required in circumstances such as:

- assessment of profit by the inland revenue;
- support for an insurance claim;
- where a small business requires a bank overdraft;
- assessment of the value of a business, where it is to be sold or where a new partner is being introduced.

Procedures for Dealing With Incomplete Records

The procedures for dealing with these situations will, of course, vary depending on the extent and nature of the problem causing the lack of proper information. In some situations virtually no records will be available, with (for example) cash receipts and payments made without recording details of the transactions. This state of affairs is typical of how many individuals conduct their day-to-day activities and it may not constitute a problem until for some reason a formal record is required. However, in a business context the more usual situation is where something similar to single-entry records exist, perhaps with a cash book and a bank statement available. The role of the accountant is to attempt to construct a set of double-entry records using whatever evidence is available. Typical examples of such evidence are bank statements, cash book, paid cheques, invoices or receipted bills. In addition, there may be valuable information to be obtained from discussions with the owner and employees of the business.

The process of preparing financial statements from incomplete records is rather like a detective story where the available evidence is used as clues to fill in the missing information in order to solve the problem. Figure 11.1 is an adaptation of Figure 1.5 and illustrates the basic building blocks of necessary **accounting information** which may have to be **reconstructed**.

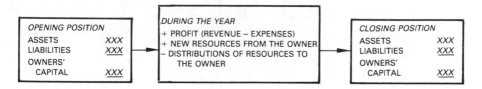

Figure 11.1

A typical series of stages to follow when dealing with incomplete records would be:

(1) Reconstruct the **opening position**.
(2) Use the cash book and bank statements to reconstruct **activity during the year**, for example, to identify:

   − cash and credit sales
   − cash and credit purchases
   − expenses paid
   − receipts of new capital from the owner
   − distributions to the owner by means of drawings
   − purchase and sale of assets.

(3) Identify relevant **end of period adjustments**.
(4) Construct the **financial statements**.

Before we look at a typical example of incomplete records in Ex.11.2, further explanations of the procedures involved in the steps set out above will be useful.

Stage 1 – Reconstruct the Opening Position

What is required is a list of **assets and liabilities**. If financial statements were produced for the previous accounting period then the end of period balance sheet will provide the necessary information. Otherwise estimates of the opening value of, for example, fixed assets, stock, debtors, creditors and cash will have to be made from available data.

Stage 2 – Analysis of Cash Book and Bank Statements

The cash book and bank statements will provide information useful for the **opening and closing balance sheets**. In addition an analysis of cash and bank receipts and payments may reveal:

Receipts
- information on sales made for cash
- amounts received from debtors in respect of credit sales' (* see below)
- new capital introduced
- proceeds of the sale of fixed assets.

Payments
- cash purchases of stock
- amounts paid to creditors in respect of credit purchases (* see below)
- payment of expenses (* see below)
- purchase of fixed assets
- amounts withdrawn by the owner for his own use.

For the items marked * it is important to distinguish payments and receipts which are in respect of transactions which originated in a **previous accounting period**, from transactions of the **current accounting period**. Areas where particular problems may occur are credit sales, credit purchases, stock and cost of sales. These problem areas are discussed below.

Credit Sales
It is likely that part of the amounts received from debtors (credit customers) will be in respect of sales **made in a previous period**. Where a business does not keep a record of its credit sales, the figure can be estimated by adjusting the amounts received from credit customers as follows:

	£
Amount received from debtors (derived from an analysis of cash book and bank statement)	10360
Less	
Debtors at the beginning of the period (the associated credit sales will have been included in a previous profit and loss account)	2480
	7880

Add

Debtors at the end of the period (i.e., credit sales
for the current period which were not included
in the £10 360)   3600

Credit sales for the current period   £11480

Credit Purchases

The same approach can be applied to the calculation of credit purchases:

	£
Amounts paid to creditors	8640
Less	
Creditors at the beginning of the period	2850
	5790
Add	
Creditors at the end of the period	3280
Credit purchases of the current period	£9070

In the case of both sales and purchases, cash sales or purchases need to be
added to compute the **total sales or purchases for the period**.

Stock and Cost of Sales

Once the purchases total is known it is usually possible to calculate the **cost of
sales figure** by adjusting for the opening and closing stock:

		£
Opening Stock	(1)	5680
Add Purchases	(2)	9800
		15480
Less Closing Stock	(3)	6480
Cost of Sales	(4)	£9000

There are **four** elements in the above calculation of cost of sales. It was
possible to calculate cost of sales (4) because elements (1). (2) and (3) were
assumed to be already known from other calculations or other sources of
information. In general, this sort of calculation will be possible provided any
three of the elements are known (or can be discovered from other data). For
example, if the firm's stock had been destroyed by fire before it was valued, it
might be necessary to estimate the value of the loss for insurance purposes. In

the above calculation element (3) (closing stock) was used to arrive at the cost
of sales figure. It might thus appear that if element (3) and (4) are not known
it would not be possible to discover the value of the stock destroyed.
However, it might be possible to arrive at an estimate of the cost of sales by
an alternative method – for example, if the sales figure for the period is
known and the business has an idea of the average mark-up they used in
calculating their selling prices, then it is possible to estimate the cost of sales:

If the average mark-up is 20% on cost and total sales are £10 800, then:

	£
Sales (120% of cost)	10800
Profit (20% of cost)	1800
Cost of Sales	£9000

Knowing the value of element (4), we can thus calculate the missing figure of
£6480 for stock destroyed.

Stage 3 – Identify the Necessary End of Period Adjustments

It was explained in Sect. 4.4 that end of period adjustments can be used to
correct errors or to improve the quality of the information in the profit and
loss account and balance sheet. Typical areas for adjustment will usually be:

(1) *Stock*
    The amount of stock left over at the end of the accounting
    period should be included in the balance sheet as a **current
    asset**, and will reduce the amount of purchases which are
    included in cost of sales as having been sold during the period.
(2) *Depreciation*
    Part of the opening value of most fixed assets will need to be
    allocated to the profit and loss account as an **expense**.
(3) *Provision for bad debts*
    The closing debtors' figure should be scrutinised and reduced
    if any debts are deemed to be **doubtful**. The amount of
    provision (or the increase in an existing provision) is written
    off in the profit and loss account as an **expense**.
(4) *Accruals*
    A check should be made to ascertain if any payments in
    respect of goods or services already received are **unpaid** at the
    date of the balance sheet. Typical examples are wages, tele-
    phone, electricity, etc.; these items should be included as

expenses in the current profit and loss account, and in the balance sheet as **current liabilities**.

(5) *Prepayments*

These are the opposite to accruals in that they represent payments for goods and services made but where the full benefit of the goods and services has **not been received or used up** at the balance sheet date. Typical examples are items where payment is in advance of the services, such as rent or insurance. Any part of such payments which are identified as being in respect of a period **after** the balance sheet date should be **deducted** from the relevant expense in the profit and loss account and included as a **current asset** in the balance sheet.

(6) *Dividends*

It is unlikely that a company which has issued share capital would also have incomplete accounting records except in the case of a fire or a burglary. However, in companies where share capital has been issued, the dividend is usually determined by the **level of profit earned**. It follows that the level of dividend will normally be decided only after the end of the accounting period when the profit for the year will be known. In such cases, dividends will be one of the end of period adjustments, shown as an **appropriation of profit** and as a **current liability** in the balance sheet.

Incomplete Records – Example

Example 11.2
Sarah Sharp, who runs a newsagent's shop, has asked for help in preparing her financial statements for the year 19X0. Her accounting records consist of a cash book, bank statements and a file of invoices and receipts. Most of her customers pay cash, but some are allowed credit.

A preliminary analysis of the available records is as follows:

(1) Summary of entries in the cash book

19X0		£	19X0	£
Jan. 1	Balance	80	– Cash purchases	850
–	Cash takings	23560	– Wages (assistant)	3500
			– Shop expenses	1650
			– Drawings	2600
			– Cash banked	14500
		23640		23100
Dec. 31	Balance	540		

(2) Summary of entries in bank statements

19X0		£	19X0	£
Jan. 1	Balance	2250	– Payments to creditors	7500
	Cash banked	14500	– Rent	1860
	Receipts from		– Shop expenses	1250
	credit customers	2600	– Purchase of cash register	3800
			– Drawings	1000
		19350		14960
Dec. 31	Balance	4390		

(3) Other information

	Jan. 1 19X0	31 Dec. 19X0
(a) Value of:	£	£
Stock	1250	1480
Debtors	520	640
Creditors	1480	1650
Fixtures and fittings(1)	2800	2300

Note: (1) No fixtures or fittings were bought or sold during the year.

(b) The cash register was bought on 31 December 19X0.
(c) The owner estimates that she consumed, for her own use, £2000 worth of stock during the year.
(d) The rent payment was made on 1 January 19X0 and covers a period of 18 months.
(e) The shop assistant is owed a month's wages of £350 at the end of the year.

Suggested Solution

Stage 1 – Reconstruct the Opening Position
From the information provided, the assets and liabilities of the shop on 1 January 19X0 appear to be:

Assets	£
Fixtures and fittings	2800
Stock	1250
Debtors	520
Bank	2250
Cash	80
	6900

Liabilities

Creditors	1480
Net worth of the shop (which constitutes the owner's capital at 1 Jan. 19X0)	£5420

Stage 2 – Analyse the information provided by the cash book and bank statements

In Ex.11.2 the information will enable us to calculate the amount of sales, purchases, cost of sales and drawings:

Sales

	£
Calculation of credit sales involves:	
Amount received from debtors	2600
Less Opening debtors (in last period's sales)	520
	2080
Add Closing debtors (this period's unpaid sales)	640
Credit sales for 19X0	2720
Add Cash sales (from cash book)	23560
Total sales for 19X0	£26280

Purchases

	£
Calculation of credit purchase involves:	
Amount paid to creditors	7050
Less Opening creditors (in last period's purchases)	1480
	5570
Add Closing creditors (this period's unpaid purchases)	1650
Credit purchases	7220
Add Cash purchases (from cash book)	850
Total purchases for 19X0	£8070

Cost of Sales

Calculation of cost of sales uses information from Note (3) above and the purchases total as follows:

	£
Opening Stock	1250
Add Purchases	8070
	9320
Less Closing stock	1480
	7840
Less Stock drawings(1)	2000
Cost of sales for 19X0	£5840

Note:

> (1) The £2000 of stock used by the owner should be classed as **drawings** rather than cost of sales. If she had not used the stock the closing stock would have been £3480 making the cost of sales £5840, which agrees with the above calculation.

Drawings
The owner withdraws assets for her own use in the form of cash both from the shop till and from the shop bank account in addition to the stock withdrawals:

	£
In cash	2600
From bank	1000
In stock	2000
Total drawings for 19X0	£5600

Stage 3 – Identify end of period adjustments
From the 'other information' provided in point (3) above, adjustments are required to reflect the prepayment of rent, the wages owed to the assistant and the information that the value of fixtures and fittings has depreciated over the year. As the business does not have double-entry accounting records, the adjustment can be expressed as:

Rent
Reducing the rent expenses for 19X0 by 1/3 from £1860 to £1240.
Recording the £620 prepayment for 19X1 in the balance sheet as an **asset**.

Wages
Increasing the wage expenses for 19X0 from £3500 (amount actually paid) to £3850 (£3500 + £350) which is the amount that **should have been paid in 19X0**. The £350 owing to the assistant is also shown in the balance sheet as a **liability**.

Depreciation
The fall of £560 in the value of the fixtures and fittings is shown in the profit and loss account as a **depreciation expense** and the reduced value of £2300 is shown in the balance sheet.

Note: If the business did have a proper double-entry book-keeping system, the adjustments could have been recorded as formal entries:

Dr Prepaid Rent	£620	
Cr Rent Expense		£620

Dr Wages Expense	£350	
Cr Accrued Wages		£350
Dr Depreciation Expenses	£500	
Cr Accumulated Depreciation		£500
(Fixtures and Fittings)		

Stage 4 – Construct the Financial Statements

We now have sufficient information from Steps 1, 2 and 3 to prepare a profit and loss account and balance sheet for Sarah Sharp's business:

Sarah Sharp – Newsagent

Profit and Loss Account for the Year Ended 31 December 19X0

		£
Sales		26280
Cost of Sales		5840
Gross Profit		20440
Expenses:		
Wages (3500 + 350)	3850	
Rent (1860 − 620)	1240	
Shop Expenses (1650 + 1250)	2900	
Depreciation	500	
		8490
Net Profit		£11950

Balance Sheet as at 31 December 19X0

	£	£	£
Fixed Assets			
Fixtures and fittings			2300
Cash Register			3800
			6100
Current Assets			
Stock		1480	
Debtors		640	
Prepaid Rent		620	
Bank		4390	
Cash		540	
		7670	
Current Liabilities			
Creditors	1650		
Accrued Wages	350		
		2000	
			5670
Net Assets			£11770

Owners' Capital	£	£
Capital 1 Jan. 19X0		5420
Profit for 19X0	11950	
Drawings	5600	
Retained Profit		£6350
Capital 31 Dec. 19X0		£11770

11.5 Preparation of financial statements from full accounting records

Sect. 11.4 described the procedures for the preparation of financial statements where the available accounts are incomplete. Where the company has maintained a proper system of double-entry book-keeping the procedures will be similar to those illustrated in Figure 4.2 and in the nine procedural steps developed in Sect. 4.4 and set out again below.

(1) **Identify** transactions
(2) **Record** transactions in books of prime entry
(3) **Transfer** (or post) details of the transactions into relevant **ledger accounts**
(4) Periodically calculate the **balance on each ledger account**
(5) Prepare a **trial balance**
(6) Identify **end of year adjustments** (repeat stages (2), (3) and (4) to include adjustments)
(7) Prepare a **further trial balance**
(8) Use the trial balance in (7) as a basis for the preparation of the **profit and loss account** and **balance sheet**
(9) **Close** those accounts which apply only to the **current accounting period**

For the purposes of this section we are assuming that Steps (1)–(5) have been satisfactorily completed so that we can concentrate on steps (6), (7) and (8).

A typical trial balance prepared in Step (5) might be that shown in Example 11.3.

Example 11.3
The following trial balance was taken from the ledger accounts of Anaheim Plc at 31 December 19X0:

	£	£
£1 Ordinary shares		150000
8% £1 Preference shares		50000
7% Debentures		100000
Land (at cost)	113000	
Plant and Machinery (at cost)	380000	
Retained Profit at 1 Jan. 19X0		90000
Share Premium		20000
Stock 1 Jan. 19X0	35000	
Sales		300000
Discount allowed and received	4300	4600
Debtors and Creditors	48000	27000
Accumulated Depreciation – plant and machinery at 1 Jan 19X0		85300
Cash	7100	
Purchases	165000	
Wages and Salaries	31900	
Lighting and Heating	3200	
Debenture Interest	3500	
Interim dividends:		
Ordinary (5%)	7500	
Preference (4%)	2000	
Provision for doubtful debts		1500
General Expenses	27900	
	£828400	£828400

This trial balance was taken from the ledger accounts **before any end of year adjustments** had been made. The following comments can be made at this stage:

(1) As the trial balance debit and credit totals agree it can be assumed that for the transactions processed there must have been an equal value of debits and credits. However, as explained in Sect. 4.2, it does not guarantee that **all the transactions have been correctly processed**.

(2) Ignoring (for the present) the adjustments, the trial balance could be used to prepare the profit and loss account and balance sheet. First it is necessary to identify **which ledger account balances go into each of the financial statements**. Reference to the accounting equation may help in the identification:

$$\text{Assets} = \text{Liabilities} + \text{Owners' Equity}$$

– and in the expanded version used in Chapter 4:

(A)   Assets = Liabilities + Capital + Retained Profit

– and when Retained Profit consists of Retained Profit at the beginning of the accounting period plus the Retained Profit for the current period, which is:

(B) Retained Profit = Revenue − Expenses − Distributions

Equation (A) provides the content of the **Balance Sheet**
Equation (B) provides the content of the **Profit and loss account**.

Therefore if we apply this analysis to the trial balance of Anaheim Plc, we obtain the following classifications:

Balance Sheet Items

Assets	*Liabilities*	*Capital*
Land	7% Debentures	£1 Ordinary shares
Plant and machinery (accumulated depreciation)	Creditors	8% £1 Preference shares
Stock		Share premium
Debtors (Provision for doubtful debts)		
Cash		

Profit and Loss Account Items

Revenue	*Expenses*	*Distribution*
Sales	Discount allowed	Interim dividends
Discount received	Purchases	
	Wages and salaries	
	Lighting and heating	
	Debenture interest	
	General expenses	

Notes on the Classifications

(1) The credit balances in 'accumulated depreciation' and 'provision for doubtful debts' are included among the assets because they are **amounts which reduce the book value of the**

related assets – plant and machinery, and debtors.

(2) The figure of £90 000 retained profit at 1 January 19X0 could be included in the capital column as part of the opening capital. In this example we have followed the procedure adopted by many companies of adding the opening retained profit to the figures for the **current year** in the profit and loss account, as shown in the solution given on p. 227 below. In effect, the profit and loss account is a sort of end of period adjustment which **updates the retained profit figure** from 1 January 19X0 to 31 December 19X0.

(3) Similarly the trial balance figures for stock and accumulated depreciation are dated 1 January 19X0 and will be updated by specific **end of year adjustments**.

(4) In practice, the balance sheet and profit and loss account would not usually be prepared until the end of period adjustments have been dealt with, in Step 6.

Step 6 – Identify End of Year Adjustments

These adjustments are usually made to **correct errors** or to **improve the information** provided by the ledger accounts. Typical information which might require adjustment for the Anaheim Plc would be:

(a) On 30 November 19X0 the company issued bonus shares to the ordinary shareholders on a 1 for 10 basis. No entry relating to this issue has yet been made in the ledger accounts.

(b) Stock at 31 December 19X0 was valued at £41 000.

(c) The company has decided, on the advice of valuers, to revalue the land to £180 000 at 31 December 19X0.

(d) Wages owing at 31 December 19X0 amounted to £500.

(e) Depreciation is to be provided for plant and machinery for 19X0 at 10% of cost.

(f) General expenses include an insurance premium of £1200 which relates to the period 1 April 19X0 to 31 March 19X1.

(g) The provision for doubtful debts is to be fixed at 2½% of debtors outstanding at 31 December 19X0.

(h) Debenture interest has not all been paid.

(i) Corporation tax of £12 000 is to be provided.

(j) The directors wish to provide for:

– a final ordinary dividend of 5%;

– a final preference dividend.

Comments on the Required Adjustments

A basic distinction between the information in the trial balance and the information in the adjustments is that the former has been through the double-entry book-keeping system, whereas the latter has not. The adjustments must therefore be incorporated into the financial statements by following the principles of double-entry. Each adjustment will effect **two balances**, usually one relevant to the balance sheet and one in the profit and loss account. A common error which results in balance sheets which do not balance is to process the adjustments on a single entry basis only.

Notes on the Journal Entries for the Adjustments

(A) Assuming that the balance on the share premium account is to be used as the basis for the bonus shares, the relevant journal entry would be:

　　　Dr Share Premium　　　　　　　　£15000
　　　　　Cr £1 Ordinary Shares　　　　　　　　£15000
　　　Bonus issue of 1 for 10 on 150 000 £1 Ordinary shares.

(B) The inclusion of the value of stock for 1 January 19X0 in the trial balance for 31 December 19X0 suggests that the company uses a **periodic stock system**. It was explained in Chapter 7 that with this system the balance of stock in the ledger account remains constant until it is updated by a periodic valuation. In this example, the value of stock at 31 December 19X0 has been valued at £41 000.
　　　The required journal entries would therefore be:

　　　　　Dr Cost of Sales　　　　　　　　£35000
　　　　　　　Cr Stock　　　　　　　　　　　　£35000

This uses a **FIFO assumption** to transfer the opening stock to cost of sales.

　　　　　Dr Cost of Sales　　　　　　　　£165000
　　　　　　　Cr Purchases　　　　　　　　　　£165000

This similarly transfers the **purchases total into cost of sales**:

　　　　　Dr Stock　　　　　　　　　　　　£41000
　　　　　　　Dr Cost of Sales　　　　　　　　£41000

This records the **closing stock balance in the stock account** and reduces cost of sales by the **value of unsold stock**.

If the company used a perpetual system the Stock Account would be updated for each amount of stock purchased, sold or used in production. The stock value in the trial balance would then represent the up-to-date value at 31 December 19X0 and no end of period adjustment may be necessary. An adjustment may, however, be necessary even with a perpetual system if an end of year physical check of stock levels reveals a **discrepancy with the book value** in the Stock Ledger Account.

(C) As discussed in Chapter 6, many companies have in recent years adopted the practice of **revaluing assets**. The provisions in the Companies Act 1985 for the application of 'alternative accounting rules' provide the statutory regulations for the treatment of revaluation in published accounts. The appropriate journal entry here is to:

  Dr Land   £67000
   Cr Revaluation Reserve   £67000

The **historical cost of the land** should be disclosed either in the balance sheet or in the notes to the financial statements.

(D) The appropriate journal entry is:

  Dr Wages   £500
   Cr Accrued Wages   £500

This increases the **wage expense** in the profit and loss account and the accrued wages is included as a **creditor** in the balance sheet.

(E) Dr Depreciation Expense   £38000
  Cr Accumulated Depreciation –   £38000
  plant and machinery
 Being 10% of cost of £380 000

(F) Dr Prepaid Insurance   £300
  Cr General Expenses   £300

The insurance premium of £1200 covers 9 months of 19X0 and 3 months of 19X1. This entry reduces the general expenses for 19X0 by £300 (1/4 of £1200) and transfers that sum to the current assets in the balance sheet where it is shown as a **prepayment**. Note that considerations of materiality have been ignored in this example.

(G) The trial balance shows that the company already has a provision for doubtful debts of £1500. They have decided that a provision of 2½% of debtors is adequate to cover potential bad debts from the £48 000 outstanding debtors. The required provision is thus £1200 (2½% of £48 000) which is £300 less than the existing provision which will have been created out of the previous year's profit and loss accounts. The required journal entry is thus:

Dr Provision for Doubtful Debts   £300
     Cr Bad and Doubtful Debts Expense   £300

This reduces the provision to £1200 and credits the excess provision to the profit and loss account.

(H) Dr Debenture Interest   £3500
     Cr Accrued Debenture Interest   £3500

The total debenture interest for 19X0 should be £7000, 7% of £100 000. It can be seen from the trial balance that an **instalment of £3500** has already been paid. This journal entry brings the expense up to £7000 and shows the unpaid £3500 in the balance sheet as a creditor.

(I) Dr Taxation Expense   £12000
     Cr Accrued Taxation   £12000

This journal entry records the estimate of **corporation tax** which will be paid on profit earned in 19X0. The debit will appear as an **expense** in the profit and loss account and the credit in the balance sheet as a **creditor**.

In practice, the estimate of corporation tax payable will be calculated by applying the prevailing rate (in recent years between 30% and 40%) to the company's **taxable profit**. 'Taxable profit' will normally be different to the profit shown in the profit and loss account which has been calculated using accounting principles; taxable profit is based on the rules determined by the inland revenue which may **disallow** certain expenses incurred by the company and included in the normal profit and loss account. On the other hand, they may provide **special deductions allowable for tax purposes**: the most notable example is **depreciation**, which must be added back to accounting profit when calculating taxable profit but special 'capital allowances' are allowed as deductions in place of depreciation.

(J) The trial balance shows that the company has already paid interim dividends to their shareholders during 19X0. Because the final dividend for the year, at least for Ordinary shareholders, is usually related to the current year's level of profit, it follows that the size of the dividend cannot be determined until the profit for the year has been calculated. It is usual therefore for the final dividend to be declared after the end of the accounting year and consequently the end of year adjustments usually include a journal entry for **dividends**:

Dr Final Dividend – ordinary shares   £8250
               – preference shares   £2000
     Cr Dividends Payable   £10250

The ordinary dividend is 5% of £165 000 Ordinary share capital (including the bonus shares). The Preference dividend is 4% of £50 000 which, when added to the interim 4%, constitutes the 8% due to the Preference shareholders. The debit of £8250 and £2000 will be **added to the interim dividends** and shown in the profit and loss account as an **appropriation of profit**. The £10 250 credit will appear as a **current liability** in the balance sheet.

Processing the Adjustments

The information provided by the adjusting journal entries must now be amalgamated with the data in the initial trial balance. In practice, this would be achieved by posting each journal entry to the relevant ledger account and then preparing another trial balance (i.e., Step 7) based on the adjusted ledger account balances. The financial statements can then be prepared (Step 8) from the adjusted trial balance. An alternative method of showing how the adjustments are processed is by means of an **extended trial balance**.

The Extended Trial Balance

The extended trial balance is used here to explain how adjustments can be processed. In practice, it may be used by a firm who wishes to produce financial statements without waiting until the ledger accounts are completed. They are also often used by auditors as part of their working papers for auditing end of period adjustments.

The form of the extended trial balance using the data from Ex.11.3 is shown in Figure 11.2.

The extended trial balance in Figure 11.2 shows how the adjustments column lists the adjusting journal entries **alongside the ledger account balance** which they will affect. Note also that the total debit figure of £387 850 equals

	Trial Balance		ADJ	Adjustments		Profit and Loss Account		Balance Sheet	
	Dr £	Cr £		Dr £	Cr £	Dr £	Cr £	Dr £	Cr £
£1 Ordinary Shares		150000	A		15000				165000
8% Preference Shares		50000							50000
7% Debentures		100000							100000
Land	113000		C	67000				180000	
Plant and Machinery	380000							380000	
Retained Profit – 1 Jan. 19X0		90000					90000		
Share Premium		20000	A	15000					5000
Stock	35000		B	41000	35000			41000	
Sales		300000					300000		
Discounts allowed and Received	4300	4600				4300	4600		
Debtors and Creditors	48000	27000						48000	27000
Accumulated Depreciation – Plant and Machinery		85300	E		38000				123300
Cash	7100							7100	
Purchases	165000		B		165000				
Wages and Salaries	31900		D	500		32400			
Lighting and Heating	3200					3200			
Debenture Interest	3500		H	3500		7000			
Dividends:									
Ordinary	7500		J	8250		15750			
Preference	2000		J	2000		4000			
Provision for Doubtful Debts		1500	G	300					1200
General expenses	27900		F		300	27600			
Cost of Sales			B	165000 35000	41000	159000			
Revaluation Reserve			C		67000				67000
Accrued Wages			D		500				500
Depreciation Expense			E	38000		38000			
Prepaid Insurance			F	300				300	
Decrease in Provision for Doubtful Debts			G		300		300		
Dividend Payable			J		10250				10250
Debenture Interest Accrued			H		3500				3500
Taxation			I	12000		12000			
Taxation Payable			I		12000				12000
Retained Profit – 31 Dec. 19X0 – Balancing Figures						91650			91650
	£828400	£828400		£387850	£387850	£394900	£394900	£656400	£656400

Figure 11.2

the **total credit figure**. This is a confirmation that double-entry procedures have been followed. Some of the adjustments necessitate opening **new ledger accounts**: in Figure 11.2, all the accounts after general expenses are new. The adjusting entries are processed by debiting or crediting the existing trial balance figure as appropriate, and by sorting the amended figures into the profit and loss account and the balance sheet columns.

The profit and loss columns are **credited with revenue** and **debited with expenses and appropriations of profit**. The inclusion of the retained profit of £90 000 at 1 January 19X0 means that the balancing figure of £91 650 represents the retained profit at the end of year. This figure is carried across to the balance sheet to be included in the owners' equity which is described as Share Capital and Reserves. With the inclusion of the £91 650, the debit and credit columns of the balance sheet will agree if the adjustments have been properly processed.

Step 8 – Preparation of the Financial Statement[1]
The profit and loss account and balance sheet columns of the extended trial balance include all the information necessary to prepare the final financial statements. If the statements are to be published (i.e., for external presentation), their format is specified by the Companies Act 1985 and details of these requirements are discussed in Sect. 11.6. For internal financial statements, the format can be decided by the company; however, in many respects, the externally required format is now adopted extensively for all financial statements produced by companies.

A typical set of internal financial statements based on Ex.11.3 would be as follows:

Anaheim Plc
Profit and Loss Account for the Year Ended 31 December 19X0

	£	£
Sales		300000
Cost of Sales		159000
Gross Profit		141000
Plus Discount Received(1)	4600	
Decrease in Provision for Doubtful Debts(1)	300	4900
		145900
Less Expenses:		
Wages and Salaries	32400	
Lighting and Heating	3200	
Discounts Allowed	4300	
Debenture Interest	7000	
Depreciation	38000	
General Expenses	27600	
		112500
Net Profit		33400
Taxation		12000
Profit After Taxation		21400
Dividends:		
Ordinary	15750	
Preference	4000	
		19750
Retained Profit for 19X0		1650
Retained Profit at 1 January 19X0		90000
Retained Profit at 31 December 19X0		£91650

Note: (1) These two credits could alternatively have been deducted from the £112 500 expenses total.

As can be seen from the example in Sect. 11.6 the required format for the published profit and loss account is not radically different from that shown above. There is an attempt in the UK Companies Act format, which in turn is based on EC requirements, to standardise the format by requiring (for example) that all expenses are classified under the sub-headings of **Distribution Cost** and **Administrative Expenses**.

Anaheim Plc
Balance Sheet as at 31 December 19X0

Fixed Assets	£	£	£
Land (at Valuation)			180000
Plant and Machinery (at Cost)		380000	
Less Accumulated Depreciation		123300	
			256700
			436700
Current Assets			
Stock		41000	
Debtors	48000		
Less Provision for Doubtful Debts	1200	46800	
Prepaid Insurance		300	
Cash		7100	
		95200	
Current Liabilities			
Creditors	27000		
Accrued Wages	500		
Debenture Interest Payable	3500		
Dividends Payable	10250		
Taxation Payable	12000	53250	
Net Current Assets			41950
			478650
Long Term Liabilities			
7% Debentures			100000
			£378650
Capital and Reserves			
Called up Share Capital			
Ordinary Shares £1		165000	
8% Preference Shares £1		50000	
			215000
Reserves:			
Share Premium		5000	
Revaluation Reserve		67000	
Retained Profit		91650	163650
			£378650

As with the profit and loss account, the required Companies Act format for the balance sheet does not differ significantly from that shown above. There are some differences in terminology: for example, Current Liabilities is replaced by 'Creditors: amounts falling due within one year' and Long Term Liabilities by 'Creditors: amounts falling due after more than one year'.

For both the profit and loss account and balance sheet, the Companies Act allows the use of alternative formats such as a **horizontal** (or two-sided) rather than the vertical presentation which was used in Ex.11.3. In practice, however, virtually all firms now use a vertical presentation.

11.6   Presentation of financial statements for external publication

Sect. 5.2 considered what determined the **form** and **content** of financial statements; Sect. 5.3 dealt with theoretical issues, Sect. 5.4 with legal requirements and Sect. 5.5 with other forms of regulation such as 'Statements of Standard Accounting Practice'. Section 11.6 considers further the legal regulations, particularly those now contained in the Companies Acts 1985 and 1989. Among those regulations is the requirement that the company present to the annual general meeting of shareholders:

- a **profit and loss account**
- a **balance sheet**
- a **director's report**
- an **auditor's report**.

We are concentrating in this Sect. 11.6 on the requirement relating to the profit and loss account and the balance sheet; examples of a director's report and an auditor's report can be seen in the Marks and Spencer annual report in Appendix B.

The Companies Act 1985 introduced new regulations governing the **format** of published accounts, and much of the remainder of this chapter is based on the content of these formats. The Companies Act 1989 included, among other provisions on consolidated accounts and auditing, two aspects of relevance to external publication. One is a relaxation of reporting requirements in respect of **private companies**. (See Chapter 10, n. 1 for definition of a private company). The other is the potentially very significant concession that allows listed companies to send shareholders **summary financial statements** if they do not wish to receive the full statements.

The Profit and Loss Account

The Companies Act 1985 provides for two methods of analysing the data in profit and loss accounts. **Format 1** analyses expenses by **type of operation**, and is often termed the 'Operational Format; **Format 2** analyses expenses by **type of expenses**, and is termed the 'Type of Expenditure Format'. In Sect. 4.5 we introduced the concept of a 'Natural Classification' and 'Functional Classification' of expenses in the profit and loss account. In effect, Format 1 adopts the functional classification and Format 2 adopts the natural classification as described in Sect. 4.5. As the Act provides a horizontal and a vertical form for both Format 1 and Format 2; there are in effect **four** possible alternatives. In practice few firms use a horizontal presentation and we will consider only the vertical form. An example of Format 1 is shown in Figure 11.3 and on Format 2 in Figure 11.4. It appears that in practice most firms have adopted Format 1 in their published accounts.

The profit and loss account must be presented **in the order and under the headings** shown in the formats. The arabic numbers (1, etc.) denote that these items may be **amalgamated or amended** where the nature of the company's business requires. (The arabic numbers themselves need not be shown in the published accounts.) The Act requires also that the **corresponding previous year's figures** must be shown.

Figure 11.3

Companies Act 1985

Profit and Loss Account – Formats

Format 1 – Operational Format

	£	£
1. Turnover		X
2. Cost of sales		(X)
3. Gross profit (or loss)		X
4. Distribution costs	X	
5. Administrative expenses	X	
		(X)
		X
6. Other operating income		X
		X
7. Income from shares in group companies	X	
8. Income from shares in related companies	X	
9. Income from other fixed asset investments	X	
10. Other interest receivable and similar income	X	
		X
		X
11. Amounts written off investments	X	
12. Interest payable and similar charges	X	
		(X)
Profit or loss on ordinary activities before taxation		X
13. Tax on profit (or loss) on ordinary activities		(X)
14. Profit (or loss) on ordinary activities after taxation		X
15. Extraordinary income	X	
16. Extraordinary charges	(X)	
17. Extraordinary profit (or loss)	X	
18. Tax on extraordinary profit (or loss)	(X)	
		X
		X
19. Other taxes not shown under the above items		(X)
20. Profit (or loss) for the financial year		X
Dividends paid and proposed		(X)
Transfers to (from) reserves		(X)
Retained profit (or loss) for the financial year		X
Retained profit (or loss) brought forward		X
Retained profit (or loss) carried forward		£X

The lines after line 20 are not included in the Companies Act 1985 standard format. They are included here to provide a complete picture of the profit and loss information for the company.

Figure 11.4

Companies Act 1985
Profit and Loss Account – Formats
Format 2 – Type of Expenditure Format

	£	£	£
1. Turnover			X
2. Change in stocks of finished goods and in work in progress			(X)
3. Own work capitalised			X
4. Other operating income			X
			X
5. (a) Raw materials and consumables	X		
(b) Other external charges	X		
		X	
6. Staff costs:			
(a) Wages and salaries	X		
(b) Social security costs	X		
(c) Other pension costs	X		
		X	
7. (a) Depreciation and other amounts written off tangible and intangible fixed assets	X		
(b) Exceptional amounts written off current assets	X		
		X	
8. Other operating charges		X	
			(X)
			X
9. Income from shares in group companies		X	
10. Income from shares in related companies		X	
11. Income from other fixed asset investments		X	
12. Other interest receivable and similar income		X	
			X
			X
13. Amounts written off investments		X	
14. Interest payable and similar charges		X	
			(X)
Profit or loss on ordinary activities before taxation			X
15. Tax on profit (or loss) on ordinary activities			(X)
16. Profit (or loss) on ordinary activities after taxation			X
17. Extraordinary income		X	
18. Extraordinary charges		(X)	
19. Extraordinary profit (or loss)		X	
20. Tax on extraordinary profit (or loss)		(X)	
			X
			X
21. Other taxes not shown under the above items			(X)
22. Profit (or loss) for the financial year			X
Dividends paid and proposed			(X)
Transfers to (from) reserves			(X)
Retained profit (or loss) for the financial year			X
Retained profit (or loss) brought forward			X
Retained profit (or loss) carried forward			£X

The Balance Sheet

The Companies Act 1985 permits either a vertical or a horizontal format for the balance sheet. As with the profit and loss account, most firms now adopt the vertical format and for this reason we do not include examples of horizontal balance sheets. An example of the vertical format is given in Figure 11.5.

Figure 11.5

Companies Act 1985

Balance Sheet Format 1

	£	£	£
A CALLED UP SHARE CAPITAL NOT PAID*			X
B FIXED ASSETS			
I Intangible assets			
1 Development costs	X		
2 Concessions, patents, licences, trade marks and similar rights and assets	X		
3 Goodwill	X		
4 Payments on account	X		
		X	
II Tangible assets			
1 Land and buildings	X		
2 Plant and machinery	X		
3 Fixtures, fittings, tools and equipment	X		
4 Payments on account and assets in course of construction	X		
		X	
III Investments			
1 Shares in group companies	X		
2 Loans to group companies	X		
3 Shares in related companies	X		
4 Loans to related companies	X		
5 Other investments other than loans	X		
6 Other loans	X		
7 Own shares	X		
		X	
			X
C CURRENT ASSETS			
I Stocks			
1 Raw materials and consumables	X		
2 Work in progress	X		
3 Finished goods and goods for resale	X		
4 Payments on account	X		
		X	

II Debtors
    1 Trade debtors   X
    2 Amounts owed by group companies   X
    3 Amounts owed by related companies   X
    4 Other debtors   X
    5 Called up share capital not paid*   X
    6 Prepayments and accrued income*   X
        X

III Investments
    1 Shares in group companies   X
    2 Own shares   X
    3 Other investments   X
        X

IV Cash at bank and in hand   X
        X
D PREPAYMENTS AND ACCRUED INCOME*   X
        X

b/f   X   X
E CREDITORS: AMOUNTS FALLING DUE
WITHIN ONE YEAR
    1 Debenture loans   X
    2 Bank loans and overdrafts   X
    3 Payments received on account   X
    4 Trade creditors   X
    5 Bills of exchange payable   X
    6 Amounts owed to group companies   X
    7 Amounts owed to related companies   X
    8 Other creditors including taxation and
        social security   X
    9 Accruals and deferred income*   X
        (X)

F NET CURRENT ASSETS (LIABILITIES)   X

G TOTAL ASSETS LESS CURRENT LIABILITIES   X

H CREDITORS: AMOUNTS FALLING DUE AFTER
MORE THAN ONE YEAR
    1 Debenture loans   X
    2 Bank loans and overdrafts   X
    3 Payments received on account   X
    4 Trade creditors   X
    5 Bills of exchange payable   X
    6 Amounts owed to group companies   X
    7 Amounts owed to related companies   X
    8 Other creditors including taxation and
        social security   X
    9 Accruals and deferred income*   X
        X

Figure 11.5   continued

I PROVISIONS FOR LIABILITIES AND CHARGES
1 Pensions and similar obligations   X
2 Taxation, including deferred taxation   X
3 Other provisions   X
                                                              X
J ACCRUALS AND DEFERRED INCOME*   X
                                                                   (X)
                                                                   £X

K CAPITAL AND RESERVES   £   £
I   Called up share capital   X
II   Share premium account   X
III Revaluation reserve   X
IV   Other reserves:
     1 Capital redemption reserve   X
     2 Reserve for own shares   X
     3 Reserves provided for by the articles
       of association   X
     4 Other reserves   X
                                                            X
V   Profit and loss account   X
                                                            £X

* These items may be shown in either of the positions indicated.

It can be seen from Figure 11.5 that the major headings such as 'Fixed Assets' are prefixed by letters A, B, C, etc, with major subdivisions such as 'Intangible Assets' being denoted by roman numerals (I, etc.). Minor subdivisions such as 'Development Costs' are denoted by arabic numerals (1, etc.). The significance of these distinctions is that although the prefixes themselves do not have to be shown on the balance sheet, they denote **what headings** must be shown: any item preceded either by a letter or roman numeral prefix **must be disclosed** in the company's published balance sheet; a company which wishes to disclose the minimum number of headings on the face of its balance sheet, would therefore present a balance sheet as in Figure 11.6 with the details denoted by the arabic numerals shown in the notes to the financial statements.

In practice, most companies have decided that the format in Figure 11.5 produces a balance sheet which is **too detailed for easy comprehension**, and they have adopted the format as in Figure 11.6, or a version which is close to it. The Marks and Spencer balance sheet in Appendix 3 is a typical example.

Figure 11.6

Format for Modified Published Balance Sheet

	£	£
A Called up share capital not paid		X
B Fixed assets		
I Intangible assets	X	
II Tangible assets	X	
III Investments	X	
		X
C Current assets		
I Stocks	X	
II Debtors	X	
III Investments	X	
IV Cash at bank and in hand	X	
	X	
D Accruals and deferred income	X	
	X	
E Creditors: Amounts becoming due and payable within one year	(X)	
F Net current assets (liabilities)		X
G Total assets less current liabilities		X
H Creditors: Amounts becoming due and payable after more than one year	X	
I Provisions for liabilities and charges	X	
J Accruals and deferred income	X	
		(X)
		£X
K Capital and reserves		
I Called up share capital	X	
II Share premium account	X	
III Revaluation reserve	X	
IV Other reserve	X	
V Profit and loss account	X	
		£X

Summary

Chapter 11 has been concerned with explaining the factors which influence the form and content of financial statements. These influences include the forms of ownership and whether the statements are for internal use or external publication. A further major theme of the chapter was an analysis of methods which can be used to prepare financial statements in situations where only incomplete records are available and where proper double-entry records have been maintained.

Note and Reference

1. We have omitted Step 7 which would be the preparation of a new trial balance from the ledger accounts which include the effect of the end of period adjustments. We could alternatively have included two extra columns in the extended trial balance in Figure 11.2 to show the 'adjusted trial balance'.

Questions and Problems

11.1   What do you understand by the following terminology:

Incomplete records	Taxable profit
Capital account	Capital allowances
Current account	Interim dividend
Single entry records	Extended trial balance
Horizontal accounts format	Vertical accounts format

11.2   What are the main reasons for having different types of ownership such as a sole trader, a partnership and a limited company?

11.3   If you were asked to prepare a set of financial statements for your family, what records would probably be available for you to use?

11.4   What do you consider to be the relative advantages or disadvantages of the two alternative profit and loss account formats permitted by the Companies Act 1985.

11.5   Can you identify any ways in which the Marks and Spencer accounts in Appendix B do not seem to conform to the requirements of the Companies Act 1985.

11.6   Stelling and Hudgill are in partnership sharing profits and losses 3:2. Under the terms of the partnership agreement the partners are entitled to interest on capital at 5% per year and Hudgill is entitled to a salary of £4500 per year. Interest is charged on drawings at 5% p.a. and the relevant amounts of such interest is given below. No interest is charged or allowed on current accounts.

The partners' capital are:

	£
Stelling	30000
Hudgill	10000

The net trading for the firm before dealing with the partners' interest or Hudgill's salary for the year ended 30 June 19X9 was £25 800. Interest on drawings for the year amounted to Stelling £400, Hudgill £300.

At 1 July 19X8 there was a credit balance of £1280 on Stelling's current account while Hudgill's current account showed a debit balance of £500. Drawings for the year to 30 June 19X9 amounted to £12 000 for Stelling and £15 000 for Hudgill.

Required: Prepare for the year to 30 June 19X9:

  (i) the firm's profit and loss (appropriation) account;
 (ii) the partners' current accounts.

11.7 Elliott and McDonald, partners in a book publishers, wish to convert their partnership into a limited company, 'Roker Park' Ltd. The abbreviated partnership balance sheet before the formation is as follows:

	£
Capital Accounts	
Elliott	10000
McDonald	12000
	£22000
Net Assets	£22000

The partnership agreement states that Elliott and McDonald share net income in the proportion 2:1.
The agreed valuation of the partnership assets for the purposes of forming the company is £310 000. Share capital issued was 310 000 Ordinary shares at £1 each.

Required:

(a) Show the distribution of shares to Elliott and McDonald
(b) Show the balance sheet of Roker Park Ltd immediately after its formation.

11.8 Mr Alfred Tubbs commenced business as a retail florist and greengrocer on 1 January 19X7 with an initial capital of £40 000 which he paid into his business bank account. He employed Miss Prism to manage the shop at an annual salary of £5000 plus commission of 10% of the net profit before charging the commission.
Mr Tubbs did not maintain proper accounting records, but the following information is available:

1. An analysis of the business bank statement for 19X7 shows:

Receipts	£	Payments	£
Capital Introduced	40000	Lease	20000
Takings Banked	135000	Shop Fittings	9000
Loan From Bank	15000	Motor Van	4800
		Payment to	
		Suppliers	114600
		Interest	1000
		General Expenses	8400
		Rent	3800
		Balance	29200
	£190800		£190800

2. All sales were for cash and each day's taking were banked at the end of the day. However the shop maintains a petty cash balance of £200 in the till.
3. During the year the following payments were made in cash out of the daily takings before they were banked:

	£
Salary payments to Miss Prism	4400
Drawings – Mr Tubbs	2600
Payments to suppliers	1800
General expenses	900

4. The 5 year lease on the shop was purchased on 1 January 19X7 for £20 000. In addition there is an annual rental of £4500.
5. By 31 December 19X7 cheques totalling £2600 which had been sent to suppliers had not been presented to the bank for payment.
6. The loan from the bank was received on 1 July 19X7 and the interest rate was fixed at 20% per annum.
7. Invoices from suppliers which have not been paid amount to £7400 and an invoice for general expenses of £200 is also unpaid.
8. Stock at 31 December 19X7 is valued at £34 200.
9. The shop fittings have an estimated life of 5 years and no residual value. The motor van will be retained for 3 years at which time its estimated selling price would be £1500.
10. During the year Mr Tubbs used goods from the shop, for his own use, which had cost £250.

Required: Prepare a profit and loss account for Mr Tubb's business for 19X7 and a balance sheet as at 31 December 19X7. Make what assumptions and adjustments you feel are necessary to prepare the accounts under generally accepted accounting principles. State clearly the basis for any calculations you make.

11.9 Terry Small and Bert Long are in partnership sharing profits and losses 3:2. Under the terms of the partnership agreement the partners are entitled to interest on capital at 5% per year, and Long is entitled to a salary of £4000 per year.

The Partners' Capital Accounts on 31 March 19X6 showed equal balances.

You ascertain that on 31 March 19X6 the firm had premises that were valued at £15 000, equipment at £2000 and a motor van at £500. The stock was valued at £6700 and debtors, all of which were considered good, amounted to £5500. The partnership owed £6250 to trade creditors, and had a bank overdraft of £2100. Prepaid insurance was £50.

The cash book summary for year ended 31 March 19X7 is as follows:

Cash Book Summary

	£		£
Cash From Sales	14250	Balance	2100
Sale of Old Motor Van	250	Creditors	7100
		Wages	6800
		Drawings, Small	2500
		Long	2000
		Rates and Insurance	500
		Telephone	150
		Lights and Heating	180
		Motor Van	1800
		Motor Expenses	850
		Stationery and Post	330
		Bank Interest and	
		Charges	140
Balance as at 31 March			
19X7 c/d	£9950		
	£24450		£24450

1 April 19X7 Balance b/d
£9950

At the end of the financial year, 31 March 19X7, stock was valued at £6400, debtors £5800 and creditors £6100.

Other Information:

(1) On 1 July 19X6, the annual payment of £150 was made for insurance.
(2) Write off the loss on the sale of the old motor van to expenses.
(3) Depreciation: equipment by 10% per year, straight-line.
            new motor van by 20% per year, straight-line.
(4) Current accounts were not used, and no interest is charged on drawings.

Required: For the year ended 31 March 19X7 prepare the partnership's profit and loss account and balance sheet as at 31 March 19X7.

11.10 Martin Hansen runs a general store but does not keep proper accounting records. With his help you have been able to compile the following information.

	1 July 19X7	30 June 19X8
	£	£
Freehold Land and Buildings – cost	20000	20000
Delivery Van (cost £6000)	4500	?
Stock at Cost	3000	3500
Debtors	750	900
Creditors	950	1300
Cash at Bank	650	1350
Cash in Hand	150	250
Loan	8000	4000

In addition, Hansen informed you that he owned £400 for van expenses at 30 June 19X8 (and £300 at 1 July 19X7) and that his property insurance is paid in advance on 1 April; the payment in 19X7 was £1200 and in 19X8 it was £1600.

Extracts from his store cash book and bank statements show:

Cash Book	£
Cash receipts From Customers	90500
Cash Payments : for purchases	19000
: for Hansen's own use	30400
: general store expenses	450
: wages	5000

Bank Statement	
Cash Banked	39550
Cheques Received From Customers	9500
Loan Repayment (including interest)	4800
Cheque payments for – suppliers	35000
– electricity	500
– van expenses	1200
– telephone	400
– rates	850
– property insurance	1600

Note: Depreciation is to be provided on the delivery van (which is still owned at 30 June 19X8) at a rate of 25% on cost.

Required: Prepare a profit and loss account for the year to 30 June 19X8 and a balance sheet as at that date.

11.11 Mr Thomas runs a hardware store. On the night of 30 June 19X8 his shop is burgled. The thieves took all his stock and stole £130 cash from the till. He does not keep proper records and he is not sure how much stock he has lost.

He is fully insured and as support to the insurance claim the insurance company wish to see his profit and loss account for the six months to 30 June 19X8 and his balance sheet as at that date. Mr Thomas has asked for your help in providing these statements. He provides you with the following information:

(a) Assets and liabilities at 1 January 19X8:

Shop Fittings – Cost	1500
– Accumulated Depreciation	800
Net book value	700
Stock	2700
Debtors	430
Rates Prepaid (until 30 March 19X8)	130
Bank	2140
Cash in Till	30
Creditors	1650
Accrued Electricity	40

(b) His bank statements for the six months period show:

Receipts

	£
Cash Banked	9460
Cheques Banked	10600
Income From Investment	180
	20240

Payments

Trade Creditors	17850
Rent (1 Jan–30 Sept. 19X8)	1200
Electricity	160
Insurance	150
Telephone	80
	£9440

(c) Payments in cash from the shop till:

Creditors	2400
Drawings	1600

(d) The shop's average gross profit margin in recent years is 25%.
(e) The shop fittings are thought to be worth £500.
(f) A rates bill for the year beginning 1 April 19X8 for £600 has been received, but not paid.
(g) Debtors and creditors amounted to £270 and £1900 respectively on 30 June 19X8.

> *Required*: Prepare for Mr Thomas's business a profit and loss account for the six months to 30 June 19X8 and a balance sheet at that date (show your workings clearly).

11.12 The trial balance of the USC Plc on 31 December 19X6 is as follows:

	Dr £	Cr £
Ordinary Shares of £1 each, fully paid		60000
10% Preference Shares of £1 each, fully paid		20000
8% Debenture 20X3/X8		50000
General Reserve		70000
Profit and Loss Account – balance 1.1.X6		45000
Leasehold Property – Cost	40000	
– Accumulated Depreciation		12000
Plant and Machinery – Cost	180000	
– Accumulated Depreciation		45000
Fixtures and Fittings – Cost	30000	
– Accumulated Depreciation		10000

	Dr £	Cr £
Investments in Government Securities – at Cost	40000	
Sales Revenue		220000
Provision for Doubtful Debts		4000
Interest Received From Government Securities		3000
Cost of Goods Sold	90000	
Cash	59000	
Stock at 31.12.X6	25000	
Debtors	20000	
Creditors		15000
Bad Debts Written Off	5000	
Wages and Salaries	25000	
Rent and Insurance	10000	
Debenture Interest	2000	
Ordinary Share Dividend – interim	12000	
Preference Share Dividend – interim	1000	
General Administration Expenses	15000	
	£554000	£554000

In addition, the following information has to be taken into account:

(1) The leasehold property was acquired on a 20 year lease on 1 January 19X0 for £40 000. It has been agreed that the property should be revalued in the financial statements to a current value at 1 January 19X6 of £42 000. Depreciation of the lease is required for 19X6.

(2) The company decided to have, with effect from 30 September 19X6 a 1 for 1 scrip issue of ordinary shares using the general reserve to implement the issue. No adjustments have been made in respect of the issue. You should make the appropriate adjustments.

(3) A final Ordinary dividend has been declared for shareholders on 31 December 19X6 of 30p per share. The interim dividend of 20p was paid on 30 June 19X6.

(4) The provision for doubtful debts should be 5% of debtors.

(5) Stock with a cost of £10 000, which it was wrongly assumed had been sold, is discovered in the warehouse. No entries in respect of this stock have yet been made.

(6) Depreciation for the year (apart from the leasehold property) is to be based on the following:

Plant and machinery 20% on cost
Fixtures and fittings 10% on reducing balance.

(7) Wages and salaries unpaid at the end of the year amounted to £5000. Of the rent and insurance payment made in 19X6, £2000 was in respect of periods after the end of the year.

(8) It has been calculated that the investment in government securities will yield in 19X6 a return of 10% on their cost.

(9) Taxation is to be charged at 35% on net profit.

(10) Provide for any other adjustments you decide need to be included based on the evidence in the question.

> *Required*: A profit and loss for the year ended 31 December 19X6 and a balance sheet as at that date. The statements should conform to the Companies Act as far as is possible given the available information (show clearly the basis for any adjustments you make to the trial balance figures; apart from note (9) above, ignore other aspects of taxation).

11.13 The following balances have been extracted from the books of Opus Ltd at 31 December 19X7:

	£
Creditors	18000
Sales	220000
Land at Cost	52000
Buildings at Cost	110000
Furniture and Fittings at Cost	66000
Bank Overdraft	20000
Accumulated Depreciation – Buildings	24000
– Furniture and Fittings	32000
Undistributed Profit at 1 January 19X7	7000
Provision for Doubtful Debts	3500
Goodwill	36000
Cash	700
Stock at 1 January	42000
Interim Dividend – Preference Shares	1800
Wages and Salaries	26000
Rates and Insurance	12600
General Expenses	9200
Debtors	46800
Purchases	132000
Debenture Interest	1200
Bad Debts Written Off	2200
5% Debentures (19X5/X8)	48000
6% £1 Preference Shares	60000
£1 Ordinary Shares	80000
Share Premium	26000

Additional Information:

1. Stock at 31 December 19X7 was £44 000
2. Insurance paid in advance was £1400
3. Wages owing were £1200
4. Depreciation is to be provided at 10% on the cost of buildings and 20% on the written down value of furniture and fittings.
5. Provision for bad debts is to be 5% of debtors.
6. The directors propose to pay a 10% ordinary dividend.
7. Make what further adjustments you consider appropriate.

Required:

(a) Prepare the profit and loss account of Opus Ltd for the year ended 31 December 19X7 and a balance sheet at that date.

(b) Using the accounts you have prepared in (a) answer the following:

(i) What is a share premium, and how did it arise?
(ii) Which of the reserves are capital, and which are revenue reserves? What, in principle, is the difference between the two?
(iii) How could the Goodwill account have arisen?

11.14 The trial balance of Sacremento Plc on 31 March 19X9 was as follows:

Dr	£	Cr	£
Freehold Land and Buildings – Cost	90000	Ordinary Shares of 50p each, fully paid	60000
Fixtures and fittings – Cost	90000	12% Preference shares of £1 each, fully paid	20000
Cost of Goods Sold	170000	10% Debentures 20X4/X9	30000
Stock 31 Mar. 19X9 – Cost	30000	Profit and Loss Account balances 1 Apr. 19X8	42000
Trade Debtors	22000	Fixtures and Fittings	
Wages and Salaries (Salesmen)	31000	– Accumulated Depreciation to	
Directors' Salaries	12500	31 March 19X8	25000
Debenture		Trade Creditors	14500
Interest (half year to 30 Sept. 19X8)	1500	Provision for Doubtful Debts 31.3.X8.	1100
General Distribution Expenses	5700	Bank Overdraft	16200
Bad Debts	1300	Sales	270000
General Administration Expenses	9300	Dividends From Investment	500
Investment – Cost	16000		
	£479300		£479300

You are given the following further information:

(1) Depreciation of fixtures and fittings is to be provided at a rate of 10% straight-line.
(2) The provision for doubtful debts is to be adjusted to 10% of the trade debtors.
(3) A revaluation of the freehold land and buildings on 31 March 19X9 at £130 000 is to be incorporated in the accounts.
(4) On 1 April 19X8 a leasehold property was acquired for use as a

distribution warehouse for £30 000. The consideration was discharged by the issue of 40 000 ordinary shares of 50p each fully paid but no entries were made in the books. The lease lasts for 20 years.

(5) The managing director informs you that certain stock costing £3000 (and included in the £30 000 stock at 31 March 19X9) is obsolete, and its expected net realisable value is £500.

(6) The board of directors have made the following recommendations:

(i) the payment of the preference dividend for the year;
(ii) the payment of an ordinary dividend of 5p per share for the year.

(7) Taxation is to be charged at a rate of 30% on net profit.

Required: Make any adjustments to the trial balance information you think necessary and prepare, in a form which would be acceptable for UK Companies Act purposes:

(a) profit and loss account for the year ended 31 March 19X9;
(b) balance sheet as on that date.

Note: show clearly the basis for any adjustments you make to data in the trial balance.

11.15 The following trial balance was extracted from the accounts of Rens Plc at 31 Decemer 19X6:

	£	£
£1 Ordinary Shares		100000
8% £1 Preference Shares		40000
Undistributed Profit at 1 Jan. 19X6		20000
10% debentures 20×1/×6		80000
Plant and Equipment		
(net book value 1 Jan. 19X6)	220000	
Motor Vehicles		
(net book value 1 Jan. 19X6)	100000	
Bank Interest	2000	
Sales and Purchases	150000	400000
Rates and Insurance	4000	
Lighting and Heating	3000	
Carriage Inwards	5000	
Office Salaries	40000	
Salesmens' Salaries	25000	
Advertising	10000	
Motor Expenses	20000	
General Expenses	23000	
Audit Fee	6000	
Debtor and Creditors	65000	30000
Bank Overdraft		26000
Cash	4000	
Stock (1 Jan. 19X6)	15000	
Debenture Interest	4000	
	£696000	£696000

Take the following information into consideration:

(a) Stock at 31 December 19X6 was £28 000.
(b) Amounts due but unpaid at the end of the year were:

- Office salaries £3000
- Rates   £1000

(c) The advertising expense includes £8000 for a four month advertising campaign which started on 1 November 19X6.
(d) Bad debts of £5000 have to be written off. A provision for bad debts of 5% of debtors is to be made on the remaining debtors.
(e) The plant and equipment (which cost £280 000) is to be depreciated on a straight-line basis at a rate of 10% p.a.
(f) The motor vehicles (which cost £120 000) are used for delivering sales and are to be depreciated using the reducing-balance method at a rate of 25% p.a.
(g) Taxation is to be provided at a rate of 35%.
(h) The company wish to provide for:

- the preference dividend
- an ordinary dividend of 12%.

Required: You are required to make any further adjustments you consider appropriate, and to prepare a profit and loss account for the year ended 31 December 19X6 and a balance sheet at that date. The statements should conform to the requirements of the UK Companies Act as far as possible, given the available information.

11.16 The Penang (Holdings) Plc has an authorised share capital of 40 million ordinary shares of £1 each and 20 million 8% preference shares of £1 each. The following trial balance was extracted from the books on 31 December 19X7:

	£000	£000
Cash	14922	
Purchases and Sales	15060	70015
Stock as at 1.1.X7	2000	
Carriage Inwards	210	
Wages	15028	
Returns Inwards and Outwards	2020	528
Freehold Premises at Cost	25000	
Debtors and Creditors	15000	1000
Carriage Outwards	210	
Rates	600	
Profit and Loss Account Balance at 1.1.X7		3060
20 million Ordinary Shares of £1 each		20000
10 million 8% Preference Shares of £1 each		10000
2 million 5% Debentures of £5 each		10000
Office Expenses	912	
Salaries	6013	

	£000	£000
Bad Debts	1000	
Provision for Bad Debts		1000
Motor Vehicles Cost	3000	
Plant and Machinery Cost	4000	
Share Premium		6500
General Expenses	1018	
Salesmen's Salaries and Commissions	5020	
Discounts	200	510
Directors' Fees	5000	
Goodwill at Cost	8000	
Debenture Interest Paid	100	
Depreciation to 1.1.X7.		
Motor Vehicles		900
Plant and Machinery		800
	£124313	£124313

Required: Prepare a profit and loss account for the year ended 31 December 19X7 and a balance sheet as at that date, presented according to the Companies Act, taking into consideration the following:

(i) Stock valued on 31 December 19X7 = £3 050 000
(ii) Office expenses owing – £100 000
(iii) Rates prepaid – £125 000
(iv) The directors decide to recommend a dividend of 15% on the ordinary shares and pay the dividend on preference shares.
(v) The provision of bad debts is to be 10% of the debtor's balances.
(vi) Depreciate plant and machinery 10% per annum on cost and motor vehicles at 15% p.a. on book value.
(vii) The debentures were issued on 1 July 19X7.
(viii) The corporation tax charged for 19X7 is estimated to be £5 million.

Apportionment of Expenses:

	Cost of Sales (%)	Distribution (%)	Administrative (%)
Rent and Rates		60	40
Salaries		45	55
Wages	55	10	35
Depreciation:			
Motor Vehicles		40	60
Plant and Machinery	15	70	15

All other expenses are to be allocated according to function, and normal accounting principles.

Note: All calculations to nearest £1000

12

Statement of Source and Application of Funds

12.1 Introduction

Chapter 12 is concerned with the preparation and interpretation of the 'Statement of Source and Application of Funds' (Funds Flow Statement). Since SSAP 10 was issued in 1975 UK companies have been required to publish this statement as part of their **annual report**. The statement is intended to demonstrate, for an accounting period, how a business's activities were **financed**, and how these resources were **used**. The information necessary for the preparation of the statement can usually be derived from the information in the profit and loss account and balance sheet. However, as we shall see, the Source and Application of Funds Statement presents the information in a way which **adds to the understanding of the data in the other two financial statements**.

12.2 Nature of the funds flow statement

The nature of the statement can be most easily described by reference to Figure 9.1, which is repeated below as Figure 12.1.

Figure 12.1 shows the way that **funds flow within** a business; within the working capital cycle, cash and credit flows in and out of the business as it makes purchases and sales. Inclusion of the long term funds items – i.e., the purchase and sale of fixed assets and the acquisition and repayment of loans and other forms of finance – completes the overall picture of the funds flow.

The profit and loss account will provide some information on the flow of funds in relation to purchases and sales for a period and the balance sheet will provide a 'snapshot' of the information in Figure 12.1. However, as we demonstrated in Sects. 2.4 and 6.9, profit does not necessarily represent cash flows. It will also be necessary to have a specific statement which will analyse the flow of cash and working capital which will cause **successive snapshots** (balance sheets) **to change**.

250

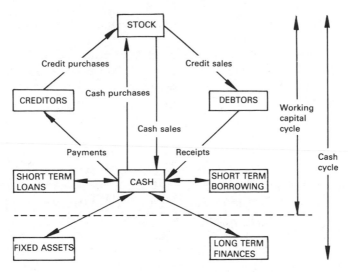

Figure 12.1

We have so far in Chapter 12 identified three types of flows which affect businesses, and which accounting is attempting to measure. The **profit** flow is shown in the profit and loss account; the other two flows are of **working capital** and of **cash**. We have earlier (see Sects 2.4 and 3.9) emphasised the significant difference between profits and cash flow, and a clear understanding of these differences is important to a proper appreciation of the use of the source and application of funds statement. A funds flow statement could in general be said to apply to either working capital or cash, or perhaps to both; however, SSAP 10 equates **funds** with **working capital**[1], and we will use this definition in the rest of this chapter. Ex.12.1 illustrates the differences between these three flows.

Example 12.1
A business starts trading with £1000 cash and no other assets. During its first month's trading a profit of £800 is generated, its profit and loss account is as follows

	£
Sales Revenue	1800
Cost of Sales	800
Gross Profit	1000
Other Expenses	200
Net Profit	£800

We will examine the different flows into and out of the business under **three** sets of assumptions:

Assumption (1) At the end of the period the business holds only **cash**, and all transactions were for **cash**.

In this situation the cash flow, funds flow and profit will all be the same – i.e., cash flow 1000 + 1800 − 800 − 200 = 1800 (**increase in cash = 800 =** profit figure). This is a simple example and the opening and closing balance sheets would be as follows:

	1 Jan. 19X1	*31 Jan. 19X1*
	£	£
Cash	1000	1800

Assumption (2) Some of the sales were made **on credit**, leaving debtors outstanding at the end of the month of £200. £1200 of stock was acquired and only £800 used, leaving a balance of £400.

The balance sheets now look like this:

	1 Jan. 19X1	*31 Jan. 19X1*
	£	£
Cash	1000	1200
Debtors	–	200
Stock	–	400
		£1800

Profit remains the same as before at £800 and the **change in funds is also the same** at £800 (£200 cash + 200 debtors + 400 stock). The **cash flow** now, however, is different, showing an **increase of only £200**, as follows:

	£
Opening cash balance	+1000
+ Cash from sales (Sales Revenue 1800 − Debtors 200)	+1600
Less Purchase of Stock	−1200
Less Other expenses (paid cash)	− 200
= Closing Cash balance	£1200

Assumption (3) All details as before, except that a **fixed asset has been acquired with cash** for £700.

The balance sheets would look as follows:

	1 Jan. 19X1	*31 Jan. 19X1*
	£	£
Fixed Assets	–	700
Cash	1000	500
Debtors	–	200
Stock	–	400
	£1000	£1800

The effect of this additional transaction is to:

- Leave profit unchanged at £800
- Show cash flow as a decrease of £500
- Show funds flow as an increase of £100 (stock 400 + debtors 200
  − cash decrease of 500)

In Ex.12.1 it has been relatively easy to identify the changes in the funds and cash, but in a more complex business situation the preparation of a 'Source and Application of Funds' statement would be the easiest way of providing an analysis. As explained earlier funds flow statements are generally associated with working capital changes, as in Assumption (3) above, and cash flow statements provide details of changes in the cash position. The principles underlying the two statements are the same, however, and in practice some companies use the term funds to mean cash.[2] The difference between the two statements lies in the treatment of **working capital**. In a funds (working capital) statement debtors, creditors and stock are included under the heading 'working capital changes', while in a cash statement they will appear either as sources or uses of funds (e.g., an increase in stock means the firm has had to finance a larger amount of stock and the increase is treated as an application of funds – i.e., cash).

12.3 Statement of source and application of funds

A convenient starting point for the analysis of the flow of working capital or cash is the accounting equation. The equation shows that changes in assets will be matched by corresponding changes in other assets, liabilities or owner's equity. These changes represent **sources** and **application of resources**, as shown in Figure 12.2.

Assets	≡ Liabilities	+ Owners' Equity
APPLICATION	SOURCE	SOURCE
Purchase of Fixed assets	Increase in long term liabilities	Proceeds from new share issues
		Proceeds from trading
SOURCE	APPLICATION	APPLICATION
Proceeds from sale of fixed assets	Repayment of long term liabilities	Payment of cash dividends
		Payments for trading operations

Figure 12.2

A source and application of funds statement provides an **organised framework** in which to represent this information.

Design and Presentation

The statement can be designed in either of the following ways:

(a)

	£
Sources (Flows in)	80
Application (Flows out)	60
Net-In-flow	£20
Changes in Working Capital (or Cash)	£20

(b)

	£
Opening Working Capital (or Cash)	10
Sources	80
Applications	(60)
Closing Working Capital (or Cash)	£30

Both (a) and (b) are presenting **the same information**. In both statements the details of Sources and Applications will explain how the business has been **financed**, and why the total funds (or cash) have **increased** or **decreased**. A more detailed breakdown of the analysis to be included in a funds flow statement is provided in Figure 12.3.

Figure 12.3

Source and Application of Funds Statement for year to 31/X/19XX

SOURCE OF FUNDS	£ 000
Profit before tax	XXXX
Adjustment for items not involving the movement of funds e.g.	
Depreciation	XX
Loss/Profit on Sale of Fixed Asset	X
Funds Generated From Operations	XXXX

Figure 12.3

		£000
FUNDS FROM OTHER SOURCES		
Issue of Shares for cash		XXX
Issue of Debentures		XX
Long Term Loan		XX
Dividends Received		XX
Proceeds From Sale of Fixed Assets		XX
Total Sources		XXXX
APPLICATION OF FUNDS		
Dividend paid	XX	
Tax Paid	X	
Purchase of Fixed Assets	X	
		XX
NET CHANGE IN FUNDS		XXX
MOVEMENT IN WORKING CAPITAL		
Increase/Decrease in Stock	X	
Increase/Decrease in Debtors	XX	
Increase/Decrease in Creditors	X	
	XX	
CHANGES IN LIQUID FUNDS		
Increase/Decrease in Cash	X	
Increase/Decrease in Overdraft	XX	
Increase/Decrease in Investment	X	
		XX
Net Changes in Working Capital		XXX

Figure 12.3 provides a framework, based on SSAP 10, within which a detailed funds flow statement can be presented. We will now examine the procedure for producing a fund flow statement, using the information in the profit and loss account and balance sheet of Matthew & Son Ltd.

Example 12.2

Balance Sheet of Matthew & Son Ltd as at 31 December

		19X0		19X1
		£000		£000
Fixed Assets				
Machinery at Cost		500		700
Less: Accumulated Depreciation		300		450
		200		250
Current Assets				
Stock	120		80	
Debtors	100		280	
Cash	80		60	
	300		420	

	£	£	£	£
Current Liabilities				
Creditors	210		240	
Net Current Assets		90		180
		290		430
Long Term Liabilities				
Loan at 10%		—		40
		£290		£390
Financed By:				
Owners' Equity				
Share Capital 200000				
Ordinary Shares @ £1		200		200
Share Premium		30		30
Retained Profit		60		160
		£290		£390

Profit and Loss Account for Matthew & Son Ltd for the Year Ended 31 December 19X1

	£000	£000
Sales Revenue		1200
Less: Cost of Goods Sold		760
Gross Profit		440
Less:		
Other Expenses		
Clerical	82	
Depreciation	180	
Loss on Sale of Fixed Asset (note 1)	40	
		302
		138
Interest		4
Net Profit		134
Tax		14
Net Profit After Tax		120
Dividends		20
Increase in Retained Profits		100

Note:

1. An item of machinery which originally cost £120 000 and had a net book value of £90 000 was sold for £50 000 (i.e., a 'loss' of £40 000).

The preparation of a funds flow statement relies on a **systematic analysis** of the data presented above with a view to identifying the sources and application of funds. A variety of different approaches to the problem are possible. We could identify **each change between the two balance sheet dates**, and then show their effects in terms of funds flow or application. Alternatively we could **select a format for presentation** and then systematically examine the relevant data in the balance sheets and profit and loss account and make entries, where necessary under the **appropriate headings** in the source and application of funds statement.

We can now examine a funds flow statement showing the relevant sources and application of funds, based on the data in Ex.12.2 above.

Source and Application of Funds for the Year Ended 31 December 19X1 for Matthew & Son Ltd

	£000	£000	Analysis No.
Source of Funds			
Profit Before Tax and Dividend		134	(1)
Adjustment for items not involving the movement of funds			
Add:			
Depreciation for the Year		180	(2)
Loss on Sale of Fixed asset		40	(3)
Funds Generated From Operations		354	
Funds from other sources			
Proceeds from Sale of Machinery		50	(4)
Long Term Loan		40	(5)
Total Sources		444	
Application of Funds	£000		
Purchase of Machinery	320		(6)
Dividend Paid	20		(7)
Tax Paid	14		(8)
		354	
Net Increase in Funds		£ 90	(9)
Movement in Working Capital			
Decrease in Stock	(40)		(10)
Increase in Debtors	180		(11)
Increase in Creditors	(30)		(12)
	110		(13)
Changes in Liquid Funds			
Decrease in Cash	(20)		(14)
Net Increase in Working Capital		£ 90	

Detailed Analysis and Workings

(1) *Profit* The figure of £134 000 profit before tax is given in the profit and loss account. However, it could alternatively be calculated by **adding back** to the figure for the increase in retained profit of £100 000:

(a) £20 000 in respect of dividends. It can be assumed that this dividend had been paid: if it had not been paid at the 31 December 19X1 date it would have appeared as a **current liability** in the balance sheet.

(b) £14 000 in respect of tax which has also been paid, since no outstanding tax balance appears in the **liabilities** section of the balance sheet.

(2) *Depreciation adjustment* The depreciation in each year's profit and loss account represents an àllocation of the cost of assets purchased in earlier years. It does not involve a current cash outlay since this took place at the time the asset was purchased. We therefore need to **add back** the depreciation expense to the profit figure in order to calculate the funds generated from operations.

(3) *Loss on sale of fixed Asset:* We saw in Chapter 6, Ex.6.6, that the residual value of an asset can be over-or under-stated, leading to a difference between the **book value** and the asset's **realisable value**. In this example the asset originally cost £120 000 and has a current net book value of £90 000. However, it has had to be sold for £50 000 a short-fall of £40 000 on its book value. This is a **book loss**, as there has been no flow of funds equivalent to the £40 000; the figure would not have arisen at all if the asset had been depreciated by an additional £40 000 over the period it had been held. The 'loss' is thus really an adjustment to the earlier depreciation figure for the asset and as such does not constitute an outflow of funds; like depreciation, it must be **added back** to profits.

(4) *Proceeds from sale of fixed asset:* Although the loss which has arisen in relation to the sale of this asset did not involve a funds flow, the actual sale itself produced proceeds of £50 000 which do need to be included as a **source of funds**.

(5) *Long term loan:* During the year, Matthew & Son Ltd have **raised additional funds** by way of a long term loan of £40 000.

(6) *Purchase of Machinery* The balance sheet each year shows the value of machinery at cost. In 19X0 the figure was £500 000 which had grown to £700 000 by 19X1. The change in the cost of machinery held is therefore £200 000. However, we already know from (3) and (4) above that machinery which had cost £120 000 has been sold. If there had simply been a sale of fixed assets and no replacement the effect would be to reduce the value of fixed assets at cost from £500 000 to £380 000, however, as the closing balance is actually £700 000 the total acquisitions can be assumed to be worth £320 000 – i.e.

	£
Opening balance of Fixed Assets at cost	500000
Less Sale	(120000)
	£ 380000
Plus Additions	320000
Closing Balance of Fixed Assets	£700000

(7), (8) *Dividend and tax* Any amounts which are outstanding at the end of an accounting period appear in the balance sheet as **creditors**. Since the balance sheet at 31 December 19X1 of Matthew & Son shows neither tax or dividend as creditors, we can assume that they have **both been paid during the year**.

(9) *Net increase in funds* The year's activities both from operations and other transactions have generated a net increase in funds of £90 000. The next section of the funds flow statement will explain how and where the increase in funds have been **used by the organisation**.

(10) *Decrease in Stock* During the period the value of stock held has gone down from £120 000 to £80 000, a decrease of £40 000. This has in effect **released additional funds** within the organisation for use elsewhere.

(11) *Increase in debtors* The sum tied up in debtors has increased from £100 000 in 19X0 to £280 000 in 19X1, an increase of £180 000 which has to be **financed** by Matthew & Son Ltd.

(12) *Increase in creditors* The sum owing to creditors at the year end has increased from £210 000 to £240 000, an increase of £30 000. This **increase in credit available** helps to offset some of the increased credit given to debtors. The full extent of the relationship between the different elements of working capital were dealt with in Sect. 10.11.

(13) *Movement within working capital* During 19X1 funds of £90 000 were generated. These funds were then used to facilitate an **increase in the value of working capital**. However, the total increase in stock and debtors **less** creditors during the period was £110 000, thus producing a shortfall of £20 000 which had to be **financed** from cash resources (see 14 below).

(14) *Decrease in cash* The shortfall in funds to finance the increase in the other elements of working capital has been identified above. The **decrease in cash** between the two periods from £80 000 to £60 000 (i.e. £20 000) was the source of the additional working capital funding necessary. By separating the 'liquid funds' from the rest of working capital the movement of, and explanation of, the movement in cash and 'near cash' items can be highlighted.

The funds flow statement provides users of accounting information with an alternative view of the firm's performance for the period in question. The data is presented and emphasised in a form which is significantly different from that shown in the balance sheet and profit and loss account.

12.4   Interpretation of a funds flow statement

The information contained in the funds flow statement is relatively straightforward; it provides an analysis of the funds generated by the business during the period, together with information on **where** and **how funds have been used**. A greater insight into how a firm is funded and its use of funds can be observed by the comparison of **consecutive funds flow statements**, as in Ex.12.3.

Many of the users of accounting information are concerned not only with what has happened in the business during previous years, but how it will perform **in the future**: more particularly they are concerned with how well it will **generate funds in the future**. By examining a number of consecutive funds flow statements it may be possible to highlight **significant trends**, and to use these trends as a basis for predicting likely future funds flows.[3] This will be demonstrated in Ex.12.3 below, using the information from Ex.12.2, together with an additional year's figures.

Example 12.3

Balance Sheet of Matthew & Son Ltd as at 31 December

		19X0 £000		*19X1* £000		*19X2* £000
Fixed Assets						
Machinery at Cost		500		700(1)		1200
Less: Accumulated						
Depreciation		300		450		725
		200		250		475
Current Assets						
Stock	120		80		155	
Debtors	100		280		250	
Cash	80		60		—	
	300		420		405	
Current Liabilities						
Creditors	210		240		140	
Overdraft	—		—		125	
Dividend Due	—		—		25	
Tax Due	—		—		10	
	210		240		300	
Net Current Assets		90		180		105
		290		430		580
Long Term Liabilities						
Loan at 10%		—		40		40
		£290		£390		£540
Financed By:						
Owners' Equity						
Share capital						
Ordinary shares @ £1		200		200		300
Share premium		30		30		80
Retained profit		60		160		160
		£290		£390		£540

Note:

1. See page 254.

Profit and Loss Account for Matthew & Son Ltd for the Year Ended

		31/12/19X1		31/12/19X2
		£000		£000
Sales Revenue		1200		1400
Less: Cost of Goods Sold		760		945
Gross Profit		440		455
Less:				
Other Expenses				
Clerical	82		100	
Depreciation	180		275	
Loss on Sale of Fixed asset	40			
	—		—	
		302		375
		138		80
Interest		4		4
Net Profit		134		76
Tax		14		16
Net Profit After Tax		130		60
Dividends		20		60
Increase in Retained Profits		£100		

Source and Application of Funds for Matthew & Son Ltd for Years Ended:

	31/12/19X1			31/12/19X2	
	£000	%		£000	%
Source of Funds					
Profit Before Tax and Dividend	134			76	
Adjustment for items not involving the movement of funds					
Depreciation for the Year	180			275	
Loss on Sale of fixed Asset	40			–	
Funds Generated from Operations	354	79.7		351	70.1
Funds from other sources					
Proceeds from Sale:					
Machinery	50	11.3		–	
Shares[2]	–			150	29.9
Long Term Loan	40	9.0		–	
Total Sources	444	100.0		501	100.0
Application of Funds					
Purchase of Machinery	320		72.1	500	99.8
Dividend Paid	20		4.5	35	7.0
Tax Paid	14		3.1	6	1.1
		354	79.7	541	107.9
Net Change in Funds		90	20.3	(40)	(7.9)
Movement in Working Capital					
Increase (Decrease) in Stock	(40)			(75)	
Increase (Decrease) in Debtors	180			(30)	
(Increase) Decrease in Creditors	(30)			100	
	110			145	
Changes in Liquid Funds					
Increase (Decrease) in Cash	(20)			(185)	
Net change in working capital	90	20.3		(40)	(7.9)

The funds flow statements for the two years 19X1 and 19X2 are shown above, together with a calculation of the percentage which the various elements represent. (The percentages are found by making the total source of funds for the period equal to 100%.) The individual sources of funds are then expressed as a **proportion of this 100%**, (i.e., in the example above a loan of £40 000 in 19X1 provided 9% of that year's funds). The application of funds, and the equivalent change in working capital, is also then equal to 100%.

Users of accounting information will generally be concerned with examining a variety of different points about an organisation, in order to evaluate its performance. A more detailed analysis of the interpretation of accounting information is provided in Chapter 13. As was stated earlier, a selection of consecutive funds flow statements might provide some indication of the trend of future fund flows; however, when interpreting the information in only two statements it is possible to draw limited conclusions. The percentages do, however, indicate important facts relating to the source and application of funds for the company over the two year period.

The amount of funds generated from operations were similar in both periods, but **declined in 19X2 as a proportion of total funds**. In 19X1 additional funds were generated from sale of machinery and by increasing the gearing of the company by raising a loan of £40 000. The level of gearing still appears to be relatively low, suggesting a potential future source of funding for the company. In 19X2 the company financed its expansion by raising a further £150 000 of equity finance. This has been used to finance the purchase of new assets, as perhaps the most significant event in both periods is the **acquisition of new machinery**. In 19X1 72% of funds generated were used in this way, while in 19X2 almost all of the funds generated were used to acquire additional machinery. As a result, any additional funds required within the business (for example, for dividends and taxation) had to be funded directly from cash sources, and by means of an overdraft. In addition to the investment in new machinery the company continued the build up of working capital (other than cash) by £145 000 in 19X2 (£110 000 in 19X1). This has also put a strain on cash resources, contributing to the overdraft of £125 000.

The financing of expansion in the future could be accomplished out of resources provided by operations and/or by funds from borrowing or new equity issues. The choice of the alternative adopted depends largely on company policy – for example, a conservative approach might restrict expansion to that which could be financed out of retained profit. Whatever policy is adopted the use of forecast source and application of funds data should assist in planning future developments.

12.5 Summary

The funds flow statement provides users of accounting information with an additional view of the firm and its performance during a period. The process of preparing a funds flow statement requires detailed analysis of the information contained in the profit and loss account and balance sheet. The inclusion of the statement in published annual reports improves the quality of the available information.

As with all accounting information, the intepretation of the funds flow statement should be undertaken in the light of the other information contained in the annual report.

Notes and References

1. ED 54 'Cash flow statements' issued by the Accounting Standards Committee in July 1990 proposed the adoption of cash flows as the basis for a new standard which would be developed to replace SSAP 10.
2. See, for example, the Marks and Spencer Source and Application of Funds in Appendix B.
3. It cannot, of course, be assumed that all past trends can be extrapolated into the future; they must be interpreted in the context of **other available information**.

Questions and Problems

12.1 What do you understand by the following terminology?

Flow of funds   Working capital cycle
Liquidity   Liquid funds
Depreciation adjustment

12.2 Identify the different 'flows' which affect a business.
12.3 Examine the Source and Application of Funds Statement in Appendix B. Comment on:

(a) The style of the presentation.
(b) What it reveals about the financing of the Marks and Spencer Plc operations.

12.4 Given that a company produces a profit and loss account and balance sheet, why is it required to also provide a source and application of funds statement?

12.5 Balance sheets of Claymore Engineering Ltd are as follows: (all figures in £000)

	31.1.19X2			31.1.19X3		
Fixed Assets	*Cost*	*Depn*	*Net*	*Cost*	*Depn*	*Net*
	£	£	£	£	£	£
Freehold Land	440	–	440	520	–	520
Plant and Machinery	480	180	300	604	216	388
Fixtures and Fittings	96	52	44	116	60	56
	£1016	£232	£784	£1240	£276	£964
Current Assets						
Stock	148			204		
Debtors	172			176		
Bank	–			64		
		320			444	
Less Current Liabilities						
Creditors	136			188		
Bank Overdraft	56			–		
Proposed Dividends	60			80		
Taxation	40			100		
	292	28		368	76	
		£812			£1040	
Issued Share Capital		400			600	
Share Premium		60			140	
Profit and Loss Account		112			280	
		572			1020	
14% Debentures		240			20	
		£812			£1040	

Additional Information:

1. A machine which had cost £32 000, and on which £24 000 depreciation had been provided, was sold for £12 000. The profit was transferred to the profit and loss account.
2. Fixtures which had cost £20 000, and on which £8000 depreciation had been provided, were sold for £4000. The loss was transferred to the profit and loss account.

Required: Prepare a statement of source and application of funds for the year ended 31.1.X3, explaining how the company has improved its cash position (all workings should be shown).

12.6 Robolo Plc had the following balance sheet:

	At 31.12.X0 £000	At 31.12.X1 £000
Issued Share Capital:		
Ordinary Shares		
of £0.25 each	200	250
Share Premium	–	10
Retained Profits	149	161
Debentures	50	–
Creditors	9	104
Bank Overdraft	–	92
Corporation Tax Owing on:		
19X0 Profits	46	27
19X1 Profits	–	21
Accumulated Depreciation:		
Buildings	30	36
Plant	62	57
Proposed Dividends	20	25
	646	783
Freehold Property at Cost	180	230
Plant and Machinery at Cost	144	172
Stocks	158	189
Debtors	145	192
Bank Balance	19	–
	£646	£783

The following additional information should be considered:

1. There has been no disposal of freehold property during the year.
2. Plant which had cost £27 000, and in respect of which depreciation of £24 000 had been provided, was sold for £7000. The profit on the transaction had been dealt with in the profit and loss account.
3. No interim dividend had been paid.

Required: Prepare a source and application of funds for Robolo Plc, and comment on your findings.

12.7 The following are extracts from the financial statements of the Carmel plc:

Balance Sheets as at 31 December

	19X8 £000	19X8 £000	19X7 £000	19X7 £000
Fixed Assets				
(NBV)				
Freehold				
Land		1200		900
Plant and				
Machinery		390		420
		1590		1320

	£000	£000		£000	£000
Investments (at Cost)		240			250
Current Assets					
Stock	650			580	
Debtors	400			500	
Short Term Investments	100			50	
Cash	80			30	
	1230			1160	

	£000			£000		
Less Current Liabilities						
Trade Creditors	400			350		
Taxation	80			40		
Proposed Dividends	40			20		
Bank Overdraft	160	680		400	810	
			550			350
			2380			1920
Share Capital						
50p Ordinary Shares			1200			1000
Reserves						
Share Premium			100			50
Land Revaluation			300			–
Retained Earnings			320			270
			1920			1320
Loan Capital						
12% Debentures			460			600
			£2380			£1920

*Profit and Loss Appropriation Account for the Year Ended
31 December 19X8*

	£000	£000
Net Profit Before Tax		185
Tax		80
		105
Dividends		
Interim (paid)	15	
Final (proposed)	40	55
Retained Profit for Year		50

Notes:

(1) Profit for the year is after charging £70 000 depreciation on plant and machinery.
(2) During the year plant with a net book value of £50 000 was sold for £98 000. The profit and loss on sale is included in the £185 000 net profit before tax.

Required:

(a) Prepare the source and application of funds statement for the year ended 31 December 19X8.
(b) Comment on what is revealed about Carmel Plc by the statement drawn up in (a).

12.8 You are given the following financial statements for the Rice Co.:

Balance sheets as at

	31/12/X7	31/12/X8
	£	£
Issued Share Capital	50000	60000
Share Premium	20000	10000
Profit and Loss a/c	4000	15500
Debentures	60000	50000
Dividends Payable	4000	5000
Current Taxes Payable	16500	6500
Creditors	25000	30000
	£179500	£177000
Fixed Asset (NBV)	67000	57000
Investments	25000	20000
Stock	45000	50000
Debtors	35000	40000
Cash	7500	10000
	£179500	£177000

Profit and Loss Account for the Year Ended 31 December 19X8

	£
Trading profit after charging depreciation of £7000	35000
Less Loss on Sale of Fixed Asset	2000
	33000
Less Provision for Taxation	16500
Net Profit for the Year	16500
Balance of Profit Brought Forward	4000
	20500
Less Dividends Proposed	5000
Balance of Profits Carried Forward	£15500

Additional Notes:

(1) A 20 % scrip issue was made during 19X8.
(2) Fixed assets with NBV of £7000 were sold for £5000 in March 19X8.

Required:

(1) Prepare a statement of sources and application of funds for the Rice Co. for the year 19X8.
(2) Comment on the information that you have presented in (1) above. What does it reveal about the company's operations?

12.9 The balance sheets of Port Vale Plc as at 31 December 19X6 and 19X7 were as follows:

	£	19X6 £	£	19X7 £
Share Capital		100000		120000
Profit and Loss Account		48166		55128
		148166		175128
Debentures		–		40000
Current Liabilities				
Creditors	28966		35522	
Taxation Payable			3000	
Dividends Payable	4000	32966		38522
		181132		253650
Plant at Cost	147000		222600	
Less Accumulated depreciation	61000		89400	
		86000		133200
Vehicles at Cost	23400		30000	
Less Accumulated depreciation	7200	16200	12000	18000
		102200		151200
Stock	35348		52034	
Debtors	26574		37028	
Cash	17010	78932	13388	102450
		£181132		£253650

Notes:

(a) No dividends were proposed for 19X7.
(b) A vehicle which had cost £8000 was sold during 19X7 for £4000. The accumulated depreciation of this vehicle was £5500. The profit or loss on sale was included in the profit and loss account.

Required:

(a) Prepare a Source and Application of Funds Statement for 19X7

which explains the change in the value of working capital. Show clearly all your workings.
(b) Comment on the change in the company's position as revealed by the statement.

12.10 The following are the balance sheets of Bartrams Ltd as at 31 December 19X7 and 19X8:

	19X7		19X8	
	£	£	£	£
Fixed Assets, at				
Cost		29300		38600
Accumulated				
Depreciation		9500		13800
		19800		24800
Current Assets				
Stock	14400		16800	
Debtors	7200		8200	
Cash	4600		800	
	26200		25800	
Current Liabilities	6100		4200	
		20100		21600
		£39900		£46400
Issued Share				
Capital		30000		30000
Retained Profits		9900		16400
		£39900		£46400

Mr Samuel Bartram who owns a majority of the shares in the company has written to you asking for your advice. He is concerned that despite the fact that the business made a profit of £6500 in 19X8 and did not pay any dividend, there is considerably less cash available at the end of 19X8 than there was at the end of 19X7.

Required:

(a) Reply to Mr Bartram, explaining to him the relationship between profits and changes in cash balances. Include in your reply a statement of source and application of funds for 19X8. (Assume that no fixed assets were disposed of during 19X8.)
(b) Discuss the importance of both profits and cash flow to a business.

12.11 The balance sheets of Dent Ltd at 31 December 19X3 and 19X4 were as follows:

	19X3		19X4	
	£	£	£	£
Share Capital		50000		60000
Profit and Loss Account		24083		27564
		74083		87564
Debentures		–		20000
Current Liabilities		16483		19261
		90566		126825
Plant at Cost	73500		111300	
Less: Depreciation	30500		44700	
		43000		66600
Vehicles at Cost	11700		15000	
Less: Depreciation	3600	8100	6000	9000
		51100		75600
Stock	17674		26017	
Debtors	13287		18514	
Cash	8505		6694	
		39466		51225
		£90566		£126825

Notes:

(a) No dividends were paid in 19X4, and none are proposed.
(b) A vehicle which had cost £4000 was sold during 19X4 for £2000. The profit on this sale of £750 was credited to the profit and loss account.

Required:

(a) Prepare a sources and application of funds statement for 19X4 which explains the change in the value of working capital.
(b) Comment on the change in the company's position as revealed by the statement.

12.12 *Balance sheets at 31 December 19X1 and 19X2 for Turner Plc*

	19X2	19X1
	£	£
Share Capital	200000	150000
Share Premium and Capital Reserves	25000	20000
General Reserves	90000	47000
Profit and Loss Account	52000	35500
Debentures (Secured) interest at 9%	70000	40000
Creditors	130000	96000
Accrued Expenses	4500	2300
Corporation Tax Payable	32600	30700
Proposed Dividends	10000	9000
	£614100	£430500
Fixed Assets at Cost	526000	360500
Accumulated Depreciation	162700	127300
	363300	233200
Trade Investment at Cost	14350	16420
Stocks	78730	59580
Debtors	152720	119600
Cash in Hand and at Bank	5000	1700
	£614100	£430500

Notes:

1. During the year, Fixed Assets costing £14 500, book value £6900, were sold for £11 900 and additions to Fixed Assets cost £180 000.
2. Trade investments which cost £13 800 were sold for £11 600, this loss being written off to profit and loss account and further acquisitions of Trade Investments cost £11 730.

Required:

(a) Prepare the Source and Application of Funds Statement for 19X2.
(b) Comment on the value of such of statement to (1) management (2) the shareholders.
Show clearly all your workings.

13
Interpretation of Financial Statements

13.1 Introduction

In Sect. 1.1 of this text a formal definition of accounting was provided in which it was described as the communication of information to enable informed judgement and decisions to be made by users. Many of the intervening sections have concentrated on the preparation and presentation of this information. The end result is a set of financial statements which provide an **overall picture of the firm's performance for an accounting period**. The profit and loss account measures the increase in wealth which the firm has generated from operations; the statement of source and application of funds demonstrates how the funds generated from operations, together with any additional funds from other sources, have been used within the firm; and the balance sheet gives an overall picture of the closing position of the business.

There are a wide range of different user groups (see Sect. 1.6) who demand accounting information to assist them in their decision-making. Shareholders are concerned with the value of their shares, now and in the future. Potential investors will wish to select the most appropriate share to acquire. Creditors and lenders may wish to assess the level of short term liquidity and long term solvency, while management are interested in the financial statements in so far as they are a reflection of their own performance and an indication of the success of their past decisions.

Users wishing to evaluate the performance of an organisation need some gauge or criterion against which to measure it. The criterion selected will depend on the user group in question: management may gauge its performance by comparing what actually happened with what they expected to happen; they may also wish to make some comparison with **other firms**, or with some **industry norm**. Shareholders and other users might choose to compare this year's performance with that of previous years, as well as with other firms, or again with an industry norm. Potential investors will be concerned with selecting the most suitable share to purchase, and will therefore be comparing a number of different firms.

13.2 Measurement problems

Published financial statements attempt to represent the vast and varied transactions of an organisation in a compact form. This has to be achieved within the confines of current legislation, regulations and accounting conventions and bases. The financial statements end up by providing a snapshot of the business represented by a relatively small collection of numbers (with some additional information in note form). In addition, the selection of **bases used** may have a significant effect on the numbers produced; this has been demonstrated during our discussion of the measurement of depreciation in Chapter 6 and of stock valuation in Chapter 7. These factors limit the usefulness of any evaluation of performance which is based wholly on published accounting information. However, it may still be possible to illustrate many of the characteristics of the firm – e.g., its **profitability**, **growth** and **liquidity** – by examining **patterns of relationships** evident in the financial statements. This can be achieved, for example, by comparing one year's set of financial statements with other years, or comparing one firm's results in a period with that of another firm for the same period.

Because there are so many different numbers involved for each firm and because the size of firms can vary substantially, it becomes difficult to assimilate and interpret the information in its raw form. To overcome this problem a number of analytical tools have been developed which simplify the comparison by converting the information in a set of financial statements into a simpler and more understandable form. For example, the information that Marks and Spencer Plc made profits of £501.7m in 1988 while Trafalgar House Plc made £229.1m may enable us to make an initial crude comparison of the two companies. However, if we reinterpret the data to show that the £501.7m represented a 23.25% return on the amounts invested in the company and that the £229.1m represented a return of 27.66%, the conclusions of the initial comparisons are likely to be changed. By using **ratios** in this way it becomes possible to identify and examine a set of relationships, both at a point in time and over a period of time.

Before considering these analytical tools further it is necessary to draw attention to the possible **limitations** of the analysis. The user concerned with comparing performance between firms needs to recognise that basic differences between firms arise because of the **nature of the industry** they are in, and because of their **relative size**. This can be illustrated by attempting to compare the qualities of two fruits such as an apple and a pear. It is almost impossible to offer more than a personal opinion or preference when making such a comparison – the fruits are quite different. It would be easier to compare a Cox apple with a Pippin apple because you can now compare colour, size, texture, sweetness, etc. Our description of fruit is analogous with modern business. There are a large number of different organisations in business; no two firms are exactly the same, but many will be similar in some or several respects. For example, it is difficult to compare Marks and Spencer

Plc with ICI Plc because they are in different industries and are different in size. You will, of course, be able to look at their profit and say that one is bigger than the other, but what does that tell you about performance, efficiency or effectiveness? If you are making a detailed comparison of the performance of various aspects of two firms, it is important that the firms should be from the same industry – for example, you can compare one supermarket chain with another because their modes of operation will be similar. However, if it is the overall performance of a firm that is under consideration it is possible (and necessary) to compare firms from different industries.[1]

13.3   Financial analysis

Users of accounting information interpret the contents of financial statements so that they can more fully use and understand the information they contain. A number of different techniques are available which simplify the information for ease of understanding and interpretation.

If we examine a firm's balance sheet and profit and loss account over a period of years we might expect to observe **trends** and **relationships**. These can be expressed in **absolute terms**, or as **ratios**; this is illustrated in Ex.13.1.

Example 13.1
Extracts from the profit and loss account for John Doe Plc:

	19X4	19X5	19X6	19X7
	£	£	£	£
Sales	600	650	770	850
Cost of Sales	450	495	590	660
Gross Profit	£150	£155	£180	£190

In absolute terms, we can say that sales increased by £50 between 19X4 and 19X5 and then increased by £120 in 19X6 and a further £80 in 19X7. We can give a similar report on cost of sales and gross profit. However, we can also express the changes in sales as ratios – for example, 50/600 × 100 reveals an 8.33% increase in the first year, 120/650 × 100 = an 18.46% increase in the second year. This form of analysis can be carried out in respect of other numbers in the statement above. For example, the gross profit in 19X7 of £190 is an **increase of £40** on the gross profit of 19X4. However, expressed as a ratio to sales the profit in 19X4 is 25% whereas in 19X7 it is 22% – i.e., a **decrease**. Further ratios can be calculated in respect of other available financial information in order to provide a measure of the important elements of performance. These elements are discussed below in Ex.13.2.

Trends which are often disguised in absolute numbers can sometimes be highlighted through the use of ratios[2] – e.g., in Ex.13.1 the gross profit in absolute terms shows an increasing trend over the four years. However, expressed as ratios of gross profit to sales the percentage figures are:

19X4	19X5	19X6	19X7
25	24	23	22

which represents a **decreasing trend**. Areas such as profitability, liquidity, stock market performance and financial structure can each be broken down into a series of ratios which provide a summary of performance. These are easier to examine and interpret than the raw data from a set of financial statements. They must, however, be used properly – i.e., to compare **like with like**. For example, there are many different measures of profit which can be used (i.e., gross profit, net profit, profit before tax, profit after tax, retained profit, etc.). Each version of 'profit' may be useful for different purposes; in general, the selection of appropriate numbers and the usefulness of financial ratios is dependent on the ability and skill of the **preparer** and of the **interpreter** of the information conveyed by the ratios.

Ratios can best be understood in conjunction with an example. The balance sheet and profit and loss account in Ex.13.2 below will provide the basis for our introduction to some of the more commonly used ratios.

Example 13.2
The following are the balance sheets and profit and loss accounts of Pierrepoint Co. Ltd:

	Balance Sheets			
		at 31 December		*at 31 December*
		19X0		*19X1*
		£000		£000
Fixed Asset				
Machinery, at Cost		300		320
Less: Accumulated				
Depreciation		50		60
		250		260
Current Assets				
Stock	20		60	
Debtors	20		30	
Cash	20		10	
	60		100	
Current Liabilities				
Creditors	40		40	
Net Current Assets		20		60
		270		320

	£000	£000
Long Term Liabilities		
Loan at 10%	–	20
Net Assets	£270	£300
Financed by:		
Owner's Equity		
Share Capital (220,000		
ordinary shares @ £1)	220	220
Retained profit	50	80
	£270	£300

Profit and Loss Accounts for the Years Ended:

	31 December 19X0 £000	31 December 19X1 £000
Sales Revenue	200	300
Less: Cost of Goods Sold	100	120
Gross Profit	100	180
Less: Interest	–	2
Other Expenses	40	98
Net Profit Before Tax	60	80
Less: Corporation Tax	30	40
Net Profit After Tax	30	40
Dividends (4.5 p per share)	10	10
Profit Retained	£20	£30

Market Share Price: at 31 December	19X0 p	19X1 p
	200	200

Ratio Analysis

The advantages of using ratios rather than the raw absolute numbers has been explained earlier in this section. The types of ratios used will depend on the **objectives** of the analysis. The ratios used to analyse the data in Ex.13.2 would typically be used by someone concerned about the **profitability** of the organisation, the **security** of its future and the **financial risk** implied by its financial structure. Profitability ratios measure the efficiency with which the firm has **used its resources to generate sales with a satisfactory profit margin**. It is

difficult to evaluate whether management have used the available resources to
maximum efficiency; their comparative efficiency can, however, be evaluated
by reference to other companies. The security of future profits and the
survival of the organisation can be evaluated by ratios concerned with **short
term liquidity and long term solvency**.[3] The third consideration (i.e., financial
risk) is measured by examining the company's **financial structure** and its
gearing ratios.[3]

Profitability Ratios

ROCE (Return on Capital Employed)
This commonly used ratio relates **profit** to the **resources used to earn it**. There
are several versions of ROCE used in practice, and we have described some
of these below.

			19X0			*19X1*	
(1)	*Return on Equity*	$\dfrac{\text{Profit After Tax}}{\text{Shareholders' funds}}$ =	$\dfrac{30}{270}$	=	11%	$\dfrac{40}{300}$	= 13%
(2)	*Return on Equity*	$\dfrac{\text{Profit before tax}}{\text{Shareholders' Funds}}$	$\dfrac{60}{270}$	=	22%	$\dfrac{80}{300}$	= 27%

These before and after tax measures of profitability relates the **shareholders'
profit** to the amount they have **invested in the business**.

			19X0			*19X1*	
(3)	*Return on Total Finance Employed*	$\dfrac{\text{Profit Before Tax and Interest}}{\text{Shareholders' Funds + Loans}}$ =	$\dfrac{60}{270}$	=	22%	$\dfrac{82}{320}$	= 26%

Ratio (3) provides a measure which reflects the **profitability of the firms
activities, irrespective of how they are financed**. Comparison of ratio (3) with
ratio (2) should reveal the effect of **gearing** on the returns of the ordinary
shareholders. In 19X0 both (2) and (3) show a return of 22%. This is because
the company has no debt in 19X0; the introduction of the 10% loan in 19X1
creates gearing and results in a higher return for the shareholders (27%) in
ratio (2) compared with the overall return to the company of 26% in ratio (3).
In this instance, the shareholders have benefited from the introduction of

gearing. The differential is small because the gearing levels are low (see ratios (12) and (13) below. The advantage to the shareholders arises because the company is earning 26% on all its finances but is paying only 10% to the long term debt holders, leaving a **surplus** to be shared by the shareholders.

			19X1	19X2
(4)	*Return on Assets*	$\dfrac{\text{Profit Before Interest and Tax}}{\text{Assets Employed}}$ (Total Assets − Current Liabilities)	$\dfrac{60}{270} = 22\%$	$\dfrac{82}{320} = 26\%$

This ratio expresses the **return on assets employed by the firm**. It will usually give the same result as ratio (3) as the total finances (equity + loans) is equivalent to the assets (total assets − current liabilities) acquired by that finance. The use of ratio (4) to compare different firms should be undertaken with caution. We have seen in Chapters 6 and 7 the problems of valuing fixed and current assets in the balance sheet; for example, if Company A regularly revalues its assets and Company B does not the comparison of profitability using ratio (3) could be significantly affected.[4] For ratio analysis to be effective requires **consistency** in the preparation of the accounting data: comparing two balance sheets in which assets are valued at different times could result in misleading conclusions.

Evaluating ROCE
The ROCE is perhaps the most important ratio for evaluating a firm's performance. It is in turn the result of two factors – i.e., the generation of sales and the profit margin on sales. This relationship in the form of ratios is as follows:

$$\text{ROCE} \quad = \quad \text{Asset Turnover} \quad \times \quad \text{Profit Margin}$$

$$\frac{\text{Profit}}{\text{Capital Employed}} \qquad \frac{\text{Sales}}{\text{Capital Employed}} \qquad \frac{\text{Profit}}{\text{Sales}}$$

'Capital employed' is used here as meaning the finances (or capital) invested in assets. It is equivalent to the version of ROCE used in ratio (4).
Applying the numbers in Ex.13.2 we obtain:

			19X0	19X1
(5)	*Asset Turnover*	$\dfrac{\text{Sales}}{\text{Assets Employed}}$	$\dfrac{200}{270} = 0.74$	$\dfrac{300}{320} = 0.94$

The asset turnover ratio is a measure of how effectively the company is using the assets at its disposal to **generate sales**. In this case, the ratio has improved from 0.74 times to 0.94 times: this means that for every £1 invested in assets it is generating £0.74 and £0.94 of sales in each year.

$$\begin{array}{cccc} & & 19X0 & 19X1 \\ (6)\ \textit{Profit Margin}\ \dfrac{\text{Profit}}{\text{Sales}} & = & \dfrac{60}{200} = 30\% & \dfrac{82}{300} = 27.3\% \end{array}$$

This ratio shows how much **profit**, on average, is being made on **sales**. To be consistent with ratio (4) the profit figure being used here is **before tax and interest**.

By combining ratios (5) and (6) we can obtain:

Asset Turnover		×	Profit Margin	=	ROCE
19X0	0.74	×	30%	=	22%
19X1	0.94	×	27.3%	=	26%

Liquidity and Solvency

These concepts were also examined in Section 10.10. The ratios used here attempt to provide investors, lenders and creditors with some indication of the **solvency and liquidity of a business**. It is appropriate, however, before preparing these particular ratios to draw attention to the fact that the accounting data which is used to generate them is to be found in financial statements which will be **some months old**, and relate to a **previous trading period**. While they may provide an indication of **trends**, they do not necessarily provide a good current measure of liquidity.

			19X0		19X1	
(7)	*Short term* (*Current Ratio*)	$\dfrac{\text{Current assets}}{\text{Current Liabilities}} =$	$\dfrac{60}{40}$	$= 1.5$	$\dfrac{100}{40}$	$= 2.5$
(8)	*Very Short Term* (*Quick Ratio*)	$\dfrac{\text{Very Liquid Assets}^{(5)}}{\text{Current Liabilities}} =$	$\dfrac{20}{40}$	$= 0.5$	$\dfrac{10}{40}$	$= 0.25$

Ratio (7) indicates the relationship between current assets and current liabilities; it is a measure of the **cover for current debt** which is provided by **current assets**. It is often stated that a satisfactory current ratio is 2:1;

however, it must be explained yet again that this will vary from industry to industry, and from company to company. Marks and Spencer Plc's balance sheet, for example, reveals that they operate on much less than a 2:1 ratio. The need for two ratios arises because in many instances stock will not easily convert to cash quickly, and so its inclusion could be misleading. In this example the inclusion of the 'quick ratio' does indicate a different signal coming from the company than would be evident by using ratio (7) alone: the quick ratio shows that the company's position has deteriorated whereas ratios (7) suggests that the liquidity position has improved.

			19X0		*19X1*	
(9)	*Stock Turnover*	$\dfrac{\text{Cost of goods Sold}}{\text{Average stock(1)}}$ =	$\dfrac{100}{40(2)}$ =	2.5	$\dfrac{120}{40}$ =	3.0

Notes:
   (1) Average stock is used because over an accounting period the level of stock may change **in line with changes in the level of sales**, so that a year end figure alone could be misleading.
   (2) In Ex.13.1 we do not have the necessary information to determine the **average stock in the first year**; it is assumed to be the same as for 19X1 in order to facilitate the calculations.

This ratio provides an indication of the **speed with which the stock 'turns over'** – i.e., how quickly it is used up or sold. This will be dependent on the nature of the business, management policy and stock control. The figures of 2.5 and 3.0 for the two years show that on average stock 'turned over' 2.5 times in 19X0 and increased to 3 times in 19X1. An alternative way of expressing this, as we saw in Chapter 10, is to say that on average stock was held for 365/2.5 = 146 days in 19X0 and 365/3 = 122 days in 19X1.[6]

			19X0		*19X1*	
(10)	*Debtors' Turnover*	$\dfrac{\text{Sales}}{\text{Debtors}}$ =	$\dfrac{200}{20}$ =	10	$\dfrac{300}{30}$ =	10

This ratio provides an indication of the **average time taken by debtors to pay**; however, our assumption here is that all goods are sold on credit and if this is incorrect, then any conclusions drawn will be misleading. We can interpret the data in a similar way to the stock turnover – i.e., on average the debtors take 365/10 = 36.5 days to pay for goods purchased on credit.

The information from ratios (9) and (10) can be combined to show how long resources are tied up from the time the **stock is purchased** to the time that **cash is received from debtors** – i.e.:

	19X0	19X1
Number of days in stock	146.0	122.0
As debtors	36.5	36.5
Overall	182.5 days	158.5 days

		19X0	19X1
(11) *Creditors' Turnover*	$\dfrac{\text{Cost of Goods Sold}}{\text{Creditors}}$	$\dfrac{100}{40} = 2.5$	$\dfrac{160}{40} = 4$

With the appropriate information it is also possible to determine **creditors' turnover** – e.g., how long the business takes to settle with its creditors; this ratio will be of particular interest to **potential trade creditors**. it requires data on the total credit purchases for the period in question, divided by the average creditors for the year. This information is not generally available in published accounts and an approximation can be made by using the **cost of goods sold**, and adding to it the value of any **increase in stock** during the period.

We have made the assumption in calculating ratio (11) for 19X0 that purchases is equal to the cost of goods sold figure. For 19X1 we have taken into consideration the increase in stock. The resulting figures show that on average in 19X0 the company took 365/2.5 = 146 days to pay their creditors. In 19X1 this had been reduced to 365/4 = 91 days.

We can now combine this information with that for ratios (9) and (10) as follows:

	19X0	19X1
Number of days in stock	146.0	122.0
As debtors	36.5	36.5
	182.5 days	158.5 days
Less: Creditor days	146.0	91.0
Net days	36.5	67.5

This shows that because of the changes in the three components of working capital it is tied up for a longer period in 19X1 than in 19X0.

Gearing – Financial Risk

This topic which was discussed in more detail in Section 10.7, is concerned with measuring the degree to which a firm relies on debt financing to undertake its activities (e.g., the level of debt to equity, in other words a firm's gearing). There are two common versions of the gearing ratio. These are described in ratios (12) and (13):

$$
\begin{array}{llll}
& & 19X0 & 19X1 \\
(12)\ \textit{Gearing} & \dfrac{\text{Long Term Debt}}{\text{Long Term Debt} + \text{Equity}} = & \dfrac{0}{270} = 0\% & \dfrac{20}{320} = 6\% \\
\textit{Ratios: 1} & & & \\
\\
(13)\ \textit{Gearing} & \dfrac{\text{All Debt}}{\text{All Debt} + \text{Equity}} = & \dfrac{40}{310} = 13\% & \dfrac{60}{360} = 17\% \\
\textit{Ratios: 2} & & &
\end{array}
$$

An alternative way of expressing ratio (12) is to use capital employed – e.g.:

$$
\frac{\text{Long Term Debt}}{\text{Capital Employed}} = \frac{0}{270} = 0\% \qquad \frac{20}{320} = 6\%
$$

Long term debt is 6% of the capital employed, or alternatively the proportion of long term debt within the organisation is 6%.

Both shareholders and lenders may be interested in these ratios. For lenders they provide some indication of the **level of debt** which an organisation is carrying. If they are contemplating lending to the firm, it indicates what prior **commitment** the firm already has. For shareholders, it provides an indication of their level of **financial risk**. All share investment is risky since it involves an outflow of funds **now**, for some expected inflow at a **later period**. The degree of uncertainty associated with the expected future inflow is a measure of the risk which shareholders bear; this risk exists in both an all-equity firm and a geared firm. However, the level of risk for shareholders is increased by the addition of debt financing; this arises because interest payments on debt are due annually and are paid before shareholders receive any dividends. Additionally a default on interest payments could result in lenders instigating bankruptcy proceedings against the organisation.

Stock Market Ratios

For organisations whose shares are quoted on a recognised stock exchange additional ratios can be calculated:

			19X0			*19X1*		
(14) *Earnings per Share*	Net Profit After Tax	$=$	$\dfrac{30}{220}$	$=$	£0.14	$\dfrac{40}{220}$	$=$	£0.18
	Number of Shares							

This ratio relates the total profit to the individual shares. The ratios which we have produced so far have been based on **book values** – i.e., the numbers which appear in the balance sheet and profit and loss account of the business.

A quoted share price provides an additional measure or 'market value' as opposed to 'book value' which can be used to assess performance.

			19X0			*19X1*		
	Dividend per Share		p			p		
(15) *Dividend Yield*	Share Price	$=$	$\dfrac{4.5}{200}$	$=$	2.25%	$\dfrac{4.5}{200}$	$=$	2.25%
(16) *Earnings Yield*	Earnings per Share / Share Price	$=$	$\dfrac{14}{200}$	$=$	7%	$\dfrac{18}{200}$	$=$	9%
(17) *Price/ Earnings Ratio*	Share Price / Earnings per Share	$=$	$\dfrac{200}{14}$	$=$	14.29	$\dfrac{200}{18}$	$=$	11.11

Ratio (15), the **dividend yield**, shows a shareholder's rate of return, in terms of cash received as dividend, in relation to his (or her) investment as measured by the market price of his share.

Ratio (16), the **earnings yield**, shows what the maximum dividend would be if the company paid all of its profits out as dividend.

Ratio (17), the **price earnings ratio** (P/E), shows how the stock market assesses the company. A **high** P/E ratio (market price of share high in relation to earnings) suggests that the market has confidence in the company, and expects it to earn higher profits in the future. A **low** P/E ratio indicates the opposite – i.e., a lack of confidence. As with other ratios the number of the P/E ratio is not of itself very revealing, except when used in comparison with other companies.

All of the ratios which have been examined should be used with care and with due consideration to any **additional information** which is available in the annual reports other than the profit and loss account and balance sheet.

13.4 Comparing financial statements

In Sect. 13.4 we are using an illustration of the use of data from financial statements to make a limited comparison of three well known UK companies.

The comparison is used to demonstrate what can be achieved and also to point out some potential weaknesses in this type of analysis.

The companies compared are:

> *Marks and Spencer Plc*,   A retail organisation.
> *Trafalgar House   Plc*,   Engaged in commercial and residential property, construction and engineering, passenger and cargo shipping and hotels.
> *Maxwell Communications Corporation Plc*, Engaged in communications, publishing and printing.

A summary of the data from the financial statements of the three companies for periods ending 31 March 1988 (Marks and Spencer), 30 September 1988 (Trafalgar House) and 31 December 1987 (Maxwell Communications) is as follows:

	Profit (before tax) £m	*Sales* (*Turnover*) £m	*Net Assets* £m
M and S Plc	501.7	4577.6	2158.0
T H Plc	229.1	2484.4	828.2
MCC Plc	166.0	884.1	1014.3

Two points should be noted about these three companies:

(1) They operate in **different sectors of the economy**, and are likely to have different types of **assets** in their balance sheets and different types of **expenses** in their profit and loss accounts.
(2) They appear to be of **varying size**, using the above data as a criterion (e.g., Marks and Spencer's profits are more than three times that of Maxwell Communications and its net assets figure twice as great).

Using the ratio analysis described in Sect. 13.3, we can represent the data as follows:

	Profit Margin %	*Ranking*		*Asset Turnover*	*Ranking*		*ROCE* %	*Ranking*
M and S Plc	10.96	(2)	×	2.12	(2)	=	23.24	(2)
TH Plc	9.22	(3)	×	3.00	(1)	=	27.66	(1)
MCC Plc	18.78	(1)	×	0.87	(3)	=	16.34	(3)

Expressing the data in this form enables us to make a more informed comparison of the three companies:

> (a) A comparison of the profit margins enables us to rank the companies in terms of the **average return they achieve on each £ of sales**.
>
> (b) The asset turnover, showing the success each company had in **generating sales from the assets at their disposal**, reveals a **reverse ranking to the profit margin**.
>
> (c) When these two ratios are **combined to produce the ROCE**, the ranking is again shown. It appears that the impact of the asset turnover has been more significant in its effect on the ROCE than the profit margin: Trafalgar House had the lowest profit margin, but the highest ROCE.

It is to be expected that because of the different natures of the respective industries and the different structures of the three companies that some aspects of their financial results will differ; it would be dangerous to take the comparison of the profit margin or the asset turnover in isolation from the other data. The ROCE does provide a better basis for comparison because it combines the effect of the other two subsidiary ratios. However, care must be taken also with the use of ROCE to compare companies' performances. This is because of two factors:

> (1) The 'return' element in ROCE is based on the reported accounting profit. We have seen in earlier chapters that profit measurement using accounting principles may not always be an adequate measure of a firm's performance. In Chapter 14 this is again explained in the context of changing price levels.
>
> (2) The 'capital' element in ROCE is based on the 'book value' of the firm as shown in the balance sheet. We have seen here also that the inclusion of assets in the balance sheet and their measurement can vary from firm to firm. This is also emphasised by the discussion in Chapter 14.

Common Size Statements

We saw above that although the three companies were of a different size it was possible to assist their comparison by the use of ratios. It is possible to take this a stage further by expressing all the balance sheet and profit and loss account in **percentage terms**. In the balance sheet, for example, the different elements could be expressed as a percentage of total assets and in the profit and loss account as a percentage of sales. In respect of the three companies in our example, this latter comparison is:

	Marks and Spencer		Trafalgar House		Maxwell Communications	
	£m	%	£m	%	£m	%
Sales	4577.6	100.00	2484.4	100.00	884.1	100.00
Cost of sales	3163.4	69.11	2089.8	84.12	625.8	70.78
Gross Profit	1414.2	30.89	394.6	15.88	258.3	29.22
Expenses(1)	912.5	19.93	165.5	6.66	92.3	10.44
Net Profit	£501.7	10.96	£229.1	9.22	£166.0	18.78

Note:

(1) As these are simplified statements we have shown this figure in a single item. Reference to the respective profit and loss accounts show that it is a net figure which includes items of income included here as deductions from total expenses.

Analysing the respective profit and loss accounts in this way reveals the following:

(1) On average when Marks and Spencer sells an item for (say) £100, that item has cost £69.11 to purchase from the suppliers. Operating their stores and other general overheads costs a further £19.93 per £100 sales, leaving £10.96 as a net profit (before taxation). A comparison of these figures over a number of years will reveal further evidence of how successful the company is in maintaining selling prices and controlling costs and the resulting **gross** and **net profit margins**.

(2) As was stated earlier, comparison of profit margins between companies must be carried out with a knowledge of the inherent differences in the operations of the companies concerned. For example, Marks and Spencer and Trafalgar House have very similar net profit margins, but show considerable differences in the percentages for cost of sales, gross profit and expenses. These differences are as likely to be caused by the fact that one company is a retail organisation and the other a conglomerate of manufacturing and service companies as by the relative efficiency of each of them.

13.5   Trend statements

This technique can be used to compare data for a sequence of years by selecting **one year as a base year** and expressing other years **in relation to that**

base year. It is a technique used to construct indices of prices, for example the retail price index used to measure inflation. This is discussed further in Sect. 14.3 in the context of accounting for changing price levels.

The technique can be demonstrated using the figures from Ex.13.1:

	19X4	*19X5*	*19X6*	*19X7*
	£	£	£	£
Sales	600	650	770	850
Cost of Sales	450	495	590	660
	=====	=====	=====	=====
Gross Profit	£150	£155	£180	£190

Using 19X4 as the base year the data can be re-expressed as:

	19X4	*19X5*	*19X6*	*19X7*
	£	£	£	£
Sales	100	108	128	142
Cost of Sales	100	110	131	147
	=====	=====	=====	=====
Gross Profit	£100	£104	£120	£127

We can now see the rate of growth of the elements in the profit and loss account of John Doe Plc; we can show that although sales have increased by 42% over the four years, cost of sales has increased by 47% thus resulting in a **deterioration of the relative gross profit return**, as shown in the discussion of Ex.13.1 in Sect. 13.3. It will be explained in Sect. 14.3 that even greater care must be taken when interpreting such trend data during periods when general price levels are changing.

13.6 Summary

Financial analysis of the type described in Chapter 13 provides users of information with a way of simplifying the volume and variety of data which financial statements contain. However, in interpreting this information it is important also to make full use of the other data available in the annual report – such as the Chairman's statement, the Directors' Report, etc. It is also necessary to recognise the **limitations**, of financial information which relates to **past events**, and which is already several months old by the time it reaches the users. Additionally the other limitations of historical cost accounting referred to in earlier chapters (and again in Chapter 14) must be taken into consideration.

Finally it should be remembered that financial analysis is undertaken to provide information for **decision-making about the future**. This information should be used to reduce the degree of uncertainty associated with the future, but should never be assumed to eliminate it.

Notes and References

1. It is true that in comparing different firms financial performance care must be taken to compare **like with like**. However, an investor (say, in ordinary shares) may simply be concerned about obtaining the best return available, in which case it may be necessary to compare the performance of companies from different industries.
2. An example of this is given in Sect. 14.3 in relation to the impact of inflation on reported trend figures.
3. Liquidity, solvency and financial risk are also discussed in Sections 10.7, 10.10 and 10.11.
4. Reference to the balance sheet of Marks and Spencer Plc in Appendix B shows that at 31 March 1989 the Revaluation Reserve of £456.5m constituted 24% of the net asset total of £1922.7m.
5. Very liquid assets is in this example interpreted as cash (plus marketable securities if there had been any in this company). In some situations debtors may also be included.
6. We have used a 365 day year in the calculations; in Chapter 10 we used a 240 working day year. Both are used in practice, but obviously care must be taken to ensure that the **same basis** has been used when making a comparison.

Questions and Problems

13.1   What do you understand by the following terminology?

Financial risk	Current ratio
Return on equity	Quick ratio
Return on assets	Liquidity ratios
Return on capital employed	Gearing ratios
Return on finance employed	Stock turnover
Asset turnover	Debtors turnover
Profit margin	Creditors turnover
Earnings yield	Performance evaluation
Dividend cover	Financial analysis
Price/earnings ratio	Financial trends
Common sign statements	Dividend yield
Trend statements	Earnings per share

13.2 What are the advantages of using ratios in relation to a business's annual accounts?

13.3 The following is the balance sheet of Pickle Co. Ltd at 31 December 19X0:

	£	£
Fixed Assets		
Machinery –		
Cost, *Less* Accumulated Depreciation		4000
Current Assets		
Inventory	800	
Debtors	1700	
	2500	
Less: Current Liabilities		
Creditors	1100	
Overdraft	300	
	1400	
Net Current Assets		1100
		5100
Financed By:		
Owners' Equity		
Share Capital		
(3000 Ordinary Shares of 50p each)		1500
Retained Profit		2100
		3600
Loan at 10%		1500
		£5100

Profit Statement for Year Ended 31 December 19X0

Sales Revenue	12000
Less: Cost of Goods Sold	8000
Gross Profit	4000
Less: Expenses	2000
Net Profit	2000
Dividends	500
Retained Profit	£1500

Calculate the ratios you would consider important in assessing whether you would buy shares in the company. What criterion would you choose in order to assess the ratios?

13.4 What are the best measures for analysing the following?

(a) Liquidity.
(b) Effective use of floor space in a retail company.
(c) The performance of a division of a company.
(d) Profitability, where the owner owns all the shares in the company.

13.5   Are there any limitations associated with using ratios to analyse a firm's performance?

13.6   Analyse the performance of Marks and Spencer Plc using the data in Appendix B. What additional information would you like to have for your analysis?

13.7   The Napa Valley Company achieved the following results in 19X8:

	£
Sales (50 000 units)	200000
Net Profit	20000
Capital Employed	50000

The company anticipates that for 19X9 it can increase its unit selling prices by 10% and that its unit cost prices will be the same as for 19X8. By the introduction of extra capital of £100 000 it expects to be able to increase its sales volume by 10 000 units.

Required: Advise the company on its prospects for 19X9.

13.8   You have been asked to advise a friend on a possible investment in Ordinary shares in two companies with financial structures as follows:

	Co. A	Co. B
Ordinary Shares of £1	£100000	£40000
10% Debentures	–	60000
Total Finance	£100000	£100000

The available information shows the same profit forecasts for the two companies – i.e.:

Optimistic forecast	£15000
Middle of the road forecast	10000
Pessimistic forecast	5000

The terms 'optimistic', 'middle of the road' and 'pessimistic' refer to views of the possible future trading conditions facing the two companies.

Required: Analyse the data provided, and advise your friend on his potential investment.

13.9   The following data is for the Alameda Co. Ltd:

Profit and Loss Account for the Year Ended December 31

	£000	19X7 £000	£000	19X8 £000
Sales		400		500
Cost of Sales:				
Direct Material	120		180	
Direct Labour	80	200	160	340
Gross Profit		200		160
Expenses		40		80
		160		80
Debenture Interest		20		20
Net Profit Before Tax		140		60
Taxation		70		30
Net Profit After Tax		70		30
Retained Profit From Previous Year		40		60
		110		90
Ordinary Share Dividend		50		55
Retained Profit		£60		£35

Balance Sheet as at 31 December

	£000	19X7 £000	£000	19X8 £000
Fixed Assets				
Land and Building		200		220
Plant and Machinery		260		320
		460		540
Current Assets				
Stock	30		70	
Debtors	50		80	
Cash	90		10	
	170		160	
Current Liabilities				
Creditors	(40)		(30)	
		130		130
		590		670
10% debentures		(200)		(200)
		£390		£470
Share Capital and Reserves				
Ordinary Shares of 50p		250		300
Share Premium Account		80		135
Profit and Loss Account		60		35
		£390		£470

Required:

(i) Prepare a ratio analysis for 19X7 and 19X8 to evaluate the company's performance and position with regard to its profitability, liquidity and solvency.

(ii) Comment on what your analysis reveals about the company's performance and position.

13.10 The Westcliff Co. has expanded its operations in 19X7 compared with 19X6. **Extracts** from the company's financial statements for the two years are shown below:

	19X6 £000	19X7 £000
Sales	1000	1500
Cost of Sales	600	800
Expenses	350	600
Net Assets	200	600

Included in the net assets were:

Debtors	60	120
Creditors	40	50
Stock	50	80
Cash	20	10

Required: Using the above data analyse the company's position and performance for the two years in question. What further information would you require to prepare a complete analysis?

13.11 The following are summaries of the published accounts of ABC Ltd, a clothes manufacturer, for the past two years:

Profit & Loss Accounts for the Year End

	31.12.X7 £	31.12.X7 £	31.12.X8 £	31.12.X8 £
Sales		5000		12000
Cost of Sales		2000		3000
Gross Profit		3000		9000
Expenses:				
General	500		400	
Interest	300	800	1500	1900
Net Profit		£2200		£7100

Balance Sheets as at	31.12X7		31.12X8	
	£	£	£	£
Fixed Assets				
Cost	9000		21750	
Depreciation	1000		3000	
Net Book Value		8000		18750
Current Assets				
Stock	500		800	
Debtors	800		1200	
Cash	350		–	
	1650		2000	
Current Liabilities				
Creditors	(1000)		(5000)	
		650		(3000)
		8650		15750
Share Capital		1000		1000
Retained Profits		7650		14750
		£8650		£15750

(a) *Calculate*: for both years:

  (1) the return on capital employed;
  (2) gross profit margin;
  (3) current ratio and quick ratio;

(b) Suppose you were a bank manager and ABC Ltd approached
    you for a loan. What questions would you ask?
    Given the above accounts and ratios, what would your findings
    suggest?
(c) How is ratio analysis useful to investors?
(d) It is often said that the results of ratio analysis must be treated
    with caution. Why is this so?

13.12 (a) It is often stated that the 'return on capital employed' is a key financial ratio. Explain the uses and limitations of this ratio.

(b) The financial results of Seattle Ltd and San Diego Ltd for the past four years are as follows:

	Seattle Ltd			San Diego Ltd		
	Sales	Net Profit	Capital Employed	Sales	Net Profit	Capital Employed
	£000	£000	£000	£000	£000	£000
19X5	400	18	87	600	40	200
19X4	330	16	75	550	28	150
19X3	300	15	70	450	20	130
19X2	250	14	62	350	15	100

Required: Analyse and compare the performance of the two companies over the four year period.

Using Appendix B:
(c) Calculate the return on capital employee for Marks and Spencer per for the years 1985 to 1989.
(d) Comment on the results in (c).

13.13 Two friends, Ken Jones and Frank Smith each start separate businesses as shopkeepers on 1 January 19X8. During 19X8 they have the following identical transactions:

1. They purchased shop fittings for £50 000. The fittings have an estimated life of 4 years and a residual value of £10 000.
2. They purchased goodwill from the previous owner at a cost of £50 000.
3. They purchased stock:
1 January 19X8	4000 units at £40 each
1 June 19X8	4000 units at £60 each
4. They sold stock:
30 September 19X8	3000 units at £100 each
5. They incurred other expenses of £20 000.

The friends adopt different accounting procedures for calculating profit as follows:

(a) Mr Jones uses straight-line, depreciation and Mr Smith uses a reducing-balance rate of 40%.
(b) Mr Jones writes off goodwill over a 10 year period. Mr Smith writes it off in the year it was acquired.
(c) Mr Jones uses the FIFO method for valuing stock and Mr Smith uses the LIFO.

Required:

(i) Prepare profit and loss accounts for Mr Jones and Mr Smith for the year to 31 December 19X8.
(ii) Compare the two profit and loss accounts you have prepared.
(iii) What are the implications of the differences in the profit and loss accounts from the perspective of an individual who wishes to evaluate the financial performance of the business?

14
Accounting Measurement and Changing Price Levels

14.1 Introduction

Accounting data is measured and recorded in **monetary terms,** and we have seen from earlier chapters that the most common measure of monetary value used in accounting has traditionally been **historical cost.** It was established in Chapter 2 that one of the weaknesses of historical cost values is that they are established at the time the asset is purchased, and therefore may become out of date. This is especially likely where price levels **fluctuate over time.**

In the past 40 years the UK has experienced periods of rapidly changing prices, and this has imposed a severe strain on historical cost accounting as a measure of value and profit which can be used in financial statements to report the performance and position of companies. This has led to a reappraisal of historical cost accounting, and to the consideration of possible means of amending or replacing it. Chapter 14, the final chapter in the book, initially analyses the impact of changing price levels on accounting measurement and reporting. It then identifies the possible limitations of historical cost accounting and considers the alternative solutions which have been proposed. The chapter then concludes with a more general re-evaluation of the historical cost accounting model which has been the basis for the content of most of the preceding chapters.

Before examining the impact of changing prices on financial statements we will consider a simple example using a single asset:

Example 14.1
A house was purchased on 1 January 19X0 for £100 000. On 31 December 19X0 it was sold for £150 000. An index of general price changes rose from 100 to 110 in 19X0 while an index of average house prices rose from 100 to 120. The house in this example was in a location where house prices rose more than the average. Ignoring all other costs and revenues, what profit was made in 19X0? The profit could be:

	V_0 (1 Jan. 19X0) £	ADJ £	$V_0(ADJ)$ £	V_1 (31 Dec. 19X0) £	Profit £
(1)	100000	–	100000	150000	50000
(2)	100000	$\frac{110}{100}$	110000	150000	40000
(3)	100000	$\frac{120}{100}$	120000	150000	30000

The profit is calculated using the model $P = V_1 - V_0$. The adjustments V_0 (*ADJ*) are an attempt to reflect the change in price levels under various assumptions: (1) no price change; (2) the general price level change; (3) the average house price change. These adjustments are made to express V_0 as an equivalent in current terms, thus facilitating better comparison with V_1.

In measure of profit (1) no adjustment to the numbers is made and the profit is simply the difference between the **purchase cost** and **selling price**. This is the profit that would be shown in conventional historical cost accounting statements. Measure (2) makes adjustment for a general price index, which is a measure of the **general rise in prices** of a wide range of items. This measure shows that £100 000 at the beginning of 19X0 is equivalent to £110 000 at the end, because the two amounts could purchase the same quantity of items in general. The profit is the **excess value** at the end of the year over the £110 000. Measure (3) makes an adjustment for the rise in the index for average house prices from 100 to 120, and indicates that the only profit is the **extra increase in the value of this particular house**.

Ex.14.1, though a relatively straightforward situation, illustrates the difficulty of measuring value and profit when there are price level changes. These changes were of two kinds – i.e., a general price rise and a rise in the price of a specific type of asset, in this example, a house. The former change can be equated to what is known as the **rate of inflation**. These differences between general and specific price changes are discussed later in the chapter, but we should note that they were expressed as **indices** rather than percentage rises; the general price change could have been expressed as 10% and the specific one for the house as 20%. In the rest of this chapter, for ease of exposition, we will continue to use indexes rather than percentages.

Our original definition of profit was explained in terms of a change in value. This could be reinterpreted as profit being the **extra value of the firm at the end of a period** over and above its **starting value**. This way of expressing profit is generally termed the **profit 'after maintaining capital intact'**. This is similar to the concept of capital maintenance introduced in Chapter 5, and it is assumed in this discussion that the value of the firm and the firm's capital are equivalent concepts. Where there is no change in price levels the agreement on a satisfactory definition of maintaining value intact may still cause problems, but where prices have changed the idea of maintaining the starting value is even more difficult to apply. In measure (2) in Ex.14.1 the £100 000 at the beginning of 19X0 could purchase the same assets in general as £110 000 at the end of 19X0. It was argued that the profit was the excess proceeds over this £100 000 expressed in the year end amount of £110 000: the profit was thus calculated after maintaining the value of the £100 000 intact at the end of the year (which was equivalent to £110 000 by the end of 19X0). Measure (3) in Ex.14.1 showed that the value to be maintained before calculation of the profit was £120 000 – that is, as measured **by the ability to buy houses in general rather than assets in general**. There are other possible definitions that could be used – e.g., the ability to buy a similar house in the same location as the one sold: because you would probably have to pay a price similar to the proceeds of the house sold, it **could be said that no profit is earned on the sale**. This idea of 'maintaining capital intact' is important, and will be discussed further below.

14.2   Maintaining capital intact

The profit of a period for an individual has been defined as '**the maximum amount that he could consume and still remain as well off at the end as he was at the beginning**'.[1] This definition can be amended to be applicable to a firm's profits for a period: 'the maximum amount that the firm could pay as a dividend and still remain as well off at the end of the period as it was at the beginning'. The interpretation of this definition revolves around the meaning of 'as well off'.

There are at least **three** possible interpretations of this phrase:

> (a) the ownership of assets with the same monetary value (measure (1) in Ex.14.1);
> (b) the capacity to purchase the same quantity of assets in general (measure (2) in Ex.14.1);
> (c) the capacity to purchase the same quantity of a specific asset (measure (3) in Ex.14.1).

The expression 'as well off as' is equivalent to the concept of maintaining capital or value intact. The profit of a period is the surplus of the value at the end of the period over the starting value, adjusted to maintain this initial value intact.

As we have seen above, the interpretation of maintaining value intact may vary. An individual's interpretation may be affected by his intended **expenditure pattern**, and as we all have different expenditure patterns a change in prices will affect some people more than others. For example, if two people each have £10 000 and one intends buying a particular car while the other does not, when the price of the car rises (everything else remaining the same), the former will be less well off while the latter will be unaffected.

There are many users of accounting information relating to the firm, but for the purposes of exposition we can divide them into two groups: those who will look at the information from the point of view of the **owners**, and those who will look at it from the point of view of the **firm** (or perhaps the managers of the firm). Owners will be interested primarily in making sure that their investment in the firm (which entailed them sacrificing consumption when the investment was made) enables them, at the minimum, **to enjoy the same consumption later**. This could be ascertained accurately only by constructing an index for each owner based on his own personal expenditure patterns. If this index increased from 100 to 150 over the investment period, then an investment of £100 would have to return at least £150 at the end of the investment period to maintain value intact. If it returned £160 then there could be said to be a profit of £10 to the investor, using the formula:

$$V - (V_0 \times I) = \text{Profit}$$

$$160 - \left(100 \times \frac{150}{100} \right) = £10$$

where I is the appropriate index of expenditure patterns for the investor.

The other viewpoint is that of the firm. An index could be calculated based on the **firm's expenditure pattern** which would depend on the pattern of the forecast acquisition of assets. Using this in the above formula the firm can calculate **its profit** after maintaining its value intact.

The UK government publishes an Index of Retail Prices (RPI) which measures the effect of price level changes on the average consumer and is the most commonly used measure of 'inflation' in the economy. This general price index could possibly be considered as a proxy for the expenditure patterns of the two groups considered above. However, the index is based on the average consumer and will not reflect exactly each individual owner's index of his expenditure patterns. Most owners would accept it, however, as a reasonable proxy for the level of inflation they are experiencing, but the expenditure patterns of most firms will be specific to the firm, being based on the purchases of the specific assets necessary to continue its particular trade. Most firms will thus find that the RPI is not a good proxy for their expenditure patterns. Firms may thus need to produce their own specific index in order to calculate whether their value has been maintained intact. The use of such an index may mean that the firm compares its end of period value (V_1) with the **replacement cost of the components of the starting value**. The use of this index is therefore sometimes called a 'replacement cost adjustment'.

It is possible to construct specific indexes for particular assets; this can be done by collecting data from the market, or from information supplied by a trade association or the government. Specific indexes are more easily constructed when assets are frequently replaced with **similar assets**, but if technology changes and replacements are not similar they may be difficult to construct.

When examining the information needs of the owners and the managers of a firm it is necessary to consider the firm's **objective(s)**. It is common to assume that the key objective is to maximise the owners' wealth (i.e., the owners' ability to purchase assets in general) and that the managers of the firm should identify with the owners' objective(s). They should thus be concerned about the expenditure patterns of the owners as well as those of the firm. The use of a general price index (as a proxy for the expenditure patterns of all the owners), **as well as** a set of specific price indexes for the expenditure pattern of the firm, may be necessary information to reflect this objective(s).

It is possible to use both types of index to make adjustments to the accounting information which is produced using the historical cost framework examined in earlier chapters. In Sect. 14.3 and 14.4 we will concentrate on **adjusting this accounting information**, rather than substituting other valuation bases which may not be acceptable within this framework. (These more radical alternatives are referred to in Sect. 14.7.) We will now examine the effect of price changes on a firm's assets and liabilities and the way this will affect financial reporting, perhaps resulting in serious limitations to reports based on historical cost accounting.

14.3   The limitations of historical cost accounting

Historical cost accounting is the most common system of reporting accounting information. It is widely used throughout the world. In recent years, many countries have attempted to amend it or replace it, in an effort to meet problems caused by changing price levels.[2] In the UK there have been several proposals during the past twenty years, the two most important being:

> 1974 SSAP 7   'Accounting for Changes in the Purchasing Power of
> Money'
> 1980 SSAP 16   'Current Cost Accounting'

Both these Standards, which adopted different types of solutions, were later withdrawn from use. After the withdrawal of SSAP 16 the Accounting Standards Committee (ASC) issued a handbook on the general guidelines on accounting for the effects of changing prices.[3] The following discussion of the limitations of historic cost accounting uses the analysis of this topic from the ASC handbook.

Profit Measurement

One of the important accounting principles used in measuring profit is the **matching principle**. As stated in Chapter 5, this is an attempt to ensure that the **revenues** recorded in an accounting period are matched with the **expenses** incurred in earning them. Thus if a firm bought stock on 1 January for £1000 and twelve months later sold it on 31 December for £1400 then ignoring other possible expense items, the £1000 would be matched as cost of sales against the sales revenue of £1400 to show a gross profit of £400. However, if the cost of stock increased over the year and was £1100 at the time of the sale we may need to question our original 'match' which produced the gross profit of £400. The issue is: should we match current revenues (i.e., 31 December) with costs incurred at an earlier date (i.e., 1 January) or should the matching be of **current revenues** and **current costs**'. The respective calculations are:

	£	£
Sales Revenues	1400	1400
Cost of Sales:		
Historic Cost	1000	
Current Cost		1100
Gross Profit	£400	£300

If we extend the above example and assume that the firm used a fixed asset which cost £2400 six years ago and is being depreciated at £240 a year over ten years, then depreciation will be based on a **six year old cost figures**. What if the current cost of a similar fixed asset had risen to £3600? The respective calculations will be:

	£	£
Gross Profit	400	300
Depreciation based on:		
Historical Cost	240	
Current Cost		£360
Net Profit (Loss)	£160	£(60)

We can see from this example that the net profit based on historical cost is £160, whereas the equivalent results using current cost is a net loss of £60.

It was explained earlier that a firm's profit is the 'maximum amount that the firm could pay as a dividend and still remain as well off at the end of the period as it was at the beginning'. One definition of 'well off' for this firm might be the ability to continue to purchase and sell the same amount of stock and to be able to replace its fixed asset when it is necessary to do so. However, if the firm use the historical cost net profit as a basis for deciding its dividend distribution, it could give a maximum dividend of £160. In so doing, it would not be retaining sufficient funds within the business to replace its stock now costing £1100, and it would not be charging the current cost of fixed assets consumed during the period. In fact, we can see that as the firm is making a current cost net loss, then under the current cost approach any dividend paid would be paid out of capital. An analysis of the performance of UK companies during the early 1980s when inflation was high shows that many dividend payments were in fact higher than the current cost profits earned.[4]

Balance Sheet Values

Although there have been moves in recent years to include the value of **internally generated assets**, such as brand names or newspaper titles, the balance sheet has traditionally included only those assets acquired by external transactions.

Most of these assets are recorded in the balance sheet at their **original cost**. As such, they will probably represent out of date values and may not report a **realistic measure of the resources employed in the business**.

Return on Capital Employed (ROCE)

We saw in Chapter 13 that the ROCE is an important performance indicator for a firm. This ratio measures the firm's **profits** against its **balance sheet value**. As we have seen above, in times of rising prices profit is likely to be **overstated**, whereas balance sheet values are likely to be **understated** in relation to current costs. Consequently the ROCE based on historic cost data is likely to be higher than the ROCE based on current cost data. Actual data for UK companies reveals that in the early 1980s historic cost ROCE was on average twice that of current cost ROCE.[5]

Gain/Loss on Holding Monetary Items

Some assets and liabilities held by a firm have a **fixed monetary value**, and are often termed 'monetary items'. Examples of such items are cash, debtors, creditors and loans. The characteristics of these assets and liabilities is that their **monetary value remains constant**, even if prices of other items are changing. If the market price of, say, motor vehicles (a non-monetary asset) is increasing, the value of a motor vehicle held as an asset also changes, but if £1000 cash is held as an asset, its value is fixed at £1000 whatever happens to other prices.

However, although such assets' monetary value is fixed, their **purchasing power** may change – if there is a general increase in prices, for example, the £1000 cash will **buy less as time passes**. Similarly if a firm owes £1000 during a period of rising prices, the burden of the debt in terms of the purchasing power the firm must sacrifice to repay the debt is **decreasing**. A key criticism of historical cost accounting is that it fails to measure these 'purchasing power' gains and losses because it states assets and liabilities in historical monetary values (i.e., cost) and ignores current price levels.

Ex.14.2 may help to explain this issue:

Example 14.2
A firm holds cash £1000, debtors £500 and creditors £600 during a period when an index of general prices increases from 100 to 120. The position of this firm can be explained as follows:

Historical Cost

	Actual Monetary Value		Price Rise	Recognising Change in Prices Restated Values (ii)	Monetary Gain/Loss(iii)
	Beginning Of Period	End Of Period			
Cash	1000	1000	120/100	1200	200 (Loss)
Debtors	500	500	120/100	600	100 (Loss)
	1500	1500		1800	300
Creditors	600	600	120/100	720	120 (Gain)
	£900 (i)	£900 (i)		£1080	£180 (Net Monetary Loss)

Notes:

(i) Historical cost accounting does not incorporate the effect of changes in price levels, and thus there is **no gain or loss recognised** during the period.

(ii) This restated value represents what these items would have risen to if they had **kept pace with the rise in prices**.

(iii) This represents the **gain or loss in purchasing power** because the monetary items have not kept pace with the rise in prices. Monetary assets (cash and debtors) will thus buy less after the rise in prices and the monetary liability (creditors) can be repaid in 'inflated £s' and it thus represents a smaller sacrifice in terms of purchasing power.

If the example of gain on holding a liability is difficult to follow, consider the example of someone buying a house by taking on a 25 year mortgage of £50 000. Assuming no change in interest rates, the monetary value of the interest payments will be the same in the 25th year as in the first. However, we can assume that the borrower's salary will have increased considerably over 25 years and the **comparative burden** of the interest payment will have decreased considerably.

Misleading Performance Trends

A common feature of accounting reports in recent years has been the inclusion of five or ten year **summaries of performance**. If these summaries merely give the historical cost data pertaining to each year in the summary without adjustment then the **trends** revealed can give misleading information. Take a firm who reported the following over a five year period:

Year	1	2	3	4	5
Profit (£m)	200	230	260	290	320
Trend (%)	100	115	130	145	160

The profit performance shows a **steady increase**, which is confirmed by the percentages calculation which reveals a 60% increase over the five-year period. However, if we incorporate the following data on inflation which would have been typical of a five year period in the 1970s or 1980s, and restate the profit and percentage trend; we get:

Year	1	2	3	4	5
Inflation index	100	121	140	159	178
Profit (all expressed in year five price levels)	356	338	330	324	320
Adjusted % trend	100	95	93	91	90

The profits have been restated at the price level ruling in year five, and this reveals that in real terms profit have **fallen** over the period: the adjusted percentage trend confirms this showing that instead of increasing by 60% profits have fallen by 10%.

Comparing Financial Statements

An important need of users of financial statements is the possibility of making **comparisons between firms**, and **between years**. Conventional accounting statements, prepared for periods of changing prices, do not provide a good basis for either type of comparison because firms may have: (1) different proportions of **non-monetary** and **monetary assets** and **liabilities**; (2) different **financial structures**; and (3) different **age structures** of assets. Items in (1), (2) and (3) may further vary from year to year.

(1) *Different proportions of assets and liabilities* We have seen the effect that price level changes have on monetary as opposed to non-monetary assets and liabilities. Unless adjustments are made to allow for firms holding different proportions of these (e.g., a bank holding a lot of cash as compared with a property company holding a lot of land) **inter-period** and **inter-firm** comparison will be difficult.

(2) *Different financial structure* The amount of **debt** a firm has will influence the way price level changes affect it. The balance between equity and debt-financing will produce different effects (e.g., the more debt a firm has the more the firm may gain in times of general price level rises through holding liabilities); conversely, the more it may lose in time of general price level falls.

(3) *Different age structure of assets* The different age structure will also affect comparisons. A firm can hold a mixture of non-depreciating fixed assets, depreciating fixed assets and other assets. The longer an asset is held before realisation the **more out of date will be the depreciation expense** in the conventional profit statement. Ex.14.3 illustrates this.

Example 14.3
Two firms sell an identical product at the same price. In 19X0 their total sales were £100 000 each. Their expenses, excluding depreciation, were £50 000. Both produced the product on a similar machine, but one firm purchased its machine thirteen years ago for £150 000, the other two years ago for £300 000. Both machines are depreciated on a straight-line basis assuming no scrap value and a fifteen year life. The conventional profit statements for 19X0 are:

	First Firm £	*Second Firm* £
Sales Revenue	100000	100000
Less: Depreciation Expense	10000	20000
Other Expense	50000	50000
Profit	£40000	£30000

Because the price level changes in the cost of machinery have been ignored by these conventional profit statements, one firm looks more profitable because it purchased its machine earlier than the other. By 19X2 when the first firm replaces its machine the second firm may appear more profitable because the first firm will then have a higher depreciation expense. If adjustments were made to the depreciation expense, as discussed in Sect. 14.3 above, to show it at the level it would be if the machine had been purchased at current costs, the profits would be reported as being the same for each firm.

14.4   Proposed remedies

Despite the considerable amount of time and effort devoted to the problems of reporting accounting information during times of changing prices, there is no one solution which has been universally accepted. In the UK, the debate has frequently centred round what has been seen as two alternative methods. These are exemplified in the two SSAPs referred to at the beginning of Sect. 14.3. SSAP 7, which proposed what was known as Constant (or Current) Purchasing Power (CPP) accounting included adjustments for changes in the **general level of prices**. In SSAP 16, Current Cost Accounting (CCA) adjustments were made for **specific price changes**. Neither of these approaches has proved on their own to be generally acceptable.

The reasons why both SSAP 7 and SSAP 16 were not successful are complex, and trying to explain the reasons will inevitably be based on subjective judgments. SSAP 7 was issued in 1975 at a time when the government were concerned about rising inflation. Many commentators have suggested that the eventual withdrawal of SSAP 7 was due to government pressure because it was felt that the use of a general price index to adjust accounts could lead to a demand for general indexation of **other elements of the economy** such as wages, pensions, loans, etc., if this occurred, it might make it extremely difficult to control and reduce inflation. The failure of SSAP 16 seems to have been caused by its rejection by the companies who were required to implement it in their annual reports. It may have been too complex and not well understood, or it was not seen as essential to the reporting requirements of many companies. During the period when these inflation accounting measures were being proposed the historical cost system was in continual use, and to some extent it could be that the failure of these measures is due to the resilience of historical cost accounting. This point is considered further in Sect. 14.5.

In Ex.14.4 below the two basic approaches are illustrated; this simple example is not intended to include all the elements of the respective standards.

Example 14.4
A new company commenced business on 1 January 19X0 with £500 000 capital and a £500 000 loan with an interest rate of 15%. On 1 January the company purchased machinery for £400 000 and stock for £500 000. At the end of 19X0 the company sold half its stock for £1 000 000 in cash and incurred expenses on credit (including the loan interest), of £200 000. Assume

that the machinery will have a four year life, and will have no residual value. The relevant price indices during the period are:

	General	*Specific Stock*	*Specific Machinery*
1 January 19X0	100	100	100
31 December 19X0	110	120	150

The balance sheet and profit and loss account under historical cost accounting (HCA), (2) adjusted for general price changes (CCP), and (3) adjusted for specific price changes (CCA) are shown below:

Balance Sheet at 31 December 19X0

		HCA £000		CPP £000		CCA £000
Fixed Assets						
Machinery		400		440		600
Accumulated Depreciation		100		110		150
		300		330		450
Current Assets						
Stock	250		275		300	
Cash	1100		1100		1100	
	1350		1375		1400	
Current Liabilities						
Creditors	200		200		200	
		1150		1175		1200
		1450		1505		1650
		500		500		500
		£ 950		£1005		£1150
Capital and Reserves						
Capital		500		550		500
Current Cost Reserve		–		–		300
Retained Profit		450		455		350
		£950		£1005		£1150

Profit and Loss Accounts for the Year Ended 31 December 19X0

	HC £000		CPP £000		CCA £000
Sales Revenue		1000		1000	1000
Cost of Sales		250		275	300
Gross Profit		750		725	700
Depreciation	100		110		150
Expenses	200		200		200
		300		310	350
				415	
Gain on Holding Loan			50		
Loss on Holding Cash		—	(10)	40	—
Net Profit		£450		£455	£350

CPP Results

In the restated balance sheet the machinery and stock are increased in line with the rise in the general price index. This procedure has been criticised because it results in a figure which is **difficult to explain and justify**: it is not the original cost, nor is it the asset's replacement cost, nor what the firm could realise from selling the asset. Most people consequently prefer to use the **relevant specific price indexes** for the restatement of non-monetary assets.

The owners' initial capital of £500 000 is adjusted to £550 000 using the general price index. This illustrates that the firm's capital has to rise to £550 000 to merely keep pace with inflation, and protect the purchasing power of the owners' invesment.

In the profit and loss account the cost of sales and depreciation expenses are adjusted in line with the increase in the general price level. The gain on holding a loan calculates the gain as 10% of the loan owing during the period when general price levels have increased by 10%. The loss on holding cash is based on 10% of the £100 000 cash held throughout the year. The £1 000 000 cash from sales was received at the end of the year and this does not give rise to a loss in this period. Similarly the creditors were assumed to be incurred at the end of the year and also do not create the need for an adjustment in the profit and loss account.

CCA Results

In the CCA balance sheet non-monetary assets are revalued using the increases in price **specific to each asset**. This results in a replacement cost figure which has more defensible value than those in the CPP balance sheet.

The capital and reserves section includes a figure of £300 000 shown as a Current Cost Reserve. This reserve includes the balancing entry for the revaluation of the machinery (by £200 000) and the cost of sales and stock (by £100 000 in total).

In the profit and loss account the cost of sales and depreciation are adjusted using the specific price increases showing the replacement cost of the assets consumed in earning the sales revenue for the period. The profit figure is £100 less than the historical cost accounting profit because of the increase in current cost over historical cost of the assets used in the business. In terms of capital maintenance this is explained by the fact that extra funds must be retained in the business if capital is to be maintained. In this case, 'capital' is defined as the ability of the firm to **maintain its operating capability by purchasing and replacing the specific assets** shown in its balance sheet.

Current Developments

As was stated earlier, no single system of accounting for inflation has been proposed and found to be generally acceptable in the UK. However, some elements of the two systems illustrated above have met with general approval. The **CCA adjustments to cost of sales (COSA) and to depreciation** have in recent years met with general acceptance. The adjustment for monetary items has usually been proposed as two separate adjustments – i.e., the '**Monetary Working Capital Adjustment' (MWCA)** for 'short term items, and the **gearing adjustment** for long term debt. Both of these are more controversial and have thus not become generally accepted as being necessary and useful.

The opinion on the revaluation of balance sheet items generally focuses on the use of some form of **current value**. However, there is no unanimity as to whether this should mean replacement cost, realisable values or the concept of value to the owner as described in Chapter 2.

14.5 Historical cost accounting – a postscript

At the beginning of Chapter 1, we defined accounting as the 'identifying, measuring and communicating of economic information to permit informed judgement and decisions by the users of the information'. The theme of this book has been an explanation and analysis of how accounting performs these three tasks of **identifying, measuring** and **communicating**. We have been concerned with the consideration of internal accounting systems of book-keeping and recording, as well as with the external disclosure of accounting information.

The analysis throughout the book has concentrated on accounting information prepared using what are known as **generally accepted accounting principles**. This model of accounting is also termed 'historical cost accounting', or 'traditional accounting', or 'conventional accounting'. In Sect. 14.4 we considered alternatives in the context of inflation accounting. Sect. 14.6 and 14.7 conclude our analysis by evaluating the strength and weakness of the historical cost model, and refer briefly to other possible alternatives.

14.6   Evaluation of historical cost accounting

If we accept the definition in Sect. 14.5 as being the objective of accounting then an evaluation of the success of an accounting system will have to consider whether the 'judgement' and 'decision-making' needs of the users of the information are being adequately catered for.

Sect. 1.6 introduced the issue of identifying potential users of accounting information and also listed the questions which might concern those users. Two potential difficulties were also identified in that section. One was whether it was possible for accounting information about a firm to cope satisfactorily with such an apparently **wide variety of needs**. The other was that in making economic decisions the users are by definition concerned with the **disposition of resources in the future**; they would therefore like to be provided with information which either predicts what is going to happen to the firm or enables them (the users) to make their own predictions using the accounting information.

In Sect. 14.3 we analysed the limitations of historic cost accounting during times of changing price levels. We will not repeat that analysis here; instead, we will concentrate on the system's strength and weaknesses which are apparent even when price levels are stable.

Strength of Historical Cost Accounting

The defenders[6] of the historical cost system state that its greatest strength is that it is based on the recording of **actual events** (i.e., transactions that have taken place at the values recorded at the time); these values can be **objectively** supported by **documentary evidence** of the transactions. This quality minimises the economic and social cost of operating the system. It is less costly in economic terms because the figures are relatively easy to obtain, and the audit process is facilitated by the existence of documentary evidence; it is less costly in a social sense because it is less likely to lead to disputes over the values resulting from the accounting process unlike other systems of valuation proposed. The alternatives discussed in Sect. 2.2, for example – replacement cost, realisable value or value to the owner – are all based on **hypothetical possibilities** rather than actual completed transactions, and are thus more likely to lead to dispute over their calculation.

Another popular defence is that the role of accounting is to provide information which records the stewardship of the resources entrusted to the firm by owners and lenders. According to this argument, a historical record of how these resources have been used should form the basis of reports to the owners and creditors. Ijiri[7] also states that by providing a record of the actual external transactions of the firm, historical cost accounting provides a unique **control function**; that is, it enables the owners or creditors to exert control on those in the firm managing the resources the owners and creditors have provided.

A further argument is that as historical cost accounting has been in continuous use throughout the world for several centuries it must have been providing a satisfactory service. It follows that any system which has 'stood the test of time' should be replaced only when there is universal agreement about the alternative. One of the reasons why historical cost accounting is retained, despite the criticisms outlined below and in this Chapter, is that it has proved extremely difficult to reach general agreement about its replacement.

Weakness of Historical Cost Accounting

The weakness of historical cost accounting during inflation has been categorised in Sect. 14.3. it should be emphasised that even when there is no general change in price levels (inflation or deflation) there will always be some commodities whose price will change. It is not conceivable that all prices in an economy could be stationary for any significant length of time; historical cost values of most assets will thus eventually become out of date.

One of the strengths of historical cost accounting suggested above was that it was based on actual transactions; however, this is also considered to be one of its potential weaknesses. This was initially referred to in Sect. 2.2, where it was pointed out that the reliance on the existence of a transaction cost as evidence of value leads to the exclusion of assets which have **not been acquired by transaction**. Assets which are undoubtedly valuable to a firm, but which have been generated or developed within it, would thus be excluded from the balance sheet, whereas similar assets which had been purchased could be included. Examples of such 'internal' assets would be goodwill, product brand names, the results of research and (in a sporting context) professional footballers. This weakens the balance sheet's potential use as a valuation of a firm, and makes it difficult to compare balance sheets of different companies.

Another suggested weakness results from the application of the concept of prudence, which incorporates realisation and conservatism. (These concepts were introduced and discussed in Sects 5.7 and 5.8.) This criticism is also related to the reliance on **completed transactions** as evidence of changes in value, and follows from the presumption that the value of an asset remains at its historical cost until it is changed by a further transaction. The realisation concept thus prevents recognition of increases in an asset's value until that increase is **realised**. Realisation is assumed to exist when a transaction has generated a **new asset** in exchange for the asset disposed of; the interpretation of this concept has been amended in recent years in that firms are now allowed to **revalue** assets in the balance sheet. However, any resulting increase in value must be regarded as **part of capital**, and cannot be included in profit. It is suggested that this conservative approach can lead to misleading information which conceals a company's true performance. Suppose a company owned property which increased steadily in value over a five year period and was then sold for a profit of £10m. The balance sheet would not necessarily record an increase in the first four years, but certainly nothing would be recorded in the profit and loss account until year five when the full £10m would normally be included. It could be argued that the effect of management's decisions to buy the property started in year one, and that the profit and loss account is concealing significant information during years one – four; this is particularly so for so-called 'value based' companies such as property companies or investment trusts, for whom such **capital growth** is at least as important as the income from their assets.

A further criticism of the historical cost model is the measurement of profit by a process of **matching costs** with **revenues** for an accounting period. The revenue earned in a period usually results from **current sales of goods and services** and (apart from adjustments to allow for debtor balances) will approximate to the **operating cash inflow** for the period. Costs will, however, be a combination of current cash out-flows and past cash outflows which have been 'smoothed out' for purposes of matching; depreciation is the most obvious example of such a 'smoothed out' cost. We saw in Chapters 6 and 7 that the end of period valuation of fixed assets and stock constitutes a series of more or less arbitrary inter-period allocations of costs. Although the problems of matching is included here as a criticism of historical cost accounting, it is more a criticism of the requirement to calculate an **annual profit** for an **on-going** organisation. (This issue of the difficulty of periodic profit measurement was raised initially in Sect. 2.3.)

14.7 Alternatives to historical cost accounting

Sect. 14.3 discussed the limitations of historical cost accounting during periods of changing prices, and in Sect. 14.4 we outlined some of the proposals that have been suggested to remedy these limitations. In general, the proposals have been to remain essentially within the principles of the existing reporting system, for example to continue to produce a profit and loss account and a balance sheet. Many of the proposals have favoured some form of **current value** instead of historic cost. References to some of these proposals are given at the end of this chapter.[8]

A more radical alternative has been the proposal for systems of **cash flow accounting**. These systems concentrate on the underlying cash flows in and out of a firm, and avoid the necessity for accrual and matching. Some versions suggest that they should replace historical cost accounting completely while others propose more cash flow information as a supplement to the more traditional statements.[9]

14.8 Summary

This final chapter has been concerned with a reappraisal of the historical cost accounting system of recording and reporting. An important problem has been the strain imposed on the system during periods of changing prices levels. It is possible because of these problems and the other criticisms referred to in the chapter that the accounting reporting model will undergo change. It is likely however that the historical cost system will be at least partially retained as it still seems to meet many of the needs of the users of accounting information.

Notes and References

1. This quotation is from J. R. Hicks, *Value and Capital* (Oxford: Clarendon Press, 1946) 2nd edn, pp. 171–81.
2. For a survey of these developments, see G. Whittington and D. Tweedie, *The Debate on Inflation Accounting* (Cambridge: Cambridge University Press, 1984).
3. 'Accounting for the effects of changing prices a Handbook' (London: Accounting Standards Committee, 1986).
4. 'Accounting for the effects of changing prices a handbook'.
5. 'Accounting for the effects of changing prices a handbook'.
6. See, for example, Y. Ijiri, 'A defense of historical cost accounting', in R. R. Sterling (ed.), *Asset Valuation and Income Determination* (Houston, Texas: Scholars Book Co., 1971).
7. Ijiri, 'A defense of historical cost accounting'.
8. A selection of these proposals would include:
   ASSC, 'The corporate report' (London: Accounting Standards Steering Committee, 1975).
   D. Solomons, 'Guidelines for Financial Reporting Standards' (The Solomons Report) (London, ICAEW, 1989).
   Sandilands Committee, 'Inflation Accounting: Report of the Inflation Accounting Committee', Cmmd 6225 (London: HMSO, 1975).
   Institute of Chartered Accountants of Scotland, 'Making Corporate Reports Valuable', ICAS, 1988. Kogan Page London.
   IASC, 'Framework for the preparation and presentation of Financial Statements (London: International Accounting Standards Committee, 1989).
9. See, for example T. Lee, *Cash Flow Accounting* (London: Van Nostrand Reinholt, 1984).

Questions and Problems

14.1 What do you understand by the following terminology?

General price level changes   Monetary assets and liabilities
Specific price level changes   Current cost reserve
Inflation   Inflation accounting
Maintaining capital Intact   Stewardship
RPI   Cash flow accounting
Constant purchasing power   Current cost accounting

14.2 Discuss whether the effect of price level changes on value and profit of a firm would be of interest to:

(a) creditors
(b) trade unions
(c) customers
(d) the government.

14.3 What problems would arise in trying to construct a price level index for the following:

(a) An individual's consumption?
(b) The whole population?
(c) Cars?
(d) A firm's expenditure pattern?

14.4 A trader in lawnmowers begins a period with one lawnmower which he bought for £100 and which constitutes his opening capital. He sells the lawnmower for £160. During the period, general inflation is 10% but the replacement cost to the trader of lawnmowers increases by 20%. Explain to the trader how much profit he can withdraw from the business. Give a full explanation of the possible alternative concepts of capital maintenance which you think relevant to your answer.

14.5 Explain how price level changes can reduce the usefulness of financial statements prepared on the basis of historical cost accounting.

14.6 If financial statements used replacement cost as the basis of value rather than original cost, would there be any need to consider other price level changes when reporting to owners and managers?

14.7 Why is it that price level changes affect the ability meaningfully to compare the financial statements of one company with another?

14.8 A firm has £1000 in its bank account during March 19X0. It has no transactions affecting the bank account in this month. During the month the index of retail prices rose from 100 to 105, but the specific index relating to the assets normally traded by the firm decreased from 200 to 180. Explain whether the firm is better or worse off. (You should quantify the amounts involved.)

14.9 If both taxation and dividends are paid out of the conventional historical cost accounting profit, what problems does this raise in times of price level changes?

14.10 A firm commences business on 1 January 19X0 by purchasing a car for £1000 and inventory for £200 using the initial capital of £1200. On 30 June 19X0 it sells half the inventory for £300 cash. At the end of 19X1 it sells the rest of the inventory for £600 cash. The firm has no other transactions. The relevant indexes are:

	1 Jan 19X0	31 Dec 19X0	31 Dec 19X1
Stock	100	100	100
Car	100	105	110
General Price Index	100	100	105

The car is expected to have a ten year life, with no residual value at the end of its life. It is depreciated on a straight-line basis.

Calculate the profit for 19X0 and 19X1. What problems do you foresee in the reporting of the profit in 19X1? Will the firm be able to replace the car at the end of the tenth year?

14.11 Brady sets up business on 1 January to deal in metals. His initial capital is £10 000 with which he buys a quantity of copper. On 31 December 19X1 he sells half of it for £8000 cash, and he estimates that the batch sold will cost £7000 to replace.

(a) Prepare Brady's balance sheet at 31 December and a statement of the profit for year 1 on each of the following principles:

(1) Historical cost accounting.
(2) Replacement cost accounting.
(3) Current purchasing power accounting (at 1 January the general purchasing power index stood at 100; on 31 December it was 120).

(b) If the firm's profit for the year is 'the maximum value which the company can distribute and still be as well off at the end of the year as it was at the beginning', consider which of the above measures of profit – (1), (2) or (3) – you would regard to be the most appropriate:

(i) From Brady's point of view, as owner/manager.
(ii) From the viewpoint of a potential equity investor.

Explain your reasons.

14.12 Consider the needs of the users of accounting information identified in Sect. 1.6. Discuss how adequately those needs are being catered for by the current provision of reported accounting information.

14.13 Discuss the apparent conflict in accounting reporting between the provision of objective historical information and subjective future oriented information.

14.14 It has been suggested that the use of historical cost accounting minimises the economic and social costs of operating an accounting reporting system. Discuss this suggestion.

14.15 Explain what is meant by 'stewardship' in the context of accounting, and identify possible alternative interpretation of the stewardship concept. Why is it such an important concept in accounting?

14.16 Examine the weaknesses of historical cost accounting in the absence of inflation. Start by defining what you understand by 'in the absence of inflation'.

Appendix A Statements of Standard Accounting Practice

Appendix B Marks and Spencer Plc
Extract From the 1989 Annual Report and Financial Statements

Summary of Group Results

	1989 52 weeks £m	1988 53 weeks £m	1987 52 weeks £m	1986 52 weeks £m	1985 52 weeks £m
Turnover					
Clothing	**2522.3**	2249.9	2118.4	1866.0	1613.3
Homeware	**611.7**	551.6	516.6	439.8	366.9
Foods	**1923.0**	1730.2	1549.1	1410.0	1216.2
Financial activities	**64.5**	45.9	36.6	19.0	11.7
	5121.5	4577.6	4220.8	3734.8	3208.1
Operating profit	**563.7**	508.5	434.6	361.0	306.0
Profit on ordinary activities before tax	**529.0**	501.7	432.1	365.8	304.1
Tax on ordinary activities	**185.1**	178.4	156.2	141.3	120.6
Profit for the year	**342.9**	323.3	276.0	222.4	181.4
Shareholders' funds	**1918.6+**	2158.0+	1578.8	1452.4	1325.3
Earnings per share	**12.9p**	12.2p	10.4p	8.4p	6.9p
Dividend per share	**5.6p**	5.1p	4.5p	3.9p	3.4p
Dividend cover	**2.3 times**	2.4 times	2.3 times	2.2 times	2.0 times
Ordinary shareholders' interests per share	**71.7p+**	81.1 +	59.4p	54.9p	50.1p

+ including the effect of the property revaluation at 31 March 1988.

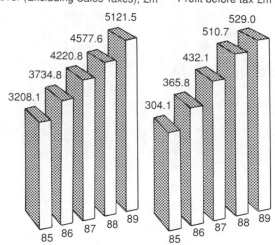

Figure B1

Financial Ratios

PROFITABILITY			1989 52 weeks	1988 53 weeks	1987 52 weeks	1986 52 weeks	1985 52 weeks
Gross Margin	Gross profit / Sales	%	**32.5**	30.9	30.2	28.4	28.8
Net Margin	Operating profit / Sales	%	**11.0**	11.1	10.3	9.7	9.5
Return on equity	Profit after tax and minority interests / Shareholders' funds	%	**17.9+**	15.0+	17.5	15.3	13.7
INTEREST COVER	Operating profit less profit sharing / Net interest charge	times	**25**	Not applicable – net interest receivable			
GEARING RATIO	Net borrowings						
	Shareholders' funds plus minority interest (i) including financial activited	%	**26.9+**	3.1+	6.8	1.9	–
	(ii) excluding financial activities	%	**16.6+**	Not applicable – no net borrrowings			

+ including the effect of the property revaluation at 31 March 1988.

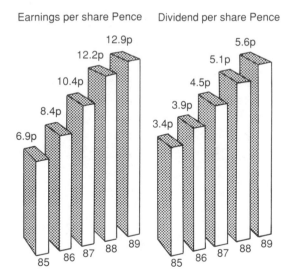

Earnings per share Pence   Dividend per share Pence

Figure B2

Operating Summary

	1989 £m	1988 £m	1987 £m	1986 £m	1985 £m
Geographical contribution to turnover					
UK	4488·6	4218·5	3844·9	3413·8	2911·5
Europe (including the Channel Islands)	128·7	132·7	120·2	94·7	82·8
North America and Far East	458·4	179·9	210·7	181·5	175·6
Export	45·8	46·5	45·0	44·8	38·2
	5121·5	4577·6	4220·8	3734·8	3208·1
Geographical contribution to operating profit					
UK	535·3	488·0	416·8	341·7	289·7
Europe (including the Channel Islands)	12·0	17·3	12·4	9·6	6·8
North America and Far East	16·4	3·2	5·4	9·7	9·5
	563·7	508·5	434·6	361·0	306·0
Number of stores					
UK	281	282	274	269	265
Europe	13	11	10	9	9
North America and Far East	371	271	263	243	227
	665	564	547	521	501
Selling area 000'sq ft					
UK	8781	8487	7942	7486	7216
Europe	402	341	308	276	268
North America and Far East	3936	2594	2545	2394	2304
	13119	11422	10795	10156	9788

	1989 £m	1988 £m	1987 £m	1986 £m	1985 £m
Employee statistics					
Average number of F.T.E.*					
UK	40476	40320	39671	38004	35909
Europe	1532	1476	1343	1241	1223
North America and Far East	8887	3896	4075	3987	3911
	50895	45692	45089	43232	41043

* Full-time equivalent

Report of the Auditors
TO THE MEMBERS OF MARKS AND SPENCER, p.l.c.

We have audited the financial statements on pages 42 to 63 in accordance with Auditing Standards.

In our opinion the financial statements give a true and fair view of the state of affairs of the Company and the Group at 31 March 1989 and of the profit and source and application of funds of the Group for the year then ended and have been properly prepared in accordance with the Companies Act 1985.

DELOITTE HASKINS & SELLS
Chartered Accountants
London 9 May 1989

Financial Calendar
FOR THE YEAR TO 31 MARCH 1990

Annual general meeting .... 13 July 1989

Final ordinary dividend for the year to
31 March 1989 to be paid .... 18 August 1989

Half-yearly results to be announced .... 31 October 1989

Interim ordinary dividend to be paid .... February 1990

Preliminary announcement of results for the year .... May 1990

Report of the Directors

The directors have pleasure in submitting their report and the financial statements of the Company and its subsidiaries for the year ended 31 March 1989.

Principal activities
Retailing
The Group sells clothing, household goods and foods under the St Michael trade mark in its chain of stores in the United Kingdom, France, Belgium, Ireland and Hong Kong. It also sells a range of St Michael merchandise and other consumer goods through a chain of stores in Canada. St Michael merchandise is also sold for export.

Following the US acquisitions, the Group sells quality clothing through Brooks Brothers in the United States and Japan, and foods through Kings Super Markets in the United States.

Financial activities
These comprise the operations of Marks and Spencer Financial Services Limited and Marks and Spencer Unit Trust Management Limited together with treasury and insurance activities.

Review of activities
The Group undertook significant expansion of its activities during the year ended 31 March 1989, both in the United Kingdom and overseas.

In April 1988, the Group acquired Brooks Brothers in the United States. Brooks Brothers primarily sells quality men's clothing and operates through 50 stores in the US and also holds 51 per cent of a joint venture company in Japan with 27 outlets. The total consideration for Brooks Brothers and certain preferential rights for food and clothing retail space in North America amounted to US $750 million.

The Group's second US acquisition was made at the end of August with the purchase of Kings Super Markets, a food chain with 16 stores, at a cost of US$110 million.

In Europe, the total number of stores was increased to 13, following the opening of two new stores in Dublin and Cork.

The Group also opened its first two stores in Hong Kong in May and October 1988.

In the United Kingdom the Company opened a further three stores, including one satellite store, and now has a total of 281 outlets. Together with extensions at existing stores, sales area has now increased from 8,487,000 square feet to 8,781,000 square feet.

Within the increasingly profitable financial activities, there are now 2.5 million cardholders and 15.5 per cent of UK sales are made using the Chargecard and Budget Account. The Group has continued to expand the range of financial services offered, through the introduction of Cardsafe, extension of personal loans and entry into unit trusts with the launch of the Marks and Spencer Investment Portfolio in October 1988.

Future developments
The Group will continue to expand into new areas of merchandise where these are considered appropriate and plans to continue its physical expansion. In the United Kingdom, capital expenditure for the year to 31 March 1990, mainly relating to new stores and extensions, is expected to be in the region of £230 million.

Profit and dividends
The profit for the financial year as shown in the financial statements amounted to £342.9 million. The directors recommend that this be dealt with as follows:

Dividends	£m
Preference shares	0·1
Ordinary shares:	
Interim dividend paid, 1·7p per share (last year 1·55p)	45·3
Final dividend proposed, 3·9p per share (last year 3·55p)	104·3
Total ordinary dividends, 5·6p per share (last year 5·1p)	149·6
Undistributed surplus	193·2

The proposed final dividend will be paid on 18 August 1989 to shareholders whose names are on the Register of Members at the close of business on 2 June 1989.

Scrip dividend scheme
Subject to passing the resolution to alter the Company's Articles of Association, referred to on page 41, it is proposed to introduce a scrip dividend scheme, enabling shareholders to choose whether to take dividends in shares instead of cash. Full details will be sent by letter to shareholders in June.

Directors
The present directors of the Company are shown on pages 6 and 7.

In accordance with Article 85 of the Company's Article of Association, Mr R Greenbury, Dr D V Atterton, Mr R A E Herbert, Mr J A Lusher and Mr D R Susman retire by rotation, being eligible, offer themselves for re-election.

Mr P H Spriddell retired on 31 August 1988.

Directors' interests in shares and debentures
The beneficial interests of the directors and their families in the shares of the Company and its subsidiaries, together with their interests as trustees of both charitable and other trusts, are shown in note 27 on page 63. Further information regarding share options is given in note 11 on pages 52 and 53.

Transactions with directors
Directors' interests in contracts or arrangements with the Company during the year are shown in note 26 on page 62.

Ordinary share capital
During the year ended 31 March 1989, 12,881,699 ordinary shares in the Company were issued as follows:

a 6,496,063 to the Trustees of the United Kingdom Employees' Profit Sharing Schemes at 176p each, in respect of the allocation from the profits of the year ended 31 March 1988.
b 662,168 under the terms of the 1977 United Kingdom Senior Staff Share Option Scheme (as adjusted for scrip issue in July 1984) at prices between 68.325p and 137p each.
c 506,607 under the terms of the 1984 United Kingdom Senior Staff Share Option Scheme at prices of 115.667p and 137p each.
d 5,216,861 under the terms of the United Kingdom Employees' Savings-Related Share Option Scheme.

At 9 May 1989, Prudential Corporation p.l.c. and its subsidiaries held 171,328,100 ordinary shares which represented 6.4 percent of the issued ordinary share capital of the Company. The Company has not received notification that any other person held more than 5.0 per cent of the issued ordinary share capital.

Increase in share capital
Following the proposal to introduce a scrip dividend scheme and because of the issue of shares annually under the various employee share schemes, it is now considered desirable to increase the Company's authorised share capital. The directors are taking this opportunity to restore the level of authorised but unissued share capital to the level it would have been but for the usage outlined above.

At present the authorised ordinary share capital amounts to 2,800,000,000 shares, of which approximately 2,675,000,000 have been issued. A resolution will be proposed at the annual general meeting increasing the authorised ordinary share capital to 3,200,000,000 shares.

The directors have no present intention of issuing any part of that capital other than for the purposes outlined above. The Company is also required by Stock Exchange regulations to state that in any event, no issue will be made which would effectively alter control of the Company without prior approval of shareholders in general meeting.

United Kingdom employees' profit sharing schemes
The amount of profit which will be allocated this year in the form of ordinary shares in the Company has been fixed at £13.1 million, representing 4.5 per cent of the earnings of 41,002 eligible employees.

Employee involvement
We have maintained our commitment to employee involvement.

Staff are kept well informed of the performance and objectives of the Company through established methods of personal briefings and regular meetings. These are supplemented by our staff newspaper, *St Michael News* and video presentations.

Communication groups in stores and warehouses are meetings of management with elected representatives of the staff. They are chaired by a member of staff. These groups provide an opportunity for staff to contribute to the everyday running of their workplace. They also ensure an additional channel for comments on Company-wide issues as minutes of meetings are circulated at Head Office and to management of divisions.

Directors and executives regularly visit stores and discuss with members of the staff matters of current interest and concern to the business. Staff representatives attend the annual general meetings and all members of the staff have the Group results explained in *St Michael News*.

This year our staff have supported a major "Quality Service" campaign aimed at improving customer service.

We have long-established Employees' Profit Sharing and Savings-Related Option Schemes, memberships of which are service related.

Employees share schemes
To encourage personal saving and to promote employee share ownership this year's Finance Bill proposes to ease various limits and restrictions on employee schemes. The directors, therefore, propose to put two resolutions to the annual general meeting in respect of the following:
a Profit Sharing Scheme: The government proposes to increase the limits for tax relief for employees in approved profits sharing schemes. At present shares may be allocated tax free up to an annual limit of £1,250 or 10 per cent of salary subject to a £5,000 ceiling. This limit may be raised to £2,000 or 10 per cent of salary and subject to a £6,000 ceiling, and resolution number 4 is designed to effect these changes.

This will not affect the criteria the Board use to determine the amount to be allocated to employees by way of profit sharing, but it allows greater tax relief, where appropriate, to individual employees.
b Save As You Earn Option Scheme: Under the Bill the maximum permissible discount at which options may be issued may be increased from 10 per cent to 20 per cent. Resolution number 5 gives effect to this and represents a continuation of the Company's philosophy of promoting employee share ownership.

The limit on the total number of shares which may be issued under all employee profit sharing and share option schemes remains unaffected by these proposals.

Equal opportunities
The Company does not discriminate on grounds of age, colour, disablement, marital status, race, religion or sex. People are given the opportunity to develop and progress according to their ability.

Disabled employees
We have continued our policy of giving disabled people full and fair consideration for all job vacancies for which they offer themselves as suitable applicants, having regard to their particular aptitudes and abilities. Training and career development opportunities are available to all employees and if necessary we endeavour to re-train any member of staff who develops a disability during employment with us.

Charitable and political contributions
Direct donations to charitable organisations amounted to £3,706,000. A political contribution was made to British United Industrialists of £25,000.

Exports
The value of goods exported directly from the United Kingdom, including shipments to overseas subsidiaries, amounted to £125.4 million (last year £126.1 million).

Alterations to Articles of Association
It is proposed to alter and update the Company's Articles of Assocation. A detailed note outlining the major changes and their reasons accompanies this report and the notice of annual general meeting.

Resolution number 3 – an explanation
The Companies Act 1985 prevents the directors of a company from allotting unissued shares without the authority of the shareholders in general meeting. In certain circumstances, this could unduly restrict the directors from carrying on the Company's business to best advantage.

Authority is therefore sought for your directors to be able to allot unissued shares if it became beneficial to the Company to do so, subject to the limitations set out in the Resolution.

The Stock Exchange no longer requires shareholders' consent to each allotment of shares for cash made otherwise than to existing shareholders in proportion to their existing shareholdings, subject to shareholders approving this Resolution.

The proposed changes to the Company's Articles of Association will enable a more simple resolution to be submitted to future annual general meetings.

Income and Corporation Taxes Act 1988
The close company provisions of this Act do not apply to the Company.

Auditors
A resolution proposing the reappointment of Deloitte Haskins & Sells as auditors to the Company will be put to the annual general meeting.

BY ORDER OF THE BOARD
The Lord Rayner, CHAIRMAN
London, 9 May 1989

Consolidated Profit and Loss Account
FOR THE YEAR ENDED 31 MARCH 1989

	Notes	1989 52 weeks £m	1988 53 weeks £m
Turnover	2	**5121·5**	4577·6
Cost of sales		**3458·5**	3163·4
Gross profit		**1663·0**	1414·2
Other expenses	3	**1099·3**	905·7
Operating profit	5	**563·7**	508·5
Net interest payable/(receivable)	4	**21·6**	(5·6)
Profit on ordinary activities before profit sharing and taxation		**542·1**	514·1
Profit sharing		**13·1**	12·4
Profit on ordinary activities before taxation	5	**529·0**	501·7
Tax on profit on ordinary activities	6	**185·1**	178·4
Profit on ordinary activities after taxation		**343·9**	323·3
Minority interests		**1·0**	—
Profit for the financial year	7	**342·9**	323·3
Dividends			
Preference shares		**0·1**	0·1
Ordinary shares:			
Interim of 1·7p per share		**45·3**	41·3
Final of 3·9p per share		**104·3**	94·4
		149·7	135·8
Undistributed surplus		**193·2**	187·5
Earnings per share	8	**12·9p**	12·2p

Balance Sheets
AT 31 MARCH 1989

	Notes	The Group		The Company	
		1989	1988	**1989**	1988
		£m	£m	**£m**	£m
Fixed assets					
Tangible assets:	12				
Land and buildings		**1947·7**	1840·9	**1841·1**	1756·1
Fixtures, fittings and equipment		**320·4**	301·3	**276·7**	275·5
Assets in the course of construction		**15·8**	8·6	**15·3**	7·6
		2283·9	2150·8	**2133·1**	2039·2
Investments	13	**—**	—	**407·5**	170·4
Net assets of financial activities	14	**71·6**	81·4	**—**	—
		2355·5	2232·2	**2540·6**	2209·6
Current assets					
Stocks	15	**364·4**	287·9	**261·4**	236·1
Debtors	16	**192·6**	130·4	**443·8**	533·3
Investments	17	**13·9**	15·5	**13·5**	15·5
Cash at bank and in hand	18	**88·2**	276·1	**25·4**	24·0
		659·1	709·9	**744·1**	808·9
Current liabilities					
Creditors: amounts falling due within one year	19	**743·1**	623·5	**615·9**	561·5
Net current assets/(liabilities)(excluding financial activities)		**(84·0)**	86·4	**128·2**	247·4
Total assets less current liabilities		**2271·5**	2318·6	**2668·8**	2457·0
Creditors: amounts falling due after more than one year	20	**343·7**	160·6	**295·0**	295·0
Provisions for liabilities and charges	21	**5·1**	—	**—**	—
Net assets		**1922·7**	2158·0	**2373·8**	2162·0
Capital and reserves					
Called up share capital	22	**669·6**	666·4	**669·6**	666·4
Share premium account	23	**34·7**	22·2	**34·7**	22·2
Revaluation reserve	23	**456·5**	468·7	**479·4**	479·5
Profit and loss account	23	**757·8**	1000·7	**1190·1**	993·9
Shareholders' funds		**1918·6**	2158·0	**2373·8**	2162·0
Minority interests		**4·1**	—	**—**	—
Total capital employed		**1922·7**	2158·0	**2373·8**	2162·0

Approved by the Board
9 May 1989
The Lord Rayner, CHAIRMAN
J K Oates, FINANCE DIRECTOR

Consolidated Source and Application of Funds
FOR THE YEAR ENDED 31 MARCH 1989

	Notes	1989 £m	1988 £m
Cash and short-term funds at 1 April		**265·9**	66·3
Source of funds			
Arising from trading			
Profit on ordinary activities before taxation		**529·0**	501·7
Depreciation		**103·4**	83·5
Sales of fixed assets		**8·0**	4·7
		640·4	589·9
From other sources			
US$ Promissory note 1998	24	**239·4**	—
9·75% Guaranteed notes 1993		—	150·0
Shares issued under employees' share schemes		**15·7**	10·3
Cash and investments in US subsidiaries acquired		**6·9**	—
Decrease/(increase) in net assets of financial activities excluding taxation (see below)		**8·9**	(19·4)
Miscellaneous		**2·7**	(3·5)
		1179·9	793·6
Application of funds			
Payment of dividends		**139·8**	123·7
Payment of taxation		**186·1**	157·5
Purchase of fixed assets		**208·2**	210·7
Transfer of fixed assets from financial activities		—	7·5
Acquisition of US subsidiaries	24	**472·2**	—
Increase in inter-company funding of financial activities		**85·0**	35·0
		1091·3	534·4
Increase/(decrease) in working capital			
Stock		**32·5**	32·5
Debtors		**29·3**	14·0
Creditors under one year (excluding taxation and dividends)		**(8·9)**	(57·5)
Group relief payable to financial activities		—	4·3
		52·9	(6·7)
		1144·2	527·7
Cash and short-term funds at 31 March		**35·7**	265·9

Cash and short-term funds comprise cash at bank and in hand and current asset investments less bank loans and overdrafts.

Decrease/(increase) in net assets of financial activities excluding taxation	1989 £m	1988 £m
Capital repayments on leases	**3·2**	6·1
Disposal of leasing activities	**19·2**	2·7
	22·4	8·8
Net expenditure on fixed assets	**(1·3)**	(3·8)
Transfer of fixed assets to fellow subsidiary	—	7·5
Depreciation	**1·5**	1·5
Increase in debtors	**(45·0)**	(86·9)
Deferred tax eliminated on sale of leasing subsidiaries	**(4·1)**	—
Decrease in group relief receivable	—	4·3
Increase in bank loans, overdrafts and inter-company funding less cash	**40·4**	43·9
(Increase)/decrease in other working capital	**(5·0)**	5·3
Net movement	**8·9**	(19·4)

Accounting Policies

Basis of accounting
The financial statements are drawn up on the historical cost basis of accounting, modified to include the valuation of certain United Kingdom properties at 31 March 1988.

Basis of consolidation
The Group financial statements incorporate the financial statements of:
a The retailing activities of Marks and Spencer p.l.c. and its UK and overseas subsidiaries for the year to 31 March. The Group balance sheet includes all the assets and liabilities of subsidiaries acquired during the year. The Group profit for the year includes only that proportion of the results arising since the effective date of acquisition.
b The financial activities of the Group's wholly owned subsidiaries to 31 March. In order to reflect the different nature of the business of the financial activities and so present fairly the Group's state of affairs, the assets and liabilities of such activities are shown as a net investment in the Group balance sheet and are analysed separately in note 14 on pages 56 and 57.

Goodwill
Goodwill arising on consolidation, which represents the excess of the consideration given over the fair value of the net tangible assets acquired, is written off on acquisition against reserves. The net assets of companies acquired are incorporated into the consolidated accounts at their values to the Group and after adjustments to bring the accounting policies of companies acquired into alignment with those of the Group.

Deferred taxation
Deferred taxation is provided on the liability method, to the extent that it is probable that a liability will crystallise. It is provided on certain items of income and expenditure included in the profit and loss account in different years from those in which they are assessed for taxation purposes.

Depreciation
Depreciation is provided to write off the cost or valuation of tangible fixed assets by equal annual instalments at the following rates:
Freehold and leasehold land and buildings over 50 years – 1 per cent (see *a* below)
Leasehold land and buildings under 50 years – Over the remaining period of the lease
Fixtures, fittings and equipment – 10 to 33⅓ per cent according to the estimated life of the asset.

a Depreciation is not provided on a freehold and long leasehold properties where, in the opinion of the directors, the residual values of those properties are such that any depreciation charge would be immaterial.
b Depreciation is charged on all additions to depreciating assets in the year of purchase.

Foreign currencies
The trading results of overseas subsidiaries have been translated using average rates of exchange ruling during the financial year.

The balance sheet of overseas subsidiaries have been translated into sterling at the rates of exchange ruling at 31 March, except for those assets and liabilities where a forward exchange contract has been arranged, in which case this forward rate is used.

Exchange differences arising between the translation into sterling of the net assets of these subsidiaries at rates ruling at the beginning and end of the year are dealt with through reserves.

The cost of the Company's investment in overseas subsidiaries and tangible fixed assets of overseas branches are translated at the rate ruling at the date of investment. All other foreign currency assets and liabilities of the Company and its United Kingdom subsidiaries are translated into sterling at the rate ruling at 31 March, except in those instances where a forward exchange contract has been arranged in which case this forward rate is used. These exchange differences are dealt with through the profit and loss account.

Transactions during the year between the Company and its subsidiaries, customers and suppliers are translated into sterling at the rate of exchange ruling on the date of the transaction. All profits and losses on exchange realised during the year are dealt with through the profit and loss account.

Pension contributions
The Group operates pension schemes for the benefit of all its UK employees and for the majority of the staff overseas. The funds of the schemes are administered by Trustees and are separate from the Group. Independent actuaries complete valuations at least every three years and, in accordance with their recommendations, annual contributions are paid to the schemes so as to secure the benefits set out in the rules and the periodic augmentation of current pensions. The cost of these is charged against profits on a systematic basis over the service lives of the employees.

Repairs and renewals
Expenditure on repairs, renewals and minor items of equipment is written off in the year in which it is incurred.

Stocks
Stocks and work in progress are valued at the lower of cost and net realisable value.

Retail stocks consist of goods for resale and cost is computed by deducting the gross profit margin from the selling value of stock.
When computing net realisable value an allowance is made for future markdowns.

The cost of work in progress comprises materials, labour and attributable overheads.

Trading results
The trading results include transactions at stores up to and including the nearest Saturday to 31 March. All other transactions are included up to 31 March in each year.

Notes to the Financial Statements

1 Trading period

The results for the year comprise store sales and related costs for the 52 weeks to 1 April 1989 compared to 53 weeks last year. All other activities are for the year to 31 March 1989. The results of Brooks Brothers and Kings Super Markets have been included from the dates of acquisition, the respective periods being 11 months and seven months.

2 Turnover

a Retailing
Turnover represents goods sold to customers outside the Group, less returns and sales taxes.

b Financial activities
Financial activities comprise treasury, insurance and financial services. Financial services include chargecard, budget accounts, personal loans and the unit trust. Turnover represents interest and other income attributable to these activities.

c Analysis of turnover – by activity and geographical market. (i) Retailing	**1989** **£m**	1988 £m
United Kingdom stores	**4425·0**	4173·6
Overseas stores:		
Europe	**127·8**	131·7
North America and Far East	**458·4**	179·9
	586·2	311·6
Export sales outside the Group:		
Europe	**37·0**	34·0
America	**3·4**	5·0
Africa	**1·8**	2·5
Far East	**3·6**	5·0
	45·8	46·5
	5057·0	4531·7
(ii) Financial activities	**64·5**	45·9
	5121·5	4577·6

Stores sales for North America and the Far East include £262.0 million in respect of the U.S. subsidiaries acquired during the year. The turnover attributable to financial activities arise wholly within the United Kingdom and the Channel Islands.

3 Other expenses

The directors consider that the nature of the business is such that the analysis of expenses shown below is more informative than that set out in the formats in the Companies Act 1985.

	1989 £m	1988 £m
Other expenses comprise:		
Staff costs (see also note 9)	594·7	502·4
Occupancy costs including rentals under operating leases	145·2	112·4
— Hire of plant and machinery of £11·0 million (last year £4·4 million)		
— Other £47·9 million (last year £39·0 million)		
Other costs including Auditor's remuneration of £0·6 million (last year £0·4 million)	208·0	170·4
	947·9	785·2
Repairs, renewals and maintenance of properties, fixtures, fittings and equipment	48·2	38·8
Depreciation of tangible fixed assets	104·9	85·0
Loss on sale of tangible fixed assets	4·6	2·0
	1105·6	911·0
Less: Other income	6·3	5·3
	1099·3	905·7

Other income includes profits on the disposal of leasing activities of £0·9 million (last year £1·9 million).

4 Interest

	1989 £m	1988 £m
Interest payable (see below)	37·9	5·8
Bank and other interest receivable	(16·3)	(11 4)
	21·6	(5·6)
Interest payable by the Group comprises:		
Bank loans and overdrafts	11·1	9·2
Debenture stocks — repayable within 5 years	0·3	0·3
Debenture stocks — repayable in more than 5 years	2·9	2·9
9·75% Guaranteed notes 1993	14·6	0·6
8·25% Guaranteed bonds 1996	9·5	9·2
US$ Promissory note 1998	20·7	—
	59·1	22·2
Classified as:		
Interest payable	37·9	5·8
Cost of sales in the trading results of the financial activities	21·2	16·4
	59·1	22·2
Included as turnover in the trading results of the financial activities:		
Bank and other interest receivable	52·6	39·1
Income from finance leases	0·4	1·4
Profit on sales of current asset investments	—	0·2

5 Profit on ordinary activities before taxation

	1989 £m	1988 £M
This arises as follows:		
United Kingdom	535.3	488.0
Europe	12.0	17.3
North America and Far East (see below)	16.4	3.2
Operating profit	563.7	508.5
Interest (payable)/receivable	(21.6)	5.6
UK profit sharing	(13.1)	(12.4)
	529.0	501.7
and can be analysed between:		
Retailing	517.6	497.5
Financial activities	11.4	4.2
	529.0	501.7

Operating profits for North America and the Far East comprise the following:

US and Far East		
Brooks Brothers	23.1	–
Kings Super Markets	3.1	–
Hong Kong	0.5	(0.9)
Corporate expenses	(1.4)	(0.7)
	25.3	(1.6)
Canada		
Marks and Spencer division	(4.6)	0.4
Peoples	(3.1)	0.4
D'Allaird's	2.9	4.8
Corporate expenses	(1.2)	(0.8)
	(6.0)	4.8
Store closure costs	(2.9)	–
	(8.9)	4.8

6 Tax on profit on ordinary activities

The taxation charge comprises:		
Current taxation		
UK corporation tax at 35%	180.3	180.8
Overseas tax	4.2	6.6
Deferred taxation	0.6	(9.0)
	185.1	178.4

7 Profit for the financial year

As permitted by Section 228 (7) of the Companies Act 1985, the profit and loss account of the parent company is not presented as part of these financial statements.

The consolidated profit of £342.9 million (last year £323.3 million) includes £346.0 million (last year £315.4 million) which is dealt with in the financial statements of the parent company.

8 Earnings per share

The calculation of earnings per ordinary share is based on earnings of £342.8 million (last year £323.2 million) after deducting minority interests and preference dividends, and on 2,667,387,290 ordinary shares (last year 2,658,358,978), being the weighted average of shares in issue during the year ended 31 March 1989.

At 31 March 1989, directors and senior employees held unexercised options in respect of 15,845,070 ordinary shares (last year 9,275,002). There were options outstanding under the Savings-Related Share Option Scheme in respect of 38,967,756 shares (last year 40,180,747). If all outstanding options had been exercised, the dilution of earnings per share would not have been material.

9 Directors and employees

a The number of directors and employees of the Company performing their duties mainly within the United Kingdom whose emoluments (excluding pension contributions) were within the following ranges, are:

Gross Emoluments £	Directors 1989	1988	Employees 1989	1988	Gross Emoluments £	Directors 1989	1988	Employees 1989	1988
420001–425000	1	–	–	–	85001–90000	–	–	3	–
345001–350000	–	1	–	–	80001–85000	–	–	5	2
320001–325000	1	–	–	–	75001–80000	1	–	4	4
260001–265000	–	1	–	–	70001–75000	–	–	3	6
245001–250000	1	–	–	–	65001–70000	–	–	13	3
200001–205000	1	1	–	–	60001–65000	–	–	14	10
170001–175000	1	–	–	–	55001–60000	–	–	32	11
160001–165000	–	1	–	–	50001–55000	–	–	47	26
150001–155000	2	–	–	–	45001–50000	–	–	80	36
145001–150000	2	1	–	–	40001–45000	–	1	93	78
130001–135000	1	4	–	–	35001–40000	–	–	182	125
125001–130000	–	1	–	–	30001–35000	–	1	326	251
105001–110000	–	–	1	–	15001–20000	5	–		
100001–105000	–	1	2	–	10001 15000	–	4		
95001–100000	–	–	3	–	5001–10000	–	1		
90001– 95000	–	–	3	–					

Included in the above is the remuneration of the Chairman £424,401 (last year £349,619). The Chairman is also the highest paid director.

Total directors' emoluments, including pension scheme contributions, were £2.8 million (last year £2.5 million). Payments to directors after leaving service amounted to £0.2 million (last year £0.5 million).

b The average weekly number of employees of the Group during the year was:

		1989	1988
UK Stores:	Management and supervisory categories	6501	6333
	Other	51768	50404
UK Head Office:	Management and supervisory categories	2275	2243
	Other	2031	2114
Financial Services:	Management and supervisory categories	48	41
	Other	529	417
Overseas		13611	6898
		76313	68450

If the number of part-time hours worked was converted on the basis of a full working week, the equivalent average number of full-time employees would have been 50 895 (last year 45 692).

9 Directors and employees continued

The aggregate remuneration and associated costs of Group employees were:	1989 £m	1988 £m
Wages and salaries	489.5	408.3
Social security costs	36.3	28.5
Pension costs	53.5	49.4
Staff welfare and other personnel costs	24.9	16.2
	604.2	502.4
Classified as:		
Other expenses – staff costs	594.7	502.4
Manufacturing cost of sales	9.5	–
	604.2	502.4

10 Pension costs

The Group operates a number of defined benefit pension schemes throughout the world.

The funds of the schemes are administered by Trustees and are separate from the Group. A complete valuation of each scheme is undertaken by independent qualified actuaries at least every three years, and the annual contributions to the schemes are paid in accordance with their recommendations.

The total pension costs charged for the year in these financial statements amounted to £53.5 million, of which £3.5 million was charged in respect of overseas schemes.

The most recent valuation of the UK scheme was undertaken as at 1 April 1986. The results of this have been projected forward to 1 April 1988.

The assumptions which have the most significant effect on the results of the valuation are the rate current salaries will increase and the return the scheme will earn on its assets. It was assumed for the 1988 projection that salaries would increase by 8.0 per cent per annum and that the scheme's investments will earn 10.0 per cent per annum.

On this basis the actuarial value of the assets of the scheme was £890 million and this was sufficient to cover all of the benefits that had accrued to members, after allowing for expected future increases in earnings.

All overseas schemes have been subject to a valuation by an independent qualified actuary within the last three years. In each case, the valuation stated that the actuarial value of the assets was sufficient to cover the benefits accrued to members, after allowing for future increases in earnings.

As shown in note 16 to the financial statements, the Company has pre-paid a contribution of £52.1 million to the UK scheme.

11 Share schemes

a Profit sharing:

The Trustees of the United Kingdom Employees' Profit Sharing Schemes have been allocated £13.1 million (last year £12.4 million) with which to subscribe for ordinary shares in the Company. The price of each share is 175p, being the average market price for the three dealing days immediately following the announcement of the results for the year ended 31 March 1989.

b United Kingdom Senior Staff Share Option Schemes:

Under the terms of the 1984 and 1987 schemes, following the announcement of the Company's results, the Board may offer options to purchase ordinary shares in the Company to directors, and senior employees at the higher of the nominal value of the shares and the average market price for three consecutive dealing days preceding the date of the offer. The 1977 scheme has now expired and no further options may be granted under this scheme. Although options may be granted under both the 1984 and 1987 schemes, the maximum option value that can be exercised under each scheme is limited to four times earnings. Outstanding options granted under all senior schemes are as follows:

Options granted	Number of shares 1989	1988	Option price	Option dates
(1977 Scheme)				
May 1982	85126	281642	75.375p	May 1985–May 1989
May 1983	900720	965010	107.475p	May 1986–May 1990
May 1984	152888	152888	127.625p	May 1987–May 1991
May 1985	2448185	2593019	137.000p	May 1988–May 1992
May 1986	1074984	1074984	211.000p	May 1989–May 1993
May 1987	1274358	1274358	232.333p	May 1990–May 1994
(1984 Scheme)				
October 1984	3041527	3414513	115.667p	Oct 1987–Oct 1994
May 1985	1509711	1643332	137.000p	May 1988–May 1995
May 1986	1000513	1000513	211.000p	May 1989–May 1996
May 1987	1270988	1270988	232.333p	May 1990–May 1997
October 1987	933157	933157	202.000p	Oct 1990–Oct 1997
May 1988	3380789	–	176.000p	May 1991–May 1998
October 1988	64234	–	158.000p	Oct 1991–Oct 1998
(1987 Scheme)				
October 1987	933157	933157	202.000p	Oct 1990–Oct 1994
May 1988	6592716	–	176.000p	May 1991–May 1995
October 1988	64234	–	158.000p	Oct 1991–Oct 1995

c United Kingdom Employees' Savings-Related Share Option Scheme:

Under the terms of the scheme the Board may offer options to purchase ordinary shares in the Company once in each financial year to those employees who enter into an Inland Revenue approved Save As You Earn (SAYE) savings contract. The price at which options may be offered is 90 per cent of the market price for three consecutive dealing days preceding the date of offer. The options may normally be exercised during the period of six months after the completion of the SAYE contract, either five or seven years after entering the scheme.

Outstanding options granted under this scheme are as follows:

Options granted	Number of shares 1989	1988	Option price
January 1982	2344797	6404827	49.0p
January 1983	1701844	2176602	88.5p
January 1984	1846209	2536961	93.5p
January 1985	6151416	6695069	103.0p
January 1986	4498688	4941086	163.0p
January 1987	8507371	9402223	175.0p
January 1988	7375912	8023979	182.0p
January 1989	6541519	–	143.0p

12 Fixed assets – tangible assets

a The Group

	Freehold £m	Long leasehold £m	Short leasehold £m	Total £m	Fixtures, fitting & equipment £m	Assets in the course of construction £m	Total fixed assets £m
Cost or valuation							
At 1 April 1988	1131.6	615.6	118.6	1865.8	507.0	8.6	2381.4
Subsidiaries acquired	13.4	–	10.6	24.0	22.4	3.1	49.5
Additions	19.5	15.5	5.0	40.0	98.4	69.8	208.2
Transfers from assets in the course of construction	35.6	18.5	8.5	62.6	3.3	(65.9)	–
Transfers	0.2	(1.4)	0.7	(0.5)	0.5	–	–
Disposals	(3.0)	(0.5)	(4.4)	(7.9)	(40.7)	–	(48.6)
Differences on exchange	(0.7)	2.2	4.4	5.9	5.6	0.2	11.7
At 31 March 1989	**1196.6**	**649.9**	**143.4**	**1989.9**	**596.5**	**15.8**	**2602.2**
At valuation	839.5	469.9	18.3	1327.7	–	–	1327.7
At cost	357.1	180.0	125.1	662.2	596.5	15.8	1274.5
	1196.6	649.9	143.4	1989.9	596.5	15.8	2602.2
Accumulated depreciation							
At 1 April 1988	4.5	1.6	18.8	24.9	205.7	–	230.6
Subsidiaries acquired	0.8	–	7.3	8.1	10.8	–	18.9
Depreciation for the year	0.1	1.3	7.0	8.4	95.0	–	103.4
Disposals	–	–	(2.0)	(2.0)	(38.6)	–	(40.6)
Differences on exchange	0.1	0.9	1.8	2.8	3.2	–	6.0
At 31 March 1989	**5.5**	**3.8**	**32.9**	**42.2**	**276.1**	**–**	**318.3**
Net book value							
At 31 March 1989	**1191.1**	**646.1**	**110.5**	**1947.7**	**320.4**	**15.8**	**2283.9**
At 31 March 1988	1127.1	614.0	99.8	1840.9	301.3	8.6	2150.8

b The Company

	Freehold £m	Long leasehold £m	Short leasehold £m	Total £m	Fixtures, fittings & equipment £m	Assets in the course of construction £m	Total fixed assets £m
Cost or valuation							
At 1 April 1988	1075.4	614.9	75.3	1765.6	455.1	7.6	2228.3
Additions	19.1	12.8	0.5	32.4	87.0	67.8	187.2
Transfers from assets in the course of construction	35.5	16.9	7.7	60.1	–	(60.1)	–
Transfers	0.7	(0.8)	0.1	–	–	–	–
Disposals	(2.9)	(0.5)	(0.7)	(4.1)	(37.4)	–	(41.5)
At 31 March 1989	**1127.8**	**643.3**	**82.9**	**1854.0**	**504.7**	**15.3**	**2374.0**
At valuation	839.5	469.9	18.3	1327.7	–	–	1327.7
At cost	288.3	173.4	64.6	526.3	504.7	15.3	1046.3
	1127.8	643.3	82.9	1854.0	504.7	15.3	2374.0
Accumulated depreciation							
At 1 April 1988	2.4	1.6	5.5	9.5	179.6	–	189.1
Depreciation for the year	–	–	3.5	3.5	85.2	–	88.7
Disposals	–	–	(0.1)	(0.1)	(36.8)	–	(36.9)
At 31 March 1989	**2.4**	**1.6**	**8.9**	**12.9**	**228.0**	**–**	**240.9**
Net book value							
At 31 March 1989	**1125.4**	**641.7**	**74.0**	**1841.1**	**276.7**	**15.3**	**2133.1**
At 31 March 1988	1073.0	613.3	69.8	1756.1	275.5	7.6	2039.2

(i) Gerald Eve, chartered surveyors, valued the Company's freehold and leasehold properties in the United Kingdom and the Isle of Man as at 31 March 1982. This valuation was on the basis of open market value for existing use. The directors, after consultation with Gerald Eve, valued those of the Company's properties as at 31 March 1988 which had been valued as at 31 March 1982 (excluding subsequent additions and adjusted for disposals). The directors' valuation was incorporated into the financial statements at 31 March 1988.

(ii) If the Company's land and buildings had not been valued at 31 March 1982 and 31 March 1988 their net book value would have been:	1989 £m	1988 £m
At valuation at 31 March 1975	360.6	361.3
At cost	756.0	668.1
At 31 March 1989	1116.6	1029.4
Accumulated depreciation	58.2	56.0
	1058.4	973.4

The Company also valued its land and buildings in 1955 and in 1964. In the opinion of the directors unreasonable expense would be incurred in obtaining the original costs of the assets valued in those years and in 1975.

(iii) The Company does not maintain detailed records of cost and depreciation for fixtures, fittings and equipment. The accumulated cost figures represent reasonable estimates of the sums involved.

13 Fixed assets – investments

The Company
a These investments comprise unlisted investments in and loans to subsidiaries.

	Shares in subsidiaries £m	Loans £m	Total £m
Cost			
At 1 April 1988	141.4	29.0	170.4
Additions	281.7	–	281.7
Disposals/repayments	(40.9)	(3.7)	(44.6)
At 31 March 1989	**382.2**	**25.3**	**407.5**

b The Company's principal subsidiaries are set out below. A schedule of interests in all subsidiaries is filed with the Annual Return.

	Principal activity	Country of incorporation and operation	Proportion of ordinary shares held by: The Company	A subsidiary
Marks and Spencer (Nederland) BV	Holding Company	The Netherlands	100%	–
Marks and Spencer (France) SA	Chain Store	France	–	100%
Marks and Spencer (Ireland) Limited	Chain Store	Ireland	–	100%
M&S Export (Ireland) Limited	Export	Ireland	–	100%
SA Marks and Spencer (Belgium) NV	Chain Store	Belgium	–	100%
Marks & Spencer Holdings Canada Inc	Holding Company	Canada	–	100%
Marks & Spencer Canada Inc	Chain Store	Canada	–	100%
Marks and Spencer Finance (Nederland) BV	Finance	The Netherlands	–	100%
MS Insurance Limited	Insurance	Guernsey	–	100%
Marks and Spencer US Holdings Inc	Holding Company	United States	100%	–
Brooks Brothers Inc	Chain Store	United States	–	100%
Brooks Brothers (Japan) Limited	Chain Store	Japan	–	51%

B. Fixed, assets – investment continued

	Principal activity	Country of incorporation and operation	Proportion of ordinary shares held by: The Company	A subsidiary
Kings Super Markets Inc	Chain Store	United States	–	100%
Marks & Spencer Services Inc	Management Services	United States	–	100%
Marks & Spencer Finance Inc	Finance	United States	–	100%
Marks and Spencer Retail Financial Services Holdings Limited	Holding Company	England	100%	–
Marks and Spencer Financial Services Limited	Finance	England	–	100%
Marks and Spencer Unit Trust Management Limited	Finance	England	–	100%
St Michael Finance Limited	Finance	England	100%	–
Marks and Spencer Property Holdings Limited	Property	England	100%	–
Marks and Spencer Property Developments Limited	Property Development	England	–	100%
Marks and Spencer Finance plc	Finance	England	100%	–
Marks and Spencer Export Corporation Limited	Management Services	England	100%	–

14   Net assets of financial activities

	1989 £m	1988 £m
Fixed assets		
Land and buildings	0.1	0.2
Fixtures, fittings and equipment	3.7	3.8
	3.8	4.0
Current assets		
Debtors	288.8	266.2
Listed investments – market value £8.5 million (last year £6.6 million)	8.8	6.5
Cash at bank and in hand	8.1	21.9
	305.7	294.6
Current liabilities		
Creditors: amounts falling due within one year	17.8	77.1
Net current assets	287.9	217.5
Total assets less current liabilities	291.7	221.5
Creditors: amounts falling due after more than one year	220.1	135.1
Provisions for liabilities and charges:		
Deferred taxation	–	5.0
Net assets	71.6	81.4

a Fixed assets	Land & buildings Short leasehold £m	Fixtures, fittings & equipment £m	Total fixed assets £m
Cost			
At 1 April 1988	0.4	6.4	6.8
Additions	–	1.5	1.5
Disposals	(0.1)	(0.7)	(0.8)
At 31 March 1989	**0.3**	**7.2**	**7.5**

14 Net assets of financial activities continued

a Fixed assets	Land & buildings Short leasehold £m	Fixtures, fittings & equipment £m	Total fixed assets £m
Accumulated depreciation			
At 1 April 1988	0.2	2.6	2.8
Depreciation for the year	–	1.5	1.5
Disposals	–	(0.6)	(0.6)
At 31 March 1989	**0.2**	**3.5**	**3.7**
Net book value			
At 31 March 1989	**0.1**	**3.7**	**3.8**
At 31 March 1988	0.2	3.8	4.0

b Debtors	1989 £m	1988 £m
Amounts falling due within one year:		
Trade debtors	**130.3**	108.8
Net investment in finance leases	–	9.5
Other debtors	**3.7**	3.7
Prepayments and accrued income	**1.5**	3.9
	135.5	125.9
Amounts falling due after more than one year:		
Trade debtors	**153.3**	127.4
Net investment in finance leases	–	12.9
	288.8	266.2

c Creditors: amounts falling due within one year:		
Bank loans and overdrafts	**8.6**	8.7
Trade creditors	**3.9**	4.1
Bills of exchange payable	–	56.0
Current taxation	**4.2**	2.4
Other creditors	–	0.9
Accruals and deferred income	**1.1**	5.0
	7.8	77.1

d Creditors: amounts falling due after more than one year:		
Payable between one and two years:		
Taxation	**0.1**	0.1
Repayable between two and five years:		
Group borrowings utilised in financial activities (see note 20)	**120.0**	–
Repayable in five years or more:		
Group borrowings utilised in financial activities (see note 20)	**100.0**	135.0
	220.1	135.1

e Total rentals receivable during the year in respect of finance leases	**3.5**	7.5

f The provision for deferred taxation arises on: The excess of capital allowances over depreciaton on assets leased to third parties	–	5.0

The decrease in the provision for deferred taxation of £5.0 million is represented by a £0.9 million transfer to the profit and loss account and a further £4.1 million eliminated on the sale of Baker Street Leasing Limited on 22 June 1988.

15   Stocks

	The Group		The Company	
	1989 **£m**	1988 £m	**1989** **£m**	1988 £m
Retail stocks	**346.5**	285.7	**253.5**	236.1
Work in progress	**10.1**	2.2	**7.9**	–
Raw materials	**7.8**	–	–	–
	364.4	287.9	**261.4**	236.1

16   Debtors

	The Group		The Company	
	1989 **£m**	1988 £m	**1989** **£m**	1988 £m
Amounts falling due withine one year:				
Trade debtors	**47.1**	16.0	**22.6**	14.5
Amounts owed by Group companies	**–**	–	**293.3**	410.3
Other debtors	**35.7**	22.0	**26.6**	18.6
Prepayments and accrued income	**81.1**	67.5	**70.0**	63.8
	163.9	105.5	**412.5**	507.2
Amounts falling due after more than one year:				
Advance corporation tax recoverable on the proposed final dividend	**34.7**	31.5	**34.7**	31.5
Deferred taxation provision arising on short-term timing differences	**(23.1)**	(21.6)	**(20.1)**	(19.8)
	11.6	9.9	**14.6**	11.7
Other debtors	**17.1**	15.0	**16.7**	14.4
	28.7	24.9	**31.3**	26.1
	192.6	130.4	**443.8**	533.3

Trade debtors include advances to suppliers of £12.4 million (last year £4.0 million) against bills of exchange drawn on the Company in respect of merchandise to be delivered between April and September 1989.

Other debtors include loans to employees, the majority of which are connected with house purchases. These include a loan to an officer of the Company, the balance of which amounted to £8,464 at 31 March 1989 (last year £10,856).

Prepayments and accrued income include £52.1 million respect of the Pension Scheme for 1989/90 (last year £50.9 million in respect of 1988/89).

The increase in the Group's provision for deferred taxation of £1.5 million (last year decrease of £0.4 million) is represented by a transfer from the profit and loss account.

17   Current assets – investments

	The Group		The Company	
	1989 **£m**	1988 £m	**1989** **£m**	1988 £m
Certificates of tax deposit	**13.5**	15.5	**13.5**	15.5
Other	**0.4**	–	–	–
	13.9	15.5	**13.5**	15.5

18   Cash at bank and in hand

Cash at bank includes short-term deposits with banks and other financial institutions.

19   Creditors – amounts falling due within one year:

	The Group 1989 £m	The Group 1988 £m	The Company 1989 £m	The Company 1988 £m
Bank loans, overdrafts and commercial paper	**66.4**	25.7	**10.1**	–
Trade creditors	**153.2**	134.6	**124.6**	124.2
Bills of exchange payable	**11.1**	5.4	**11.1**	5.4
Amounts owed to Group companies	–	–	**13.7**	1.3
Taxation	**194.7**	194.9	**194.6**	190.4
Social security and other taxes	**27.2**	26.3	**22.3**	24.1
Other creditors	**68.1**	63.8	**55.8**	52.3
Accruals and deferred income	**118.1**	78.4	**79.4**	69.4
Proposed final dividend	**104.3**	94.4	**104.3**	94.4
	743.1	623.5	**615.9**	561.5

20   Creditors – amounts falling due after more than one year:

	The Group 1989 £m	The Group 1988 £m	The Company 1989 £m	The Company 1988 £m
Repayable between one and two years:				
Debenture loan – secured				
5½%–1985/1990	**5.0**	–	**5.0**	–
Repayable between two and five years:				
Debenture loan – secured				
5½%–1985/1990	–	5.0	–	5.0
9.75% Guaranteed notes 1993	**150.0**	–	–	–
Amounts owed to Group companies	–	–	**150.0**	–
Bank and other loans	**0.5**	0.6	–	–
Other creditors	**1.6**	–	–	–
Repayable in five years or more:				
Debenture loans – secured				
6½%–1989/1994	**10.0**	10.0	**10.0**	10.0
7¼%–1993/1998	**15.0**	15.0	**15.0**	15.0
7¾%–1995/2000	**15.0**	15.0	**15.0**	15.0
8.25% Guaranteed bonds 1996	**100.0**	100.0	–	–
9.75% Guaranteed notes 1993	–	150.0	–	–
US$ Promissory note 1998	**266.6**	–	–	–
Amounts owed to Group companies	–	–	**100.0**	250.0
	563.7	295.6	**295.0**	295.0
Less borrowings utilised in financial activities (see note 14)	**(220.0)**	(135.0)	–	–
	343.7	160.6	**295.0**	295.0

Debenture loans comprise first mortgage debenture stocks which are secured on certain freehold and leasehold properties of the Company: The Company is entitled to redeem the whole or any part of each stock at par, at any time between the two dates shown above.

During the year, the Group partly financed the acquisition of Brooks Brothers with a US$450 million ten year promissory note issued by a subsidiary of, and guaranteed by, Marks and Spencer, p.l.c.

21 Provisions for liabilities and charges

The Group	£m
At 1 April 1988	–
Arising on acquisition of US subsidiaries	5.1
At 31 March 1989	**5.1**

The Company has no provisions for liabilities and charges.

22 Called up share capital

	The Company 1989 £m	1988 £m
Authorised:		
2,800,000,000 ordinary shares of 25p each	**700.0**	700.0
350,000 7.0% cumulative preference shares of £1 each	**0.4**	0.4
1,000,000 4.9% cumulative preference shares of £1 each	**1.0**	1.0
	701.4	701.4
Allotted, called up and fully paid:		
2,672,972,104 ordinary shares of 25p each (last year 2,660,090,405)	**668.2**	665.0
350,000 7.0% cumulative preference shares of £1 each	**0.4**	0.4
1,000,000 4.9% cumulative preference shares of £1 each	**1.0**	1.0
	669.6	666.4

12 881 699 ordinary shares having a nominal value of £3.2 million were allotted during the year under the terms of the Company's share schemes which are described in note 11. The aggregate consideration received was £15.7 million. Contingent rights the allotment of shares are also described in note 11.

23 Shareholders' funds

	The Group 1989 £m	1988 £m	The Company 1989 £m	1988 £m
Called up share capital (see note 22)	**669.6**	666.4	**669.6**	666.4
Reserves				
Share premium account:				
At 1 April 1988	**22.2**	13.5	**22.2**	13.5
Movement during the year	**12.5**	8.7	**12.5**	8.7
At 31 March 1989	**34.7**	22.2	**34.7**	22.2
Revaluation reserve:				
At 1 April 1988	**468.7**	86.4	**479.5**	86.7
Property revaluation	–	392.8	–	392.8
Exchange movement	**(12.2)**	(10.5)	**(0.1)**	–
At 31 March 1989	**456.5**	468.7	**479.4**	479.5
Profit and loss account:				
At 1 April 1988	**1000.7**	814.1	**993.9**	814.3
Goodwill written off	**(430.2)**	–	–	–
Undistributed surplus for the year	**193.2**	187.5	**196.2**	179.6
Exchange movement	**(5.9)**	(0.9)	–	–
At 31 March 1989	**757.8**	1000.7	**1190.1**	993.9
Shareholders' funds	**1918.6**	2158.0	**2373.8**	2162.0

24 Acquisitions

The net tangible assets acquired and consideration paid for the US subsidiaries comprised:

	Net tangible assets acquired £m	Fair value adjustments £m	Total £m
Net tangible assets acquired:			
Tangible fixed assets	46.3	(15.7)	30.6
	46.3	(15.7)	30.6
Stocks	43.4	0.6	44.0
Debtors	30.7	0.5	31.2
Cash and investments	6.9	–	6.9
Creditors: amounts falling due within one year	(50.1)	(10.2)	(60.3)
Net current assets	30.9	(9.1)	21.8
Total assets less current liabilities	77.2	(24.8)	52.4
Creditors: amounts falling due after more than one year	(2.0)	–	(2.0)
Deferred taxation	(0.9)	0.9	–
Provisions for reorganisation	–	(5.1)	(5.1)
Minority interest	(3.3)	–	(3.3)
Net assets	71.0	(29.0)	42.0
Financed by:			
Cash			232.8
US$ Promissory note 1998 (converted at rate of exchange ruling at date of acquisition)			239.4
			472.2
Goodwill			430.2

Adjustment have been made to the book values of the net tangible assets acquired to reflect their fair values to the Group and to provide for reorganisation costs arising as a consequence of the acquisitions.

25 Commitments and contingent liabilities

	The Group 1989 £m	The Group 1988 £m	The Company 1989 £m	The Company 1988 £m
a Commitments in respect of properties in the course of development	67.0	91.9	59.8	69.4
b Capital expenditure authorised by the directors but not yet contracted	243.0	253.3	235.7	249.8
c Deferred taxation not provided on the excess of capital allowances over depreciation on tangible assets	119.4	116.6	115.1	115.5
d Guarantees by the Company of the bank borrowings of subsidiaries	–	–	–	0.4
e Guarantees by the Company in respect of the Eurobonds and Promissory note issued by subsidiaries	–	–	516.6	250.0
f Guarantees by the Company of the liabilities of Marks and Spencer (Nederland) BV, Marks and Spencer (Ireland) Limited and M&S Export (Ireland) Limited	–	–	12.2	5.6

Marks and Spencer (Ireland) Limited and M & S Export (Ireland) Limited have availed themselves of the exemption provided for in s17 of the Companies (Amendment) Act 1986 (Ireland) in respect of the documents required to be annexed to the annual returns of those companies.

g In the opinion of the directors, the revalued properties will be retained for use in the business and the likelihood of any taxation liability arising is remote. Accordingly the potential deferred taxation in respect of these properties has not been quantified.

h Other material contracts

In the unlikely event of a change in the trading arrangements with certain warehouse operators, the Company has a commitment to purchase, at market value, fixed assets which are currently owned and operated by them on the Company's behalf.

i Commitments under operating leases

At 31 March 1989 annual commitments under non-cancellable operating leases were as follows:

| | The Group | | The Company | |
	Land and buildings £m	Other £m	Land and buildings £m	Other £m
Expiring within one year	1.7	1.6	0.2	0.8
Expiring between two and five years	8.1	4.6	0.6	4.4
Expiring in five years or more	39.6	–	20.5	–
	49.4	**6.2**	**21.3**	**5.2**

26 Transactions with directors

Interest-free house purchase loans were made by the Company to the following, prior to their appointments as directors. These loans, which were under the employees' loan scheme, were repaid during the year:

| | | Balance outstanding at year end | |
| | | **1989** | 1988 |
Director	Date of loan	**£**	£
Mr N L Colne	1980	**Nil**	3960
Mr D G Trangmar	1979–1982	**Nil**	4760

27 Directors' interests in shares and debentures

The beneficial interests of the directors and their families in the shares of the Company and its subsidiaries, together with their interests as trustees of both charitable and other trusts, are shown below. Further information regarding employee share options is given in note 11 on pages 52 and 53.

Interests in the Company

Ordinary shares – beneficial and family interests

| | At 31 March 1989 | | At 1 April 1988 | |
	Shares	Options	Shares	Options
The Lord Rayner	**106499**	**882506**	101396	405367
R Greenbury	**30885**	**1025346**	27865	368301
N L Colne	**72379**	**534082**	70299	275422
J A Lusher	**73033**	**583381**	25715	249927

| | At 31 March 1989 | | At 1 April 1988 | |
	Shares	Options	Shares	Options
J K Oates	6725	758816	4000	327475
A S Orton	13952	569637	11460	313465
S J Sacher	389755	543754	377055	308953
The Hon David Sieff	299838	555488	296831	231491
C V Silver	29476	760249	25830	242920
A K P Smith	150014	693756	59805	344733
D G Trangmar	25656	599621	15658	282092
Dr D V Atterton	4000	–	2000	–
R A E Herbert	7000	–	7000	–
D G Lanigan	2000	–	2000	–
D R Susman	54232	–	54232	–
The Rt Hon The Baroness Young	2000	–	2000	–

Ordinary shares – trustee interests

| | At 31 March 1989 | | At 1 April 1988 | |
	Charitable Trusts Shares	Other Trusts Shares	Charitable Trusts Shares	Other Trusts Shares
S J Sacher	391690	571998	391690	486998
The Hon David Sieff	218532	588652	228232	424300
D R Susman	570100	–	580100	–

Preference shares and debentures

At 31 March 1989 N L Colne owned 5004.9% preference shares (last year 500 shares). None of the other directors had an interest in any preference shares or in the debentures of the Company.

Interests in subsidiaries

None of the directors had any interests in any subsidiaries at the beginning or end of the year.

Between the end of the financial year and one month prior to the date of the Notice of Meeting, there has been one change in the directors' interests in shares and debentures of, and options granted by, the Company and its subsidiaries. The Hon David Seiff's trustee interest in 'other trusts' has become 528,652 ordinary shares following the disposal of 60,000 shares after the announcement of the year's results.

Providers of Group Capital

The capital of the Group arises from the following sources:

1 Preference shares

The 1,350,000 preference shares are held by 725 shareholders, who receive dividends in preference to the holders of ordinary shares at rates of 7.0% and 4.9% per annum, plus related tax credit.

2 Ordinary shares

There are 301,858 holders of ordinary shares who receive dividends at rates declared either by the directors or at the annual general meeting. Their shareholdings are analysed as follows:

Size of shareholding	Number of shareholders	Percentage of total number of shareholders	Number of ordinary shares 000s	Percentage of ordinary shares
Over 1000000	262 ⎤		1447700	54.1
500001–1000000	192 ⎥		136615	5.1
200001– 500000	344 ⎬	0.7	111779	4.2
100001– 200000	446 ⎥		65556	2.5
50001– 100000	932 ⎦		65727	2.5
20001– 50000	4151	1.4	125836	4.7
10001– 20000	10438	3.4	146241	5.5
5001– 10000	26451	8.8	187583	7.0
2001– 5000	67644	22.4	221120	8.3
1001– 2000	64527	21.4	100094	3.7
501– 1000	55755	18.5	44873	1.7
1– 500	70716	23.4	19848	0.7
	301858	100.0	2672972	100.0

Those shareholders owning more than 100,000 ordinary shares are further analysed as follows:

Type of owner	Number of shareholders	Number of ordinary shares 000s
Insurance companies	99	459145
Banks and nominee companies	612	872985
Identifiable pension funds	86	187190
Individuals	317	145345
Others	130	96985
	1244	1761650

For the purposes of Capital Gains Tax the price of ordinary shares on 31 March 1982 was 153.50p each which, when adjusted for the 1 for 1 scrip issue in 1984, gives a figure of 76.75p each.

3 Debenture stocks

These stocks, with a nominal value of £45 million, are owned by Prudential Assurance Company Limited and Prudential Nominees Limited who are entitled to interest at annual rates ranging from 5.50% to 7.75% under the terms of the debenture trust deed.

4 8.25% Guaranteed bonds 1996

US$150 million was raised in 1986 by the issue of a Eurobond at an annual interest rate of 8.25% maturing in 1996. Currency and interest swaps were arranged to provide £100 million at floating interest rates below LIBOR.

5 9.75% Guaranteed notes 1993

£150 million was raised last year by the issue of a Eurobond at an annual interest rate of 9.75% maturing in 1993. Interest swaps were arranged to provide £150 million at floating interest rates below LIBOR.

6   US\$ Promissory note 1998

A US\$450 million ten year Promissory note, bearing interest at LIBOR, was issued by a subsidiary of Marks and Spencer p.l.c. as part of the finance for the acquisition of Brooks Brothers.

7   Bank loans and overdrafts

Bank loans and overdrafts have been obtained to finance certain of the Company's subsidiaries and the overdrafts bear interest at rates varying with local bank rates.

Application of Group Sales Revenue

	1989 £m	% to total	1988 £m	% to total
To suppliers of merchandise and services	**3743.4**	**67.5**	3401.9	68.4
For the benefit of employees				
Salaries	**489.5**		408.3	
Deductions for income tax and national insurance	**105.1**		89.5	
	384.4		318.8	
Pension schemes	**53.5**		49.4	
Employees' profit sharing schemes	**13.1**		12.4	
Welfare and staff amenities	**24.9**		16.2	
	475.9	**8.6**	396.8	8.0
To central and local government				
United Kingdom	**751.4**		706.6	
Overseas	**71.6**		48.5	
	823.0	**14.8**	755.1	15.2
To the providers of Group capital				
Interest on loan capital and overdrafts	**59.1**		22.2	
Income tax deducted	**1.0**		1.0	
	58.1		21.2	
Dividends to shareholders of the Company	**149.7**		135.8	
	207.8	**3.7**	157.0	3.1
For the replacement of assets and the expansion of the business				
Depreciation	**104.9**		85.0	
Deferred taxation	**0.6**		(9.0)	
Retained profits, after adjusting for minority interests	**194.2**		187.5	
	299.7	**5.4**	263.5	5.3
Group sales revenue, including sales taxes	**5549.8**	**100.0**	4974.3	100.0

Index